THE UNIVERSE OF CREATURES

Mediæval Philosophical Texts in Translation

No. 35

Roland J. Teske, S.J., Editor

William of Auvergne

THE UNIVERSE OF CREATURES

Selections Translated from the Latin

With an Introduction and Notes

by

Roland J. Teske, S.J.

MARQUETTE
UNIVERSITY

PRESS

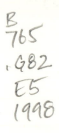
Library of Congress Cataloguing in Publication Data

William, of Auvergne, Bishop of Paris, d. 1249.
  [De universo. English. Selections]
  The universe of creatures / William of Auvergne ; selections
translated from the Latin with an introduction and notes by Roland
J. Teske.
    p. cm. — (Mediaeval philosophical texts in translation ; no.
35)
  Includes bibliographical references and index.
  ISBN 0-87462-238-7
  1. Philosophy, Medieval. I. Teske, Roland J., 1934- .
II. Title. III. Series.
B765.G82E5 1998
189'.4—dc21   97-45331

MARQUETTE UNIVERSITY PRESS
MILWAUKEE

The Association of Jesuit University Presses

For John, Jr., Melissa, Luke,
Christopher, David, and Peter

Contents

Introduction

Any work entitled *The Universe* is bound to be large, and William's work certainly measures up to its name, even though he includes in it only the world of creatures, for he had already dealt with God, one and triune, in *The Trinity, or the First Principle*, the first part of his *Teaching on God in the Mode of Wisdom* (*Magisterium divinale et sapientiale*), a truly immense work that contains in seven parts the full sweep of the philosophical and theological thought that is found in the great *Summae* of the later half of the thirteenth century. This translation of selections from the *De universo* grew out of a graduate seminar on William offered at Marquette University in the spring semester of 1995. In order to make William available to the students whose Latin was limited or non-existent, I translated large parts of the *De universo* and of the *De anima* which we read in class along with the translations of William's *De trinitate* and *De immortalitate animae*. I subsequently corrected the translation, polished it somewhat, and annotated it as best I could. I hope that it will prove useful to other students of medieval philosophy and allow them to become familiar with the thought of William of Auvergne, one of the first of the great philosopher-theologians of the thirteenth century.

I. William's Life and Works

Little is known about William's early life. He was, it is said, born in Aurillac in the Province of Auvergne. By 1223 he was a canon of Notre Dame, and by 1225 he was a professor of theology at the University of Paris, a position which normally required one to be thirty-five years old. Hence, he is assumed to have been born at least by 1190, but possibly as early as 1180. After Bartholomaeus, the bishop of Paris, died in October 20, 1227, the canons of the cathedral elected the dean of the cathedral as his successor. William was displeased with their choice, and though merely a deacon, he went to Rome and protested the election to Pope Gregory IX. Gregory was apparently impressed by William to the point that he ordained him priest and bishop and appointed him to the see of Paris where he remained as bishop until his death in 1249. Noël Valois's *Guillaume d'Auvergne évèque de Paris (1228-1249): sa vie et ses ouvrages* remains the only book-length account of William's life and works. Ernest Moody's study of William's *De anima* offers a brief account of his life in English.[1] Steven Marrone's volume on William and Grosseteste, the most important recent study of an aspect of William's philosophy, as well

---

[1]   Valois' book was published in Paris in 1880. Moody's "William of Auvergne and his Treatise De Anima" is found in *Studies in Medieval Philosophy, Science, and Logic* (Berkeley and Los Angeles: Univ. of California Press, 1975), pp. 1-109.

as my introductions to the translations of *De trinitate* and *De immortalitate animae*, provide some biographical information.[2]

The 1674 Paris-Orléans edition of William's *Opera omnia* contains the following works in the first volume: *Faith and the laws* (*De fide et legibus*), *The Virtues and the Vices* (*De virtutibus et vitiis*), *The Immortality of the Soul* (*De immortalitate animae*), *Divine Oratory* (*De rhetorica divina*), *The Sacraments* (*De sacramentis*), *Why God Became Man* (*Cur Deus homo*), *The New Treatise on Penance* (*De poenitentia novus tractatus*), and *The Universe* (*De universo*). The second volume contains: *The Trinity* (*De trinitate*), *The Soul* (*De anima*), *Supplement to the New Treatise on Penance* (*Supplementum tractatus novi de poenitentia*), and *The Conferral and Singleness of Benefices* (*De collatione et singularitate beneficiorum*).[3] Of these works *De trinitate* and *De immortalitate animae* have modern critical editions. Apart from these works there are also modern editions of William's *Grace and Free Choice* (*De gratia et libero arbitrio*), *The Art of Preaching* (*De arte predicandi*), two treatises entitled *Good and Evil* (*De bono et malo*), and *Sermon for the Eve of All Saints* (*Sermo in vigilia omnium sanctorum*).[4] Among William's other extant works there are: *The Cloister of the Soul* (*De claustro animae*), *The Faces of the World* (*De faciebus mundi*), *The Praises of Patience* (*De laudibus patientiae*), *The Mass* (*De missa*), *The Passion of the Lord* (*De passione Domini*), *Commentary on the Song of Songs* (*In Cantica Canticorum*); *Commentary on Ecclesiastes* (*In Ecclesiasten*), *Commentary on Proverbs* (*In Proverbia*), *Various Sermons* (*Sermones diversi de tempore et de sanctis*), a French Sermon, and a list of errors that William condemned as bishop.

The seven parts of William's principal work, the *Magisterium divinale et sapientiale*, were first recognized by Josef Kramp in 1920 as forming a single huge work that exemplified the systematic sweep of the great *Summae* of the latter part of the thirteenth century, beginning with God, one and triune, moving to the created world, specifically to human beings, and their souls,

---

[2]   Steven P. Marrone, *William of Auvergne and Robert Grosseteste: New Ideas of Truth in the Early Thirteenth Century* (Princeton: Princeton Univ. Press, 1983); William of Auvergne, *The Trinity, or the First Principle*, trans. Roland J. Teske, S.J. and Francis C. Wade, S.J. (Milwaukee: Marquette Univ. Press, 1989) and *The Immortality of the Soul*, trans. Roland J. Teske (Milwaukee: Marquette Univ. Press, 1991).

[3]   The 1674 edition also contains a set of sermons which, however, are not William's. There is an earlier edition of William's works (Venice, 1591), but it is not readily available.

[4]   For these editions, see Guglielmo Corti, *Il Tractatus de gratia di Guglielmo d'Auvergne*. Corona Lateranensis (Rome: Libreria editrice della Pontificia Università Laternanense, 1966); A. de Poorter, "Un manuel de prédication médiévale: Le ms. 97 de Bruges," *Revue neoscholastique de philosophie* 25 (1923): 192-209; J. Reginald O'Donnell, C.S.B., "Tractatus Magistri Guillelmi Alvernensis *De bono et malo*," *Mediaeval Studies* 8 (1946): 245-299 and "Tractatus secundus Guillelmi Alvernensis *De bono et malo*," *Mediaeval Studies* 16 (1954): 219-271. The sermon was edited by M. Davy in *Les sermons universitaires parisiens de 1230-1231: Contribution à la prédication médiévale* (Paris: Librairie philosophique J. Vrin, 1931), pp. 149-153.

the incarnation, and the means of our return to God, namely, faith, religion, the sacraments, and the virtues. William's *The Universe of Creatures* is, as William explicitly states in the first chapter of the work, the second part of the first *Teaching on God in the Mode of Wisdom*.[5] The *De universo* was, however, written late in William's career—probably around 1231 with the *De anima* following in 1236, though the absolute dating of William's works seems more a matter of conjecture than knowledge. Following the pioneering work of J. Kramp, G. Corti lists in their systematic order the following seven parts of William's *Magisterium divinale et sapientiale*: 1. *De primo principio* (*De trinitate*), 2. *De universo creaturarum*, 3. *De anima*, 4. *Cur Deus homo*, 5. *De fide et legibus*, 6. *De sacramentis*, and 7. *De virtutibus et moribus*.[6]

Corti has also called attention to the fact that William drew a distinction between his *primum magisterium* and his *magisterium* in general. The *primum magisterium* includes at least the *De trinitate*, the *De universo creaturarum*, and the *De anima*, the parts of the whole *magisterium* which are most philosophical in the sense that the argumentation in them is based upon reason rather than appeals to authority, especially to the authority of scripture. William's *Cur Deus homo* marks, I believe, a transition from the strictly philosophical works—in the modern sense of philosophical—to the final three works which clearly appeal to the Christian faith. William explicitly announces in the opening lines of *De fide* his intention to write about "the knowledge of the divine worship and of the true religion, as we have received it from above," where the phrase "*prout de sursum accepimus*" indicates that he is proceeding no longer "by way of proof and inquiry," as he had said that he would do in the beginning of *De trinitate*.[7]

The distinction between the *primum magisterium* and the *totum magisterium* needs to be stressed if one is to understand some of the problematic and even apparently contradictory things that William says about the *Magisterium divinale et sapientiale*. For example, he maintains that "the honor and glory of the creator . . . is the chief and ultimate end of the whole *Teaching on God in the Mode of Wisdom*"[8] and that "the finest goals and most excellent blessedness of the sublime and sapiential philosophy . . . are undoubtedly the exalta-

---

[5]   *De universo* Ia-Iae, ch. 1; I, 593bB. References to William's works—except for *De trinitate*—are to the Paris-Orléans edition of 1674 and give the part, chapter, volume, page, column, and section, where these are available.

[6]   Guglielmo Corti, "Le sette parti del Magisterium divinale et sapientiale di Guglielmo di Auvergne," in *Studi e Ricerche di Scienze Religiose in onore dei Santi Apostoli Pietro e Paulo nel xix centenario del loro martirio* (Rome: Pontificiae Universitatis Lateranensis, 1968), p. 298.

[7]   William of Auvergne, *The Trinity, or the First Principle* (*De trinitate*), Prologue: Switalski, p. 15; Teske-Wade, p. 63. References to *De trinitate* will include the page references to the critical edition by Bruno Switalski, *William of Auvergne. De Trinitate. An Edition of the Latin Text with an Introduction* (Toronto: Pontifical Institute of Mediaeval Studies, 1976) and well as to the English translation.

[8]   *De universo* Ia-Ia, ch. 1; I, 593bBC.

tion of the creator and the perfection of our souls."⁹ In fact, William is ada-mant that the purpose for investigating the great works of the creator is not merely that they may be known, but that "he may be exalted and acknowl-edged to be God and Lord of the ages and that human souls may be per-suaded or rather convinced to honor and worship him."[10]

On the other hand, in the Prologue of the *De trinitate*, which is often re-garded as a prologue to the whole *magisterium*, William clearly indicates that he has undertaken "to deal entirely with those who philosophize," not with those who receive a revelation as prophets or with those who are "simple subjects of the divine law." He will, he says, proceed "through the paths of proof and investigation . . . because only in this way can one take care of the errors of the educated."[11] So too, in *Cur Deus homo*, the central work of the seven parts of the *Magisterium divinale et sapientiale*, William plainly states after having cited several passages from the New Testament, "We have not, however, produced these testimonies in order to rely upon them or to use them as principles for the good, because we are not dealing with those who believe the testimonies of the scriptures, but in order to show in writing the faith which we are seeking."[12] So too, he says in *De universo*, "But understand that in all these special treatises I do not use the testimony of some law, nor is it part of my intention to defend the truth which is universal and is to be known or believed universally by human beings through testimonies, but through irrefragable proofs."[13] Even the words of Aristotle are not to be used as authoritative. "Let it not enter your mind," William warns, "that I want to use the words of Aristotle as authoritative for the proof of those things which I am about to say, for I know that a proof from an authority is only dialectical and can only produce belief, though it is my aim, both in this treatise and wherever I can, to produce demonstrative certitude, after which you are left without any trace of doubt."[14]

William is, nonetheless, quite clear that "divine authority did not choose this mode,"[15] and he denies that "belief of this sort, that is, belief persuaded and incited by proofs, has merit or favor before God."[16] And in *De fide* Wil-liam is even more explicit: "Those who intend to approach God through the path of proofs and signs alone, even if by that kind of knowledge they ad-

---

⁹ *De universo* Ia-IIae, Prooemium; I, 807aB.

[10] *De universo* Ia-Iae, ch. I, 593bC.

[11] *The Trinity, or the First Principle* (*De trinitate*), Prologue: Switalski, p. 15; Teske-Wade, p. 63.

[12] *Cur Deus homo* ch. 2; I, 556bG.

[13] *De universo* IIIa-IIae, ch. 6; I, 1028aE.

[14] *De anima*, chapter 1, part 1: II, 65b.

[15] *The Trinity, or the First Principle* (*De trinitate*), Prologue: Switalski, p. 15: Teske-Wade, p. 63.

[16] *The Trinity, or the First Principle* (*De trinitate*), Prologue: Switalski, pp. 15-16; Teske-Wade, pp. 64. I have amended the translation on the basis of Switalski's critical apparatus and of what William says in *De fide*.

vance in some sense philosophically to this point, they rightly show contempt for God by their unbelief, fall away from religion, are driven back further, and deprived of the more sublime kind of knowledge."[17] In *De fide* William is explicit that "faith is the foundation of true religion and the first root and the principle of divine worship,"[18] and he is equally explicit that this faith does not rest upon signs or proofs.

II. The Structure and Content of the *De universo*

The *De universo*, which runs from page 592 to page 1074 in the 1674 edition, is divided into two principal parts. The first principal part deals with the universe in general or the corporeal universe, while the second principal part deals with the spiritual universe. Each of the two principal parts are divided in three parts. The first part of the first principal part (Ia-Iae) has a Preface and introductory chapter and several distinct sections which a later editor has labeled treatises. The first treatise (chapters 2 through 10) argues against the Cathar dualists of William's era, whom he calls Manichees. Against them, William maintains that the universe has a single principle, the good creator, who is being necessary through himself. William's refutation of the Manichaean dualists is interesting—at times highly philosophical and at other times more at the level of common sense and dialectical arguments. For his more philosophical arguments he relies upon the Avicennian metaphysics that he articulated in the first chapters of *De trinitate*. It is curious that he never once even alludes to Augustine as a source or an authority, despite the fact that Augustine wrote so extensively against the Manichees of his own age. William's discussion of the various senses of "evil" and his argument that in none of these senses can the Prince of Darkness be evil provides an interesting discussion of the problem of evil as well as a battery of arguments against the dualist position.

The second treatise (chapters 11 through 16) argues that the universe itself is one. Here William is concerned with those people who try to maintain that there is another corporeal world separate from this world, whether the Elysian Fields of classical mythology or the paradise of the Moslems, which was portrayed as a world of bodily pleasures, at least as William understood it. William argues that the impossibility of the existence of a plurality of corporeal worlds is not due to any lack of power on the part of God, but due to the intrinsic impossibility of a plurality of such worlds. The majority of the text from these chapters has been omitted from this translation, mainly because it seemed less philosophically interesting than other chapters of this huge work.

The third treatise (chapters 17 through 27) deals with the manner of the origin of creatures from the creator. Here William deals with a wide variety of topics. First, in chapters 17 to 19 he uses a series of six images, such as water emanating from a fountain, the image of a person reflected in a mirror, the

---

[17] *De fide*, ch. 1; I, 5bC..
[18] *De fide*, Preface; I, 1bBC.

casting of a shadow by a body, the impression of a footprint by a walker, the spreading of a scent from a perfume, and the making of an artifact by a worker, to come to the meaning of creation. To a large extent he merely points to the limitations of the images as means of understanding creation, though he finds some truth or benefit in each of them. Then, after coming to the conclusion that God creates through his word, he explains in chapter 20 that the word of the creator is his art or thought, not an orally spoken word or a written word. Though William elsewhere identifies the word by which God creates as the Son of the Father, he does not here spell out the trinitarian implications of what he is teaching, perhaps because he is determined to deal with the question independently from faith in the biblical revelation or perhaps because he derived some aspects of this doctrine of the word from Avicebron.[19] In the following chapters William faces problems that arise from creation through the word of the creator. In chapter 21, for example, he argues that, though God's word is eternal, he created freely and could have created other things than he did create, though he would have created these other things by his very same word. So too, in chapter 22, he argues that, though all things were spoken at once in God's eternal word, all things were not and could not be produced at once. In chapter 23, he deals with the question of whether or not God could create things greater and better than he did create them and argues that any limitation upon what God can create stems not from a lack of his power or goodness, but from the nature of creatures. Finally, he defines creation in the proper sense as "the newness of existing or of being from the will of the creator without any means."

In chapter 24 William turns to the errors of Aristotle and his followers concerning the creation of the first intelligence and the heavens, for they maintained that from the First—an Avicennian name for the creator—there necessarily proceeded a single creature, the first intelligence and its heaven. William attacks the root of their error, namely, that "from what is one insofar as it is one there cannot in any way come anything but what is one."[20] The Aristotelians also explained that the creator did not cause the first intelligence by anything external to himself, but through his understanding of himself. Hence, they held that the first intelligence proceeded from the creator through his intellect. William explains in chapter 25 how, according to the Aristotelians, there proceed from the first intelligence a second intelligence, the matter of the first heaven, the form of the first heaven, and the soul of the first heaven.[21]

[19] See Kevin Caster, "William of Auvergne's Adaptation of Ibn Gabirol's Doctrine of the Divine Will," *Modern Schoolman* 74 (1996): 31-42.
[20] See my "William of Auvergne's Use of the Avicennian Principle: Ex Uno, In Quantum Unum, Non Nisi Unum," *Modern Schoolman* 71 (1973): 1-15. In *De trinitate* William uses this principle to show that the Father can have but one Son.
[21] William is here following Avicenna rather than Aristotle, but somehow manages to add a fourth product of the first intelligence where Avicenna has only three. See *Avicenna Latinus: Liber de Philosophia Prima sive Scientia Divina*, ed. Simone van Riet. 3 vols (Louvain-la-neuve: E. Peeters; Leiden, E. J. Brill, 1977, 1983, 1983).

In chapter 26 William begins his refutation of this Peripatetic doctrine. He points out, first of all, that the tenth intelligence, the agent intelligence, ought to be able to create another intelligence through its intellect just as the higher intelligences can. Second, according to the Aristotelians the agent intelligence is only one; hence, in causing human souls, as they claim it does, it should produce only one soul. Thirdly, the creator's intellect or act of understanding is not tied to one creature more than any other; hence, there is no reason why one intelligence should be the first effect rather than another. In a long series of arguments William rejects the doctrine that the creator produces creatures through his intellect alone and through an intellect limited to a single first effect; he points out that Aristotle and his followers have failed to understand the freedom of the creator. Here William explicitly identifies the word of God with the Word revealed in the scriptures of the Christian people, and he then continues his refutation of various other aspects of the Avicennian doctrine of the emanation of the intelligences from the First.

In Chapter 27 William lists three causes of the error of the Aristotelians. First, they failed to understand the word of the creator, especially that his word is a word that commands with ultimate power. Second, they failed to understand the freedom of the creator by which he acts, for he is unable to be prevented from acting as he wills or forced to act against his will. Third, they mistakenly thought that the creator could be at a distance from some things, though he is in fact most intimate to everything. Chapter 28 reiterates William's doctrine that the word of the creator is not merely his art and wisdom, but his word of omnipotent command by which he orders things into existence. Chapter 29 raises the question of whether the heavens and the elements were created all at once or through continuous generation. Chapter 30 presents an important insight into William's view of the being of creatures as most intimate to them, like an undergarment in William's picturesque language, so that the creator who is the sole source of being is also most intimate to each of them. The following chapters 31 through 55 are omitted from this translation; they discuss the origin of the corporeal world, such as, the heavens, and then the various elements, often following the Genesis account of creation and concluding with accounts of paradise, purgatory, and the fires of hell.

The second part of the first principal part (IIa-Iae) takes up the question of the eternity of the world. After a brief Preface in which he sketches his plan for the remainder of the first principal part, William begins by noting that some people have held that time is simply a part of eternity so that time and eternity are essentially the same.[22] William, on the other hand, insists that eternity is essentially other than time, for eternity is stable duration without beginning and without end and indivisible into before and after, while time is

References to this work will be to: Avicenna, *Metaphysics*, with the book, chapter, and page in the van Riet edition. Here see *Metaphysics* IX, 4: Van Riet, p. 483.

[22] See my "William of Auvergne on the Eternity of the World," *Modern Schoolman* 67 (1990): 187- 205.

constantly flowing, unstable, and with both a beginning and an end. William presents some of the paradoxes involved in eternity when it is conceived as indivisible, explains how eternity with its unity and simplicity has a spiritual amplitude which makes it greater than time, and points out that one should properly use only verbs of being, standing, or remaining to speak of the eternity of the creator, and these only in the present tense. William discusses the difference between perpetuity—a duration which has a beginning but is without an end, the sort of duration the human soul has—and eternity, which not merely has neither beginning nor end, but is indivisible into parts. So too, he points out that Aristotle held that time did not have a beginning or an end—a issue to which he will soon return. Finally, in this long first chapter, he turns to a discussion of the being of eternity, namely, whether it is identical with the being of the creator or something other than him or a privation.

In chapter 2 William asks whether eternity preceded time and, if so, by how much and in what way; he then turns to a discussion of the relation between eternity and time and explains the sense in which eternity or God is in time. God is when time is and whenever any part of time is, but this being in time "by concomitance" does not mean that God is in time in the proper sense so that there is succession in God's duration. William asks what it means to say that all things are in eternity and are seen in eternity simultaneously; he explains that things are said to be in eternity in much the same sense as they are said to be in God. In chapter 3 he puzzles over the claim that all things are present simultaneously in eternity. He insists that temporal things are not present in their truth in eternity. Rather, the claim that all things are present simultaneously in eternity means that God sees all things as present to himself. In chapter 4 William presents a series of images to help his reader to understand the relation of eternity and time; for example, he asks us to imagine an immense wheel, namely, eternity, with the wheel of time within it so that it touches the larger wheel only at one point. The whole of eternity stands still—whole all at once—while the wheel of time touches it point by point as it revolves. William's discussion of the relation between God's eternity and time is profound—perhaps the most penetrating discussion of divine eternity and its relation to time since Augustine. Though William never cites the famous Boethian definition of eternity as the complete possession of unending life all at once,[23] he clearly defends a doctrine of divine eternity as a duration that is all at once without any succession, a doctrine which is not found in Avicenna, but in Plotinus and, after him, in Augustine.[24]

In chapter 5 William states that Aristotle—where he seems to mean, as he often does, Avicenna rather than the Stagirite—knew nothing of such a timeless eternity and that he meant by eternity only time without beginning and

---

[23] For his definition of eternity see Boethius, *The Consolation of Philosophy* (*De consolatione philosophiae*) V, 6, 4: CCL 94, 101.

[24] See my *The Paradoxes of Time in Saint Augustine*. The Aquinas Lecture, 1996 (Milwaukee: Marquette Univ. Press, 1996).

end. In that eternity, William says, Aristotle posited the ten intelligences and located them in this eternity, because, as having no potentiality, they could not be in any flux. In chapters 6 and 7 William deals with some scriptural passages that raise difficulties for his account of eternity, for example, that "the Lord will reign for eternity and beyond" (Ex 15:18). Most of chapter 7, which continues the discussion of various temporal expressions, is omitted from the translation.

In chapter 8 William turns to the question of what he calls the newness or antiquity of the world, that is, whether the world as a whole had a beginning at some point finitely distant in the past or whether it always existed. William, first of all, presents Aristotle's opinion that the world was eternal—a view which Avicenna also held. In fact, the three arguments that William presents are each derived from Avicenna rather than from Aristotle. The first argument for the eternity of the world tries to show that the creator preceded the world either by time or only as a cause precedes an effect. The argument then goes on to exclude any temporal precedence so that God precedes the world only as a cause precedes its effect. But since cause and effect are simultaneous, there was no time when God existed and the world did not. In characteristic fashion William first "helps" Avicenna's argument and restates it in an even stronger form. The second argument for the eternity of the world is what the great Islamic thinker called the testimony of a pure and true intellect.[25] Basically, it claims that, if a cause is not now different from what it was before, no new effect has come from it. But since the creator cannot now be different from what he was before, if the world now exists, it must have existed before. Hence, the world existed as long as the creator existed. Again William bolsters the argument with considerations that Avicenna could have used to strengthen his reasoning, namely, that, if the cause is sufficient through itself alone to produce the effect, then the effect exists if the cause exists. The third argument tries to show that the creation of the world need not have been at the beginning of time, since it is possible for God to have created a body which would last up to the creation of the world and would, therefore, be in time.

In chapter 9 William replies to the Avicennian arguments. In reply to the first argument he maintains that the creator precedes the world, not by a temporal priority, but by the priority of eternity over time, as he has already explained.. He insists that the "before" of eternity and the "before" of time are not univocal and that one should not admit comparisons between eternity and time. He argues that to speak of something "before" the beginning of time is just as problematic as to speak of something in a place outside the world. To the second argument William replies with a dilemma: Either the creator cannot create a substance the creation of which does not require the help of something that already exists, or he can. William claims that the power of the creator is not limited to a particular possible, but extends to every

---

[25] See Avicenna, *Metaphysics* IX, ch. 1: van Riet, p. 440.

possible. He then argues that, if the Avicennian first intelligence and any other intelligence are considered in themselves, they are equally possible. Hence, the creator is equally powerful for creating either intelligence, and when he creates one of them, he is as he was before when he did not create it. Hence, Avicenna's strongest argument is seen not to be the testimony of a true and pure intellect.

William offers a second argument against Avicenna's proof in which he tries to show that, on Avicenna's principles, the production of anything new would require an infinite number of causes. But if an infinite number of causes had to act before anything new came about, nothing new would ever come about. But new things do come to be. Hence, Avicenna's principles are wrong. With regard to the argument from the sufficiency of the cause, William distinguishes between natural causes which act with necessity and free causes which have power over their actions and the freedom to choose either alternative. William admits that in the case of natural causes and in the case of the human will there is a change in the cause if a new effect is produced, but he argues that the creator can now will something, but could have not willed it without any change in his will.

Chapter 10 raises the question of why God created the world when he did rather than from eternity. William argues that from the side of the creator there was nothing that prevented the creation of the world from eternity, but that there is an impediment from the side of the world, as William promises to make clear in the following chapter. Another question asks whether it would not have contributed more to God's praise and glory to have created the world from eternity so that God should have created it from eternity. William replies that, when we speak of God's acting for his praise and glory, we must remember that his praise and glory is entirely for the benefit of other things. Furthermore, William insists that we should not think that God ought to have done what cannot be done.

Then William turns to Aristotle's own arguments for the eternity of the world and refers his reader to his previous refutation of the argument in *Physics* VIII for the eternity of motion.[26] He takes up Aristotle's argument from *On the Heavens* where he claimed that nature determined for some things that they would always be, just as nature determined for other things that they would never be.[27] Hence, there are, according to the argument, other things besides the creator which are eternal. In reply William claims that being is not said of the creator and of other things univocally, for the creator alone is his being, while everything else has being by participation. Furthermore, nature, William insists, determined nothing for the creator.

In chapter 11, after having refuted the arguments of Avicenna and Aristotle that the world must be eternal, William sets forth a series of arguments to

---

[26] See *The Trinity, or the First Principle* (*De trinitate*) ch. 8: Switalski, pp. 51-54; Teske-Wade, pp. 95-97.
[27] Aristotle, *On the Heavens* I, ch. 12, 281a27ff.

establish the newness of the world, that is, that the past temporal duration of the world is finite. William's arguments claim to prove that the world had a beginning in time; that is, his position differs from that of Maimonides and Aquinas who held that creation in time could not be proved by reason.[28] William's arguments range from an appeal to the authority of the scriptural narrative to quite philosophical arguments which reflect those which were developed by John Philoponus in the sixth century and are found in and best known from their formulation in the works of Saint Bonaventure.[29]

Chapters 12 through 50 are omitted from this translation. Chapter 12 asks whether time will come to an end and what will follow upon the end. Chapter 13 turns to Plato's doctrine that souls were all created eternally outside their bodies and subsequently entered bodies and migrated from one body to another. In chapters 14 and 15 William continues to combat the Platonic and Pythagorean doctrine of the transmigration of souls. Then in chapters 16 through 18 he argues against the Platonic doctrine of the Great Year, namely, that every 36,000 years everything returns to its original state. Chapter 19 argues against Origen's view that bodies are ultimately destroyed, and chapters 20 through 49 discuss the resurrection of the body, the glorification of body and soul in the next life, the properties of the glorified body, and the state of the world at the resurrection. Chapter 50 draws the second part of the first principal part to a close.

The third part of the first principal part (IIIa-Iae) takes up "the governance of the corporeal universe and especially in relation to human affairs and human beings themselves." William lists the questions he will deal with:

> Whether the blessed and sublime creator has care for all individuals or concerning all individuals. Second, whether he has care over the evils which befall just and holy persons in this life and other points related to this question, namely, how and to what purpose or benefit evil persons flourish here, I mean, flourish with powers, riches, and delights. . . . After this, concerning evil itself, whether it comes about through the providence of the creator. I shall speak here of fate and the fates. . . . I shall make you know how the foreknowledge and providence of the creator do not impose necessity upon contingent things, and how contingent events are not prevented by them or how our free will is not prevented, limited, or constrained, with regard to willing and not willing, doing and not doing, except to the extent and in the ways I shall show you.[30]

Thus the general topic of the final part of the first principal part is God's providence over the universe. Despite the obvious interest of the questions

[28] For Moses Maimonides' view see *The Guide of the Perplexed*, trans. Shlomo Pines (Chicago: Univ. of Chicago Press, 1963), II, chs. 13-18; for Thomas Aquinas's position, see *Summa Theologiae* Ia, qu. 46.

[29] See my "William of Auvergne on the `Newness of the World,'" *Mediaevalia: Textos e Estudios* 7-8 (1995): 287-302.

[30] *De universo* IIIa-Iae, Prooemium; I, 754aH.

that William deals with here, this entire part has been omitted from the translation, mainly because the present volume was becoming too long. The three-
three chapters of this part might well be translated as a separate volume.

The second principal part of the whole work is explicitly concerned with
the spiritual universe. In the Preface William express surprise at the fact that
the spiritual universe has not been treated by many authors prior to him. He
reminds his reader that "the finest goals of the sublime philosophy in the
mode of wisdom" are "the exaltation of the creator and the perfection of our
souls."[31] In chapter 1 he explains that the second principal part is also divided
into three parts. The first (Ia-IIae) deals with the separate intelligences whose
existence Aristotle and his followers maintained. The second (IIa-IIae) deals
with those substances which the Greeks called good demons and which Christians call good or holy angels. The third (IIIa-IIae) deals with those substances
which the Greeks called evil demons and which the Christians call evil angels
or evils spirits or in more ordinary language devils. The selections translated
in this volume are taken entirely from the first part (Ia-IIae).

In chapter 2 William argues that the Aristotelian intelligences cannot be
perfect simply in knowledge, but must also be perfect in their will and virtues. In chapter 3 he points out that Aristotle posited nine intelligences to
account for the movements of the nine moveable heavens. Aristotle also posited souls for those heavens and for those souls perfect intelligent substances
which the souls love and which they desire to become like. In striving to
become like the intelligences the souls move their heavens in continuous revolutions. William argues at length that such movement by which the heavens
supposedly attain new locations is ridiculous since they lose the perfection of
one location as they gain that of another. In chapter 4 William continues to
argue against the Aristotelian doctrine that souls move their heavens in order
to become like their intelligences. He points out that, if each of the souls of
the heavens has its intellect fixed upon its intelligence alone, the intellect of
the soul of the heaven is more wretched than our intellects which are not
determined to a single object. Chapters 5 through 7 continue William's argument against the Aristotelian account of the souls of the heavens. In chapter 8
William argues that the ultimate perfection of every created intellect and its
glory lies in understanding the creator, so that no intelligence can have as its
end the understanding of something less than the creator.

In chapter 9 William turns to a refutation of the Aristotelian claim that
there proceeds from the creator only a single first creature, the first intelligence, which causes a second intelligence and so on, down to the tenth intelligence. William argues that nothing on the side of the intelligences prevents
there being a multiplicity of them, for such intelligences could not fail to be
compatible with one another, and a great number of them would certainly
not be superfluous. So too, there is nothing on the side of the creator which
prevents his creating many intelligences. In chapter 10 William takes up the

---

[31] *De universo* Ia-IIae, Prooemium; I, 897aB.

problem of the individuation of human souls once they are separated from their bodies. As William understood Avicenna's teaching, souls are individuated by their bodies and other accidents, and he took that teaching to imply that human souls would cease to be many once they were separated from their bodies.[32] In this and the following chapter William argues at length against the view that bodies or anything else accidental to our souls could account for their multiplicity. Though he resolutely argues against what he takes to be the Avicennian position, he seems to offer no explanation for the multiplicity of souls except for the fact that they are created many and remain such.

Chapter 12, most of which is omitted from the translation, discusses the Aristotelian view on the location of the intelligences in the heavens, while chapter 13 discusses various errors of the philosophers about their location. William, for example, holds that, if the souls are in the heavens, they are in a most wretched state because of the rapidity of the motion of the heavens. Chapter 14 turns to the lowest of the intelligences, the agent intelligence, and points out that, though Aristotle posited the agent intelligence to escape from the Platonic doctrine of a world of species or forms, the agent intelligence forced Aristotle back into the Platonic doctrine that the real world is the world of forms. Though William knew Plato only through the Latin translation of the *Timaeus*, he reconstructs what Plato's reasons for holding the archetypal world must have been. William was also opposed to the Aristotelian doctrine that the forms by which we know are derived from abstraction, and he explains in chapter 15 his understanding of that process. For William it is not the removal or scraping away of anything from the image, but simply the shortsightedness of the intellect as a result of which it does not attain the particular details of what is seen, just as when one sees an image of Socrates from a distance and cannot differentiate it from that of any other human being.

In chapter 16 William argues against the Aristotelian doctrine of the agent intelligence, pointing out that the analogy of the agent intelligence with the light of the sun breaks down, since the sun does not bestow upon visible things colors as the agent intelligence must bestow forms upon our intellect. William is convinced that, on the Aristotelian view, the forms in the agent intelligence must be the truth of the forms which it bestows. As a result the agent intelligence contains in itself the truth of things in this world, and this world does not contain true sensible things, such as true fire and true earth.[33] William does, nonetheless, maintain an archetypal world in a Christian sense, and in chapter 17 he explains that the Son of God is the exemplar of the universe. Yet William does not agree with what he takes to be the upshot of

[32] See my "William of Auvergne on the Individuation of Human Souls," *Traditio* 49 (1994): 77-93.

[33] Steven Marrone's study of truth in William and Grosseteste is most helpful in understanding William's concerns at this point. See note 2 above.

the Aristotelian position, namely, that the agent intelligence which, according to Avicenna, creates our souls and fashions our bodies, contains the truth of particular things. William turns in chapter 18 to the reasons why Aristotle did not admit many agent intelligences, though his one agent intelligence supposedly causes our many human souls. William also points out that, if there were only nine of these intelligent substances, then the heavenly court of the creator is more deserted than the palace of most earthly kings.

In chapter 19 William argues that the agent intelligence, which supposedly causes and perfects our souls, according to the Aristotelian view, cannot account for the multiplicity or the diversity of human souls. Moreover, the diversity of souls cannot come from our bodies, since our bodies too are the work of the agent intelligence—Avicenna's giver of forms (*dator formarum*). Furthermore, William argues in chapter 20 that, when separated from their bodies, human souls do not return to the agent intelligence, for he argues that even earthly kings reward their servants with a better recompense than that, often making them the equals of their own children. The happiness of human souls cannot be the result of their union with the agent intelligence. In fact, as William argues in chapter 21, the role which the Aristotelians assign to the agent intelligence verges on idolatry. Furthermore, William argues that there is no reason why the agent intelligence should not produce another intelligence so that the emanation of intelligences would continue without end. In chapter 22 William again argues that our souls do not return to the agent intelligence for their beatitude and contrasts the Aristotelian eschatology with that of the Christian faith. In the following chapter he argues against the view that the agent intelligence created souls in itself and then cast them forth into bodies.

In chapter 24 William examines how the Aristotelians can explain the plurality of the intelligences which are separated from matter. Aristotle, William says, apparently counted the separate substances by the number of heavens and their motions—a view which, William argues, ought to introduce great multiplicity into the creator himself, since he is the source of all the motions in the universe. William argues in chapter 25 that the Aristotelian account of the creation of one intelligence by another implies that the creator is and was idle, doing nothing at all after the creation of the single first intelligence. The power to create resides, William argues in chapter 26, in the creator alone, not in the separate intelligences, and in chapter 27 he rejects the theory that these substances create through their intellects.

William turns in chapter 28 to the possibility or potentiality of the intelligences; he denies that their possibility is anything in them, but affirms that it is the power of God to create them. He goes on to argue that an intelligence or any being does not act upon something insofar as it is simply a knower; rather, it causes through the will which is a word of command. William continues in the following chapter to argue that the agent intelligence does not cause our souls by understanding and that the first intelligence does not cause the second and so on. Again in chapter 30 William argues that the first intelligence did not proceed from the creator by a natural procession, where he continues to exploit Avicenna's claim that nature acts in the manner of a servant. William returns to the meanings of "creation" and points out that with a few exceptions only God is said to create "because at the good pleasure of his will alone without any means or help he bestows being upon what he wills." In chapter 32 William points out some extraordinary powers of some creatures, a curious chapter which provides some evidence that William had not done away with the causality of creatures, as he has at times been accused of having done.[34]

In chapter 33 and following William returns to the problem of the Platonic archetypal world. William points out that predicates of the creator which indicate his magnificence and glory signify, when used of creatures, only slight shadows, nods, vestiges, or tiny signs of what they signified in the creator. For example, when "powerful" is said of a creature, it signifies only a slight trace of what it signified in God; "powerful" denominates only one who has power in the true sense. The same is true with "being," "true," "good," "beautiful," "wise," "lofty," and "noble." Such predications belong only to the creator in their proper significations and apply to other things equivocally. Plato's mistake, William explains in chapter 34, was that he supposed that all predications applied to the intelligible world in their truest sense so that there was not true fire or earth or water in this sensible world. William insists in agreement with Aristotle that each thing stands in relation to truth as it stands in relation to being[35] and develops in chapters 35 and 36 a long series of arguments to show the absurdities that follow from the Platonic position. In chapter 37 William returns to those predications, namely, being, good, true, powerful, and so on, which pertain to the creator alone according to their truth and to other things only in an equivocal sense. William at times comes close to Aquinas's doctrine of analogous predication for he does want to maintain that such predicates are truly said of creatures, though creatures do not, on the other hand, share in those names in their purified intentions in which they are proper to the creator.

In chapter 38 William reveals his awareness that Plato did not identify the archetypal world with the creator and points to the difficulties that result from making that world something apart from the creator. In any case Christians identify the archetypal world with the Son of God, "the art of the omnipotent God full of living reasons," as William describes him in chapter 39 in dependence upon Augustine's *De trinitate*.

[34] See Armand Maurer, C.S.B, *Medieval Philosophy* (New York: Random House, 1962), p. 115, where Fr. Maurer says that William "considers created being so empty and deficient that it cannot exercise true causality. As God is the sole true being, so is he alone truly a cause. It is only by an abuse of the term that a creature is called a cause."

[35] Aristotle, *Metaphysics* II, ch. 1, 993b30-31

In chapter 40 William explains that every intelligence contains a multiplicity of forms in its simplicity and indivisibility. William asks in chapter 41 whether the light of knowledge is shed upon our intellects by the agent intelligence—a view which, as we have seen, William rejects. Most of this chapter and the remaining five chapters from this part have been omitted; in them William discusses how a multiplicity of forms exists in a spiritual substance without any confusion and how the exemplar forms exist in the knowledge of the creator eternally and as one with his knowledge.

The second part of the second principal part (Iia-IIae) turns to the good spirits or good angels. William begins with the proof of the spirituality of the angels in opposition to the views of the Sadducees and of Aristotle who, according to William, denied the spirituality of the evil demons. Unlike most of his contemporaries, William rejected universal hylomorphism in creatures and argued for the strict immateriality of the intelligences or angels so that his universe included creatures that are pure forms. This part of the *De universo* is by far the largest part of the work, running to just over 170 folio pages with 163 chapters. William begins by discussing the natural or essential characteristics of the good spirits which they, of course, share with the evil spirits. Then he takes up their functions, ranks, powers, and activities, especially those regarding human beings and human affairs. In the face of the Aristotelian doctrine that matter is the principle of individuation, William argues that separation from matter does not preclude the multiplicity of pure spirits. He discusses the number and the differences of spiritual substances, which include human souls and deals with the natural knowledge and powers of the good spirits, their apparitions, the fall of some of the angels, and the roles of the good angels.

The third part of the second principal part (IIIa-IIae) begins with a discussion of the acquired dispositions of the bad angels, since William has already in the previous part dealt with their natural or essential dispositions, which the good angels share. He discusses the deterioration which they have incurred in both their desires and in their knowledge. Then he turns to the differences, ranks, and power of the evil spirits, specifically to their power to torment and deceive human beings in this life and in the hereafter. Among the other topics with which he deals there are divination, various kinds of magic, necromancy, incubi and succubi, the possibility of their generation, and the names of various demons.

III. The Translation

The translation is made from the 1674 edition of William's works. I have amended the texts in a few places where the given reading seemed impossible or improbable. I have included the page and columns numbers and letters from that edition. In general, I chose to translate long sections of text rather than to make excerpts of texts that might be considered more important since only longer sections of text can reveal the complexities of William's style and his tendency to wander off his topic for several chapters and then return to it with new insights. I have tried to balance the demands of readability against strict fidelity to the letter of William's work. I thank my students from the seminar on William who by their interest in this little known, but fascinating thinker encouraged me to complete this translation. I also wish to thank Dr. Mary Rousseau who circulated the manuscript of this translation to two readers who remain unknown to me, though I am deeply grateful to them for their suggestions and corrections which I have tried to follow in every case.

The Universe of Creatures

The First Part of the Principal Part

Preface

"The knowledge (*scientia*) of the universe" has two meanings. The first of these is philosophy made up of the aggregate of all the philosophical sciences, just as the universe is an aggregate of all the things which exist, and its totality is nothing but the collection of all of them. This, however, is evident by analogy, for, just as each of the objects of knowledge stands to the whole aggregate of all objects of knowledge, so each of the sciences stands to the science made up of all of them. But this is, as we have already said, the complete philosophy in its totality. An example of this is the science of the triangle and the science of the circle which are undoubtedly parts of the complete geometry, just as the triangle and the circle are parts of the universe mensurable or knowable through geometry. In that way number and continuous magnitude belong to the aggregate of both, and the sciences of both of them are related in the same way to the science made up of both. But in the other meaning, knowledge of the universe is knowledge of it in the way it is a universe, that is, of these things which exist and in this way, that is, insofar as it is a universe. I shall name it, determine its number, and pursue it with a detailed examination through the paths of proofs and (593b) explanations by which you will attain certitude about them, if God wills.

Chapter One
That this knowledge is the second part of the first teaching on God in the mode of wisdom for two reasons, and on the aim of the author.

Know, then, first of all, that I understand here by "universe" only the universality of creatures, and whether I say "the universe" or "everything" or simply "the world," that is, without any additional determination, there is for me one meaning for these three. Hence, the knowledge of the universe in this manner or the knowledge of everything and the knowledge of the world without qualification is the second part of the first teaching on God in the mode of wisdom.[1] There are, however, two reasons for this teaching. One of them is the honor and glory of the creator which is the chief and ultimate end of the whole teaching on God in the mode of wisdom. For only those who philosophize on these topics on account of this end correctly and truly philosophize

---

[1] The first part of the *Teaching on God in the Mode of Wisdom* (*Magisterium divinale et sapientiale*) is William's *The Trinity, or the First Principle* (*De trinitate, seu de primo principio*). References to *The Trinity* will include the pages of the critical

about them. For the great and marvelous works of the creator should not be investigated only for this reason, namely, that they may be known, but rather that he may be exalted and acknowledged to be God and Lord of the ages and that in this way human souls may be persuaded or rather led to the honor of worshiping him. We owe him not merely the knowledge and the recollection of his praises and great works, nor does that by itself perfect our souls. Rather, the truth and purity of the highest degree of veneration is owed to him because of the supereminence of his glory and loftiness, and it is owed to our souls as their noble perfection, and it is also the one ornament and supreme honor of human life.

Elsewhere you have already learned that certain wrongheaded persons among those who philosophize (594a) do not philosophize in this way, and they deceive their souls wretchedly, and they sin against the true philosophy in five ways. First, because they render it vacuous and empty of that which it ought most of all to contain, namely, the glory or glorification of the creator. Second, because they make it unable to bear its fruit, which is the reward of the eternal felicity which is hoped for on the last day. Third, because they make it deformed and truncated, cutting off in this way its end, since its chief beauty and loveliness consists in this end, just as if a peacock, the chief part of whose beauty is found in its tail, had its tail cut off. Fourth, they make it foolish in relation to themselves, since they are made fools rather than truly wise persons by it. As a result of it they live and act foolishly and not wisely. Fifth, they make it injurious and contemptuous toward God, since they most inanely apply it to their own glory, desiring foolishly to receive glory from it and not to glorify the creator with appropriate veneration. I reject such persons, not genuine philosophers, but most ridiculous apes of philosophers, which is what they really are.

The second reason is the destruction of the errors which exist concerning the universe or about the universe—errors by which one is turned from the ways of truth and paths of rectitude through which one comes to this end, namely, the end of true philosophizing. These errors are the sort by which the glory of God is opposed to the point that God is thought to be diminished even by half or not to be perfect in the ultimate degree of perfection or to be unworthy of all gratitude and all honor, as someone who could not do something else or could not act or could not have acted otherwise than he does or who does not care at all what is done somehow or other in human affairs. Those persons also involve themselves in this error who completely denied that his care and providence exists in or is concerned with human affairs. There are other errors which every law opposes, and they are opposed to

---

edition: Bruno Switalski, *William of Auvergne: An Edition of the Latin Text with an Introduction* (Toronto: Pontifical Institute of Mediaeval Studies, 1976) and to the English translation: *William of Auvergne: The Trinity, or the First Principle*, translated by Roland J. Teske, S.J. and Francis C. Wade, S.J. (Milwaukee: Marquette Univ. Press, 1989).

every law,[2] and such misguided persons were not content to diminish in that way the glory of God and to empty out the hope of his worshipers, since they dared to attribute eternity to the universe. And they have tried to be able to support this by proofs. It is clear, then, that my present goal, intention, and desire in this treatise is, if God wills it, to destroy those errors, to reply to these contrary statements of misguided persons, to resolve their questions, and to bolster the opposite truth.

Chapter Two
It is established by arguments that the author of the universe is one, and the error of the Manichees is simultaneously destroyed by metaphysical reasons.

I say, then, that the universe has a unity because of which it is and is called a universe, and that so does the author of it, who is the blessed and sublime God, for he is himself one and he does not have another opposed to him. I will make this clear to you by the paths of proofs, not as it is explained in the first part of first philosophy, but by very easy and almost pedestrian proofs.[3] For the authors and inventors of this error have seduced common folks, that is, people of small intellect and little education. And this is the first error at whose destruction I am aiming in this first chapter.[4] This error had its beginning in the region of Persia, and its author was called Manes;[5] as a result the Christian people call his followers Manichees. This error began almost with the Christian religion,[6] and it was and still is not (594b) only most destruc-

---

[2] Elsewhere, for instance, in *The Laws* (*De legibus*), William speaks of the three laws of the Jewish people, of the Islamic people, and of the Christian people.

[3] It is not clear what William meant by "the first part of first philosophy." Gilson has suggested that he meant the first part of his own *De trinitate*, which is a highly metaphysical discussion of the unity of the first principle. I have, on the other hand, argued that William may well be referring to the first book of Avicenna's *Metaphysics*, since, though the first part of his *De trinitate* might be called "first philosophy," the work as a whole cannot plausibly be so called. See my "William of Auvergne and the Manichees," *Traditio* 48 (1993): 63-75, here 65, note 13. Gugliemo Corti, on the other hand, suggests that William is referring to the whole *De trinitate*; see his "Le sette parti del Magisterium divinale ac sapientiale di Guglielmo di Auvergne," in *Studi e Ricerche di Scienze Religiose* (Rome: Lateran Univ., 1968), p. 302, note 67.

[4] William uses "small chapter: *capitulum*," though it seems that he is referring to what some later editor has called a treatise as opposed to a chapter. According to the labeling of the later editor, the first treatise (*tractatus*) includes chapters (*capita*) one through ten.

[5] In *Heresies* (*De haeresibus*), a catalogue of heresies known to him, Augustine provides a brief sketch of Manichaeism in paragraph 65; he mentions that, because "Manis" in Greek meant "madness," the followers of Mani changed his name to Manichaeus.

tive, but also most pestilential, and for this reason [the Christian religion] does not cease to pursue it with sword and fire and to exterminate it right up to today.[7] The Hebrew people and the Saracen people would do no less, if they were found among them. This seducer and liar, then, asserted that there are two principles and that there are two gods, and he called the one the god of light and the good god, but the other the god of darkness and the evil god. Thus he maintained two universes, two kingdoms, and two nations, and he called them in accord with the previously mentioned names the nation of light and the nation of darkness, the kingdom of light and the kingdom of darkness. He also divided the [separate] substances in this way, and he said that those whom the Greeks call good demons, but the Latins call good angels, come from the good god and were created by the prince of light and are his ministers. But he claimed that those the Greeks call evil demons, but the Latins call the bad angels or devils, were created by the prince of darkness or the evil god and are his ministers most ready and eager for everything evil. And he maintained an opposition and a war that was not only everlasting, but eternal between these principles, and between these kingdoms and nations. There are other mad ideas and amazing claims they make, and also many branches of this error, which it is not part of my intention to pursue at the moment.

Chapter Three
The roots of the error of the Manichees are
extirpated by metaphysical arguments.

First of all, we have to argue against the root and radical foundation of this error.[8] I say, then, that, since these misguided people assert two coeval and eternal principles, they must as a result maintain that each of them is being necessary (*necesse esse*) through itself and, for this reason, simple in the ultimate degree of simplicity.[9] For, if either one of them were in some way com-

6   William is correct on the place of origin for Manichaeism, but Mani, its founder, lived in the third century and died in either 270 or 276. For a brief introduction to Manichaeism, see Pheme Perkins, "Mani, Manichaeism," in the *Encyclopedia of Early Christianity*, ed. E. Ferguson (New York: Garland, 1990), pp. 562-563. For the Manichaeans of William's day, namely, the Albigensians or Cathars, see Bernard Hamilton, *The Albigensian Crusade* (London: The Historical Association, 1974) or Jacques Madaule, *The Albigensian Crusade: An Historical Essay*, trans. Barbara Wall (New York: Fordham Univ. Press, 1967).

7   William thinks of the Cathars or Albigensians of his own day as Manichees, though there is no certainty about the connection between the later dualism of William's century and the Manichees of Augustine's era.

8   William frequently uses "root (*radix*)" for a fundamental principle from which a position develops. The expression is common in Avicebron's *Font of Life* (*Fons vitae*).

9   William uses "being necessary through itself: *necesse esse per se*"—Avicenna's designation for the First or God. All things other than God are, if they exist, beings

posite, it would of necessity be divisible into parts (*partibile*) and, for this reason, would have parts in some sense. Hence, neither of them would be a principle without qualification, since each of them would have many elements prior to itself, namely, its parts or its components. For all parts and all components are prior to the whole which they compose.

Moreover,[10] on this account, neither of them would be being necessary through itself; in fact, each would be being possible through itself, since each of them would be caused by these parts composing its totality. After all, everything[11] composite in any way is caused in some way by its parts of which its totality consists, and it is the work of the composer who unites or brings together the parts and makes them into a totality. It has already been explained in the first part of first philosophy that every effect of this sort is possible through itself and is receptive of being (*esse*) upon itself which is other than itself and, for this reason, is in it potentially or by way of possibility, because it is an accident of it, that is, something that comes to it and is received by it upon its whole complete essence.[12] For all being which is given to an effect by a cause is separable from it at least by the intellect, and everything received [is separable] from its receiver, and in general since all being (*esse*) is other than its being (*ente*), it is separable from it in the way we said.[13] But everything whose being is separable from it has it only by way of possibility or potentially, and thus it does not have it with that necessity by which something is said to be necessary through itself. It is clear, then, that neither of these two principles is being necessary through itself.

Moreover, if each is being necessary through itself, each will be simple in the ultimate degree of simplicity. In neither, then, will there be something (595a) present essentially which is not the principle itself. Since, then, goodness and evil are present in them essentially, one of them will of necessity be its own evil. "Necessary through itself," then, will be said of both of them

---

necessary through another, but merely possible through themselves. See *The Trinity, or the First Principle* (*De trinitate*), ch. 6: Switalski, pp. 39- 40; Teske-Wade , pp. 83-84, for William's argument from the possibility of the universe to a being necessary through itself.

10   William introduces each of a series of arguments with the single word, "*Amplius*: moreover." I have retained it since it reflects his style, even though the repetition is tedious.

11   The Latin has: *omnino*, for which I have read *omne*.

12   See William's *The Trinity, or the First Principle* (*De trinitate*), chs. 5 and 6: Switalski, pp. 34-43; Teske-Wade, pp. 79-87.

13   William here anticipates the real distinction between being and essence in creatures that is more clearly found in the metaphysics of St. Thomas Aquinas. For the most recent discussion of this question, see Kevin J. Caster, "The Distinction between Being and Essence according to Boethius, Avicenna, and William of Auvergne," *Modern Schoolman* 73 (1996): 309-332, as well as Caster's *The Real Distinction in Creatures between Being and Essence according to William of Auvergne* (Marquette University dissertation, 1994).

either univocally or equivocally. But if it is said of both univocally, whatever the one has by reason of the fact that it is being necessary through itself or through its essence the other will have as well. Hence, if one has goodness by reason of the fact that it is being necessary through itself, the other will likewise have it. And with regard to evil it must of necessity be the same way. Hence, either both of them will be essentially good, or both of them will be essentially evil, or both of them will be both good and evil at the same time.

Moreover, if "being necessary through itself" is said of them univocally, it has been previously explained to you that being necessary through itself can in no way be common;[14] in fact, it is necessary that being itself be one in the ultimate degree of unity and in the ultimate degree of individuality, which can only be numerical oneness. In no way, then, will those two contraries share in it.

But if someone says that it is said equivocally of them, the error of that person is obvious, since "necessary" is derived only from "non-ceasing." After all, being necessary through itself is by the truest explanation that which does not cease to be, and this belongs to it through itself, that is, not from something else. But this means that its being is continuous, not having any interval or interruption in its being, and this belongs to it through itself, not from something else, that is, its continuity of being or of enduring. With regard to necessity, then, "necessary through itself" is not said of them equivocally, nor is it said in that way with regard to its being through itself. After all, if "through itself" conveys only a negation so that its meaning is this, namely, "not from something else," it is obvious that this negation is said of both with one meaning. But if its meaning is firmness of being, as it seems to fall in the meaning of substance or in accord with that mode, I say that it is said of them in this way only univocally. For each of them is in one meaning firm in its being, since neither of them is dependent upon another or slipping away or flowing off into corruption or into non-being. But since being itself is said of each of them only essentially, the intellect does not admit the idea that it is said of them equivocally, nor is it possible for the human intellect, however perverted and sick, to imagine or dream of equivocation in this case, unless it should choose to utter these ravings, namely, that what is said of the one to signify goodness is likewise said of the other to signify evil, as if being and good are interchangeable in one case, and being and evil are likewise interchangeable in the other.

But I shall explain for you the previous proofs, before I begin to destroy this error. For it is obvious through itself that whatever is in Socrates by reason of the fact that he is a man is also present in any other individual of the same species. Hence, whatever is present in the evil principle by reason of the fact that it is being necessary through itself is also present in the good principle for

---

14 See William's *The Trinity, or the First Principle* (*De trinitate*), ch. 4: Switalski, pp. 27-28; Teske- Wade, pp. 74-75, where William says that being cannot be common and essential or it would be a genus, a species, or a difference and that it cannot be common and accidental or it would be caused.

the same reason, if "being necessary through itself" is commonly and univocally said of both of them, as "man" is said of Socrates and other individuals of the same species. Hence, if one of them is evil by reason of the fact that it is being necessary through itself, the other will be evil for the same reason; the same thing holds with the good. Hence, each of them will be good and evil. But if being necessary through itself is singular or proper and individual, the same thing happens and in the same way. Just as, if something white is said to be a man by reason of the fact that it is Socrates, something medical will also be a man for the same reason. I have now explained for you the certitude of these proofs.

(595b)

Chapter Four
The error of the Manichees is destroyed in another way if being
is said equivocally of the two principles which they assert.

I shall return, then, in accord with my promise, to destroy this most foolish error because of which this wrongheaded fellow raves so madly, namely, that "being" is said of each of the previously mentioned principles equivocally, and in one meaning being (*entitas*) is nothing other than goodness, but in the other meaning being is nothing other than evil itself. I say, then, that, since he maintains that goodness and evil are contraries by true contrariety, it is necessary that he assign them a common genus. But if being, which is itself undoubtedly the most common of all, is not common to them, for even better reason nothing else will be common to them.

Moreover, since contraries naturally have both their being and their coming to be with respect to the same thing, if goodness and evil are contraries in the genuine sense, they will be and will come to be with respect to the same subject. I mean: a subject the same in genus, as white and black with respect to a surface, or healthy and sick with respect to the body of an animal, or a subject the same in species, as healthy and sick with respect to the same person or with respect to a subject numerically the same. Of necessity, then, goodness and evil share some genus.

Moreover, it is evident through itself that each of them shares in the definition of substance, insofar as substance is taken in its general meaning so that it is said of everything which stands with its own firmness so that it does not need a support or sustaining subject in the way in which an accident is said to need a subject. But if they share in the definition of substance, they, therefore, share in both substance and its name.

Moreover, on this account there will be no discourse between other human beings and these wrongheaded people, because they understand all words with different meanings and intentions than other human beings. For if they equivocally use or rather abuse the term "being," they will equivocate about other things with the same error; hence, they will impose meanings and intentions upon them which the intellects of other human beings neither accept nor understand.

Moreover, they will not avoid having "contrary" and "contrariety" said in common of each of those principles, and they will not avoid having "contrary" come under "being," since one of the beings is contrary to another and another to nothing. But of contraries none is non-being, and none is contrary to non-being. Since "contrary" is said in common of these, but being is superior to that which is a contrary, it is evident that "being" is said of them in common.

Moreover, "one" is of necessity said of them in common; otherwise, they would neither truly be said to be two nor be two, unless each of them were one.

Moreover, what is the definition or meaning of "one" but "undivided in itself and divided from all other things by a division which is appropriate to it"? But no one doubts that this definition belongs to each of them.

Moreover, they would not be and could not be said to be two principles or two gods, unless "principle" and "god" were said of them univocally, just as the animal that walks on the earth and a fish cannot be truly be called two dogs. For, once a name has been set, that is, with one determination, the human intellect cannot use it equivocally because it cannot actually understand at the same time diverse things. But as it is false to say that these two living things are two dogs, so they falsely claim that they are either two principles or two gods, if "god" and "principle" are used equivocally of them.

Moreover, how will everything else be univocally said of them, if "being" and "being necessary through itself" alone are said of equivocally of them? For "king" is said univocally of both of them; so is "prince"; so is "kingdom" (596a) and "principality" said of their kingdoms and principalities. So too, "nation" is said of the nation of light and of the nation of darkness. So too, "angel" is said of the good angels and of the bad angels. In the same way "substance" is said of the good substances and of the bad substances. It is necessary, then, that all those supreme terms, namely, "god" and "lord" and "being necessary through itself" be said of them univocally. But if that is so, it is evident to you that whatever we said above that they maintained is impossible, since being necessary through itself is not divided in any way nor is it common by some kind of sharing with a multitude which is many essentially, that is, which is numerically plural.[15]

Moreover, being through itself is either purely good or purely evil or neither so that it is entirely free from goodness and evil. Since it is indivisible in every way and simple in the ultimate degree of simplicity, it cannot be a mixture of good and evil, since every mixture is potentially composed of those things of which it is a mixture, just as honey-vinegar is a mixture of honey and vinegar, since every mixture is naturally posterior to each of those things from which it is mixed. It remains, then, that being necessary through itself be in one of those three ways which I mentioned to you, namely, that it be either purely good or purely evil or completely apart from good and evil. But

---

[15] William uses the Latin expression: "*hoc et hoc*," which I have translated as: numerically plural.

if it were purely good, neither of those two previously mentioned principles would, then, be purely evil or even essentially evil, since the being of each would be purely good. In the same way it is evident that, if it were purely evil, it is necessary that neither of those two mentioned principles is purely good. For since each of them is in itself and essentially being necessary through itself, each of them will necessarily be purely evil, since being necessary in itself is purely evil. But if being necessary through itself is in itself apart from goodness and evil, each of them will necessarily be by their whole being apart from good and evil, since being necessary through itself is the whole being of each of them.

Moreover, since each of them exists simply in the ultimate degree of simplicity and in no sense has many parts, it is evident that neither of them has something essential apart from being itself, both that which it is and that by which it is.[16] Hence, since they share univocally being necessary through itself, the one has nothing essential that the other does not have. If then goodness is essential to the one, it will of necessity be essential to both of them, and it is the same way with evil. Both of them, then, will of necessity be essentially good and essentially evil. It is, therefore, impossible that one be essentially good and that the other be essentially evil.

Moreover, it is evident that being does not have a contrary or opposite except non-being or one of those things which leads to non-being which is rather a mid-point between being and non-being than a contrary to being. Such things are dying, failing, being corrupted, and the like, each of which is a path to non-being and an intervening stage through which one comes to it. But you have already learned that the extreme is more worthy of the name "contrary" than one of those in-between stages, and that true contrariety exists only between extremes, because contrariety in the truest meaning and in the purest sense is complete difference and, for this reason, the greatest difference. It is, then, evident for you in this way that full and perfect being does not have a contrary except complete non-being, that is, that with which there is absolutely nothing of being. It follows, then, from this that, since the principle of the good is perfect being in the ultimate degree of perfection in itself and by itself, it does not have a contrary except non-being deprived of being in the ultimate degree of deprivation. I understand "deprived" as that which has absolutely nothing of being left. Those in-between states which (596b) we mentioned are not deprived in that way, that is, by a complete deprivation of being, nor completely diminished by a complete diminution of the same. For a complete diminution is utter destruction. It is evident, then, that the

---

[16] William was familiar with Boethius' distinction between "that which is (*quod est*)" and "being (*esse*)"; see his *De hebdomadibus* in *The Theological Treatises*, ed. by H. F. Stewart and E. K. Rand (Cambridge, MA: Harvard Univ. Press, 1946), pp. 40-43. This distinction between "being" and "that which is" is found in every creature, while in the being necessary through itself that which it is and its being are identical.

prince of darkness, according to the madness of these wrongheaded people, is truly and absolutely non-being, that is, having absolutely no being, since they set it opposite to Him Who Is,[17] and he is, also according to them, in the fullness and ultimate degree of difference from being or from a being. But if he says that he is not so far removed from being, namely, by a complete difference or by the greatest difference, but only approximates it, he will, then, be an intermediate state toward it. Hence, he will be either failing or dying or undergoing corruption or something of the sort. From each of them it is evident that he is in no way to be called either a god or a principle or a prince, since his being is feeble and weak so that he hastens toward non-being, inasmuch as he has been placed on the road to it.

Chapter Five
The destruction of the error of the Manichees, if the evil of the prince of darkness is said to be to kill.

It has already been shown to you that evil cannot be essential to him, because he is being necessary through itself and because those who maintain the principle of evil opposite and contrary to the principle of good must necessarily maintain that he is being necessary through itself. But now I shall explain to you that evil cannot be adventitious or accidental to him. I say, therefore, that, if evil is adventitious to him, it will come to him either from himself or from another. But if it would be from himself, that is, acquired by him through himself, this will necessarily be in one of the ways which I shall state, namely, it will naturally come to be in him, as rot and other such changes naturally come to be in certain things, or it will be in him as a result of his own action by which he acts upon himself or upon something else, or it will be impressed upon him by something else acting upon him. But if it naturally came to be in him, since in his being he is only good, and his entity is only goodness, there will necessarily be evil in him as a result of this good, and evil will be a result of goodness, and this will occur naturally and by itself, since evil does not come to him from another source, that is, through something else.

Moreover, on this view he begot evil in himself; hence, he begot in himself evil out of good and out of his own goodness—and did so through himself. But it is evident that neither of two contraries naturally and through itself proceeds from the other.

Moreover, the evil is contrary to his essential and natural goodness, or it is not. If it is contrary to it, then it does not exist in the same thing along with

---

[17] William alludes to Exodus 3:14 where God tells Moses that his name is: "I am who I am" or "He Who Is." See *The Trinity, or The First Principle* (*De trinitate*), ch. 4: Switalski, p. 34; Teske-Wade, p. 78, where William cites a string of similar scriptural passages and adds, "Being expresses his essence to such a degree that by it he wanted to make himself known to the sons of Israel. With knowledge of that alone, everything is known that can be said of his essence."

it, nor does it tolerate its presence with itself. Therefore, evil does not exist in him, and it cannot exist in him, since goodness is essential to and inseparable from him. But if someone says that it is not contrary, it is, then, not evil in the genuine sense; hence, nothing truly evil will come from it or through it.

Moreover, on this view it will not be contrary to the goodness of the other principle, namely, the one which is the principle of good, for they of necessity share essential goodness, just as [they share] being itself from which each of them has its essential goodness.

Moreover, such evil is either in some way opposed to his essential goodness, or not. If one says that it is in some way opposed to it, I ask once again: Is it opposed to its essence or not? But if it is opposed to its essence, it does not tolerate that essence. If it is stronger than it, it has, therefore, already destroyed it. But if its essence is less strong than the evil, it has already been destroyed by that (597a) evil. And if they are equally strong, the one, then, impedes the other and does not allow something to come from it. Hence, no evil will come from it. If no evil comes from it, it will be either good or something in between good and evil. But if it is not opposed to its essence in itself, but is opposed to it in its acts or effects, this can take place only in one of two ways which I shall mention. The first of these is that it impedes it so that it does not act at all, and then the principle of evil does nothing or will be unable to do anything through its essence. And in that way it will be utterly impotent in its essence. The second way is that it impedes it from acting, as much as it wills or in the way it wills, as much as it ought or in the way it ought, and from this another impotence and wretchedness of it is seen, namely, it cannot do as much as it wills or in the way it wills, nor can it do as much as it ought or do it in the way it ought.

Moreover, [the good principle] either undergoes this wretchedness voluntarily or involuntarily. If voluntarily, it is not naturally opposed to his essence, since he sees this most clearly and suffers no darkness in terms of ignorance. For there is nothing at all that may bring harm to its own essence; if it knows or sees it, it also suffers it voluntarily. But if he does not undergo this wretchedness voluntarily, but involuntarily suffers or endures his own evil, the impotence of his wretchedness is obvious, since he wants to repel his own evil and cannot exclude it from himself. From this one sees that he is a slave to his own evil and does evil under its coercion, as if he were oppressed by servitude to his own evil and cannot cast off or shake the yoke of this servitude from himself.

Moreover, this evil is either coeternal with him or comes to him in time. But if it is coeternal with him, since it is something other than he, it will be created or made by him and be his creature or product. Hence, it will be entirely subject to his will and unable to do anything at all contrary to him. Hence, it will only exist as long as he wills and when he wills. It does not, then, exist in him save through his will, and he can alone destroy it, as he can destroy all his other products. Since, then, his evil harms him, making him worse than he would be without it, he will not tolerate it in himself even for a moment of time.

Moreover, if he took thought when he created evil in himself, he either intended to benefit himself or to injure and harm himself by doing this. If he intended to benefit himself, his error is obvious; in fact, it is clearly a blindness, since it cannot be doubted that evil harms the one in whom it is. But error is in no sense found in God; likewise, ignorance is not found there. But these mistaken people claim that he is God. But if he intended to harm and injure himself, and did this with knowledge and foresight, since error and ignorance, as I said, have no place in him, his madness is clearly evident. For there is nothing that knowingly intends to harm or injure itself unless the upheaval of anger or of some other passion has overthrown it, as happens in those who at times strangle themselves or otherwise kill themselves. In their case it is beyond doubt that they do this out of madness. But if evil comes upon him in time, it is evident that he was corrupted and perverted and seduced. For when something becomes evil, though it was not such previously, this happens in one of the three ways I mentioned, namely, by corruption, as a horse becomes bad by a corruption of a humor or of some member, though he was not bad previously, or by perversity, as happens in human beings who become bad, when their wills are perverted so that they will evil things or in an evil way, or by seduction, as happens in those who become bad by error or ignorance, when misled by the suggestion of another. How, then, has this man dreamt that God became evil? For whichever of these three he suffered, it is evident that he is most unworthy of the name "God," for none of these can befall God in the true sense.

Moreover, change is not produced (597b) except in a substance which underlies the predicaments. Every accident is also found in it; hence, neither an accident nor change touch that which is being necessary through itself. For being necessary through itself is above and far apart from substance and accident.

Moreover, how was he changed? By himself or by another? From this you see many ways to destroy these errors. If it is by another acting upon him, it is necessary that he be passive, and that he be passive in the worst and most shameful way. For nothing is worse or more shameful than malice. One who does not see how far this is from the nature and, even more, from the nobility and supereminence of the deity or divinity sees nothing at all.

Chapter Six
The error of the Manichees is here further destroyed
through common arguments that are easy to understand.

But since the arguments which I have introduced for you thus far are metaphysical and in the mode of wisdom, I shall satisfy you in accord with my promise and introduce commonplace proofs that are easy to understand. Through these there will not be explained to you so much the impossibility of this error as its absurdity. I shall say, first of all, that evil in the proper sense is either injurious, as a bad plant or bad disease, or is harm itself. In accord with this meaning one often says: this man did me much evil. In a third way it means: something disordered, as certain things are said to be poorly situated which are not found in their place or order, as greenness on a human face. In a fourth sense evil is said to be something imperfect, that is, something deprived of its own perfection as a result of which one is said to act badly, when one does acts deprived of their appropriate perfections, and the Latins call these perfections the circumstances of actions, such as the end, the cause, the manner, the place, the time. And in this way one is said to act badly who does not act in the manner or with the end in which or for which one should act. It is the same with the other perfections or circumstances. The privation of the due measure or quantity can be reduced to this meaning; in this way too much or too little are called evils. Superfluity and lack are evils. Perhaps Aristotle meant to teach this in his Book of Topics where he says that a good amount is said to lie as in the mean, that is, in the middle point which is between the two extremes of superfluity and lack, and someone is said to have made something well on this view when his work has neither too much nor too little.[18] Of all these meanings the one most appropriate for the principle of evil is that first, in accord with which evil is said to be what is harmful.

I shall begin, therefore, with the help of God, to destroy this meaning insofar as they claim and imagine in their dreams the principle of the evil. I say, therefore, that, if the principle of the evil is not harmful, it is not evil in this way. But if it is harmful, it will be harmful without qualification and universally, or it will be harmful in particular to something. But if it is harmful without qualification and universally, it will, then, be helpful to nothing; it will, therefore, do good to nothing. How then will it be the giver of being and of life to the whole kingdom of darkness, in fact, to the whole universe of the evil? For, according to this error, he is the creator of the universe and giver of all wisdom and virtue and power which the evil spirits and other evil substances have.

Moreover, when he gives them all these things, he gives them those things either with the mind or intention of harming them, or he gives them with the mind and intention that he knows that they are good or useful or necessary for them or with the mind of harming other things in this way. But if he gives them with a mind to harm (598a) them, it is evident that he is mistaken when he believes that he harms those to whom he gives such virtues or powers, such wisdom, such arts, and being itself which is the most necessary of them all. But if he gives them all these things with the purpose of aiding or helping them, it is evident that he is beneficial and highly useful to his whole kingdom both in intention and in fact. He is not, therefore, harmful without qualification and universally. But if he gives all these things to his own with the intent of harming something else or some other things, he is, then, harmful to these others as much as he can be and to them alone, since he is clearly

---

[18] The reference to Aristotle would seem to be to *Nicomachean Ethics* II, c. 6, 1106a28-1106b16. The Latin then should probably read: *Ethicorum* instead of *Topicorum*.

beneficial to his own. Hence, he is, according to this meaning, evil for those others alone. Hence, according to this meaning he is not different from nor more evil than the principle of the good, since the principle of the good is harmful and hostile to the evil and destructive of them.

Moreover, either his intention is to destroy or to occupy the kingdom of the good or it is only to defend his own. But if his intention is to destroy and to occupy that other kingdom, he cannot do so, because the king of the good is not less powerful than he, nor is the former's kingdom weaker than the latter's. Hence, it is evident that he is wretched in the ultimate degree of wretchedness, first, because he toils with an insatiable burning of greed when he desires to acquire another's kingdom which he cannot acquire. Second, because he burns inextinguishably with hatred and envy and also with anger, since he unwillingly made the prince of the good a most hostile enemy to himself, and he does not succeed in attacking or taking him. But anger and envy and hatred and avarice belong to him in the ultimate degree, and in general whatever things are said of him are essentially in him as primordial and greatest. Because, then, these are miseries and troubles and even spiritual tortures, it is necessary that he be miserable in the ultimate degree of misery and tortured in the ultimate degree of tortures. But if he says that these things are said of him only in terms of his effects, as Christians say that the prince of the good is angry, not in terms of a turbulence of his dispositions, but in terms of the effect of his punishment,[19] it follows then that he is of necessity free and immune from anger and hatred and envy and all bad will and most quiet and peaceful in himself and that he has no misery at all in himself or within himself, but that he is called evil only by reason of his effects. But this is easily destroyed in many ways, and the first is that, if he is evil only by reason of his effects, he will not be contrary to the prince of the good, since the prince of the good is not good only in terms of his effects, but also in his essence.

Secondly, just as the prince of the good is simply the best both essentially and in terms of his effects, so it is necessary that the prince of the evil be the worst in each of these ways. Hence, he will be evil not merely by reason of his effects, but he will be evil essentially so that his very being is his malice, just as it is the case in the prince of the good that his entity is his very goodness.

Moreover, the war which they posit between him and the prince of the good and between his kingdom and the kingdom of the good is either just or not. But if it is just on his part, he, therefore, justly attacks the prince of the good and his kingdom, and hence he acts well. The prince of the good ought also to surrender to him and not resist. Hence, the prince of the good is unjust in opposing and resisting him. But if the war is unjust, it has an unjust

[19]   See William's *The Trinity, or the First Principle* (*De trinitate*), ch. 44: Switalski, p. 249; Teske-Wade, p. 261, where William says, "For Augustine says in *The Trinity* that God is said to be angry, not because of affective turmoil, but because of the effective vengeance," though there is no exact source for the citation in the *De trinitate* of St. Augustine.

cause. But this cause is only contrariety or is one of the causes mentioned, namely, ambition or avarice or hatred or envy or anger. But if only contrariety is the cause of the war, such contrariety cannot be injustice of itself insofar as it is contrariety. For (598b) then there would be injustice on both sides and iniquity as well, since there is contrariety equally on the side of the prince of the good with respect to him, and the other way around.

Besides, evil is most often found contrary to evil, even in sensible things which they claim are creatures or products of the prince of the evil, as heat and cold are related, as well as many other things of this sort. Hence, a war between such opponents would be unjust, and unjust from both sides. For since all contraries in the genuine sense are equal by the right and law of nature, it is unjust and wrong that one rule over or be above the other.

Moreover, if the prince of the evil stands to everything which has evil or is evil, just as the prince of the good stands to everything which has goodness or is good, it will follow of necessity that, just as justice, piety, benevolence, beneficence, and other things of this sort are said of the prince of the good first of all and most of all, so the contraries to these things we mentioned will be said of the prince of the evil first of all and most of all. Hence, just as the prince of the good is just first of all and most of all and so on with the rest, so the prince of the evil will be unjust first of all and most of all, and impious first of all and most of all, and malevolent first of all and most of all, and maleficent first of all and most of all, that is, most maleficent. But it is quite easy to destroy each one of these points concerning him, as it is clear to see with injustice itself. For the laws by which he rules his kingdom are either such as they should be in that kingdom or not. If they are such as they should be in that kingdom, he did not, then, give laws to his subjects save laws such as he ought to have given, and thus he did not command or decree in his kingdom anything but what he ought to have. But what he ought to have decreed ought to be observed by his subjects. But what ought to be observed it is just to observe, and everything which it is just to observe is just. Hence, he did not decree or command[20] anything but what it was just that he command or decree and that his subjects observe. From that side, therefore, he is in no way unjust.

Moreover, either he ought to do only that which is evil or he ought not. If he ought, then, by doing evil, he only does what he ought to do, but by doing what he ought to do, he is not unjust. In fact, he is just and good. In the same way it is possible to explain with regard to judgments that, if he ought to judge only unjustly, he will be just by judging unjustly. Hence, in no way will he be unjust, that is, neither by acting unjustly nor by judging unjustly, nor by decreeing or commanding what is unjust.

But if someone says that he ought to produce good, this is destroyed in many ways: first, because he is prevented by natural possibility from produc-

---

[20] The Latin has "aut praecipit, iniqua" here which I omitted because I could not construe it to make sense.

ing good, as the opponent admits. No one has within himself as an obligation any of those things which are in themselves impossible. For, just because it is good to be a man, it does not follow that an ass ought to be a man, since this is impossible for it.

Moreover, the principle or prince of the good stands related to good things proportionally, that is, similarly to the way this latter [i.e., the prince of evil] stands to evil things, and inversely, as the former stands to evil things, so the latter stands to good things. Hence, as the former ought not to produce evils, and it is not fitting for him and cannot be fitting for him, so the latter ought never to produce good things. And as the former does what is fitting for him and pertains to him by doing good, so the latter does [what is fitting for him] by producing evil. Hence, if it is true that to act well is to do what pertains to one and what is fitting for one, and the prince of the good always acts well in this way, then the prince of the evil always acts well by producing evil.

Moreover, as all the laws and statutes of the prince of the good have to do with producing good and avoiding evil, so the laws and statutes of the prince of the evil will, on the contrary, have to do with producing evil and avoiding good. As the former has the authority to establish those things in his kingdom, so the latter (599a) has the right and power to establish the opposite in his kingdom. And just as the former must be obeyed by his subjects in his kingdom, so the latter must be obeyed in his kingdom. Hence, it is evident that the laws of these two kingdoms are contrary, and when something is right in one of them, its contrary is right in the other. Hence, it is evident that each kingdom is governed by just laws and statutes and is, therefore, well and decently administered by its prince. Hence, each of them is a good administrator of his kingdom to this extent, and each of them is good in doing good to all those who are in his kingdom, that is, by giving to them being and other things which are good for them, that is, necessary and useful things. Hence, those two princes are equally good both in doing good for their own and in administering and governing those things which are subject to them. Moreover, in the same way they are equally bad, that is, harmful, since neither of them is harmful except to his contrary or to what is in part contrary to him. The situation is the same with their kingdoms.

Moreover, since these wrongheaded people maintain virtues and the contrary vices [are possessed] by the princes opposed in this way and that the prince of the evil is related in the same way to vices as the prince of the good is related to virtues, it will follow, then, that as all virtues are said first of all and most of all of the prince of the good in the way it is fitting for him, so all vices will be said of the prince of the evil in the same way. Hence, as the former is virtuous in the ultimate degree of virtuousness, so the latter is vicious in the ultimate degree of viciousness. Hence, he is laboring under every disease of vices in the ultimate degree; hence, he is laboring under falsity and infidelity; therefore, he keeps faith or truth with none of his own. So too, he does not preserve friendship with them; hence, he hates all his own and persecutes them and has peace with none of them. Hence, he implacably persecutes all his own. Since he has, then, every sort of power over them, he destroys them all; hence, he allows none of his own to be or to live. In the same way, if the prince of the good hated someone of those he made, he would immediately destroy him.

But if he says that [the prince of the evil] keeps faith, friendship, and truth toward his own and his own kingdom, but preserves none of these toward his enemies and opponents, it is evident that this is neither falsity nor infidelity, nor vicious hatred, since all these are found in their own way in the prince of the good. For he does not keep friendship or faith toward the evil; in fact, he implacably persecutes them, but maintains the truth of justice toward them by which he punishes them and takes vengeance, but not that truth which a treaty and friendship require.

Moreover, it is necessary that the prince of the evil be most wise; he knows, therefore, both what he does and how he does it in all things and in every respect. He knows, therefore, that he acts in an evil manner when he acts in an evil manner, if he ever acts in an evil manner. With knowledge and prudence, then, he acts in an evil manner, as often as he acts in an evil manner. Either, therefore, he can restrain himself so that he does not act in an evil manner, or he cannot. If he cannot, his acting in an evil manner is not voluntary, but necessary, especially since this inability is natural to him. But there is no sin that is not voluntary. I mean: a sin of action. Hence, he does not sin in that which he does in such a manner; he never, therefore, acts in an evil manner since he never sins. But if he can restrain himself from acting in an evil manner, and he yet acts in an evil manner, how is he wise?

Moreover, just as wisdom and virtue go together in a necessary combination, so foolishness or stupidity and vice go together with each other. When a vicious person is in the ultimate degree of viciousness, he will be stupid and foolish in the ultimate degree of stupidity and foolishness.

Moreover, if it is true that vices darken those in whom they exist and make them stupid and foolish, just as virtues, on the contrary, illumine and make prudent and wise those in whom they exist, since the prince of the evil has the vices in the ultimate degree and most of all, (599b) he will of necessity be darkened in the ultimate degree of darkness and will be stupid and foolish in the ultimate degree of stupidity and foolishness.

Moreover, as the prince of light is bright in the ultimate degree of brightness, so the dark prince will be dark in the ultimate degree of darkness. For as the former stands in relation to light, the latter stands in relation to darkness in every way. Just as the former is bright in the ultimate degree of spiritual brightness, so the latter is dark in the ultimate degree of spiritual darkness. For, just as temporal brightness has no place in the prince of light, since he is incorporeal in the ultimate degree of incorporeality, so bodily darkness has no place in the prince of darkness. Nor is it necessary for you that I remove corporeality from each of them, since it cannot be doubted that being necessary through itself is far removed from corporeality, inasmuch as it is simple in the ultimate degree of simplicity, since everything bodily is divisible into parts to infinity and gathered together from various parts, in fact from parts which have no number, and is composed of matter and form. The prince of darkness, then, is darkened by a spiritual darkening beyond which there is no darkening. But this is ignorance, just as knowledge is light. Hence, he is ignorant of everything and knows absolutely nothing.

Moreover, it is evident with regard to the vices that, when they grow very strong, they are not merely vices, but insanities, just as anger becomes fury because of its strength. The situation is the same with love. Hence, since all the vices are in the prince of darkness in the ultimate degree of strength and intensity, it is necessary that he be furious and insane in the ultimate degree of furiosity and insanity. But that is to say that he is most furious and most insane. Hence, he does not spare his own or others, but he necessarily kills and destroys them indiscriminately and rages indiscriminately against all and against himself. So it must also be with his nation. Hence, in his nation there is universal war both civil and internal; hence, his kingdom destroys itself. In fact, it has already destroyed itself, since a multitude of the insane raging against themselves cannot stand even for a short while. How, then, has his kingdom stood for infinite thousands of years? For, according to these people, it does not have a beginning, or if it has a beginning, thousands of thousands of years have passed since its foundation.

Chapter Seven
The destruction of the error of the Manichees, if they hold that
the principle of evil is bodily and its kingdoms are dark with bodily obscurity.

Because such wrongheaded persons are deceived to the point that they hold that this prince is bodily and his whole kingdom is dark with bodily darkness, it is good to argue against them even on this point in accord with their folly. I ask them, therefore, whether darkness of this sort impedes vision, because if it impedes vision completely, he and his whole people in his kingdom are, therefore, blind and see nothing, unless he says that he and his people are like owls, night birds, bats, and the like among us, which see in the dark, but are blind in the light. These people, then, claim that this whole nation is bodily; for bodily light and darkness neither helps nor hinders spiritual substances for spiritual vision, that is, for understanding. On this view he and his nation will see nothing by day, and on this account he will not be able to resist the prince of light and his people by day, if the prince of light and his army are able to enter his kingdom. But if one says that, if the king of light should enter the kingdom (600a) of darkness, he will there become dark, their error is evident on this point. For light entering darkness expels the darkness and illumines the place however dark it may be, nor is it possible for the darkness to repel the light, because even a small lamp overcomes great darkness, illumining a great house. Hence, the darkness of that kingdom cannot prevent or even hold back the prince of light and his nation from entering their region and illumining the darkness. Hence, the prince of darkness and his whole nation will be blinded in that way, and so they will lie exposed to the sword and plunder and destruction by the prince of light and his nation.

Moreover, on this view our region will belong neither to the light nor to the darkness, since during the day it will belong to the light and at night it will belong to the darkness. To which of these princes and to whose kingdom will it belong? But if he says that the darkness is so dense in that kingdom that it is in no way pervious to or penetrable by the light, it is evident that such a person does not understand what "dark" means. For "dark" is used in only three meanings which I shall state. The first is the privation of light, as is apparent in night and day. For night cannot be understood save as the privation of the light of the sun which the interposition of the earth causes. The air, after all, does not take on a new disposition as a result of the sun's departure which can be called darkness. The explanation of this is that, if we understand that the brightness of the sun departs from the air and no other disposition comes to it, it will, nonetheless, be dark and night, and nothing will be seen in that region from which the earth excludes and hides the brightness of the sun. For if darkness were a disposition contrary to the brightness or light in the air, since contraries are necessarily equal in power, it would necessarily resist it and become a mixture or something in between light and darkness in the air, and in that way day would not be day, but rather a mixture of day and of night. And in that way it would turn out that there would be no night and no day in the true sense.

The second meaning is that a dense body which by its density resists the light is called dark, such as the earth, clouds, or fog. The reason for this, however, is that, as often as one of two opposites is mentioned, it is necessary that the other be mentioned. Hence, if light is said to be a body, such as the sun or a flame, the body opposed to it will also be said to be dark. If, then, one says that the kingdom of darkness is a region of blackest fog or of the most cloudy earth, he necessarily has to admit what I said above, that is, that nothing can see or be seen there, except as I explained above, namely, that animals of that kingdom are night animals, such as owls, night birds, and bats. But our opponent will not escape in that way either, because such darkness, that is, a body of such darkness is either unable to be affected by any contrary or it is not. But if it is unable to be affected, then, neither motion nor division can be produced in it. From this there also result countless aberrations and problems. The first is that, since it is a body, it will be either simple or a mixture. And if it is simple, it does not have such density, since neither flame nor fog nor cloud nor smoke is a simple body. But air admits a purification from such fog and density, as from clouds and mists. Hence, it happens that a purification is produced there, or it is possible at least that a purification be produced there and that this region become receptive of light and able to be illumined. Hence, on this view it is only the region of darkness on account of the absence of light, and thus it will be the region of darkness only in the way our dwelling place is at night.

Moreover, since that region has fire and fire is a solvent of such density and grossness, it will be as it is among us, namely, that, when that heat increases among them in that region, such darkness will be vaporized and it will (600b) put off its grossness and become apt for the reception of light.

Moreover, on this view it is clearly possible to argue that around the throne of the prince of darkness there is greater darkness to the extent that the dignity and nobility of that place is greater than an inferior place and than those more removed from the throne of the prince. Hence, there will be greater density and fog there; hence, the place will be more vile and more ugly, for grossness and density are indignities and deformities in bodies.

Moreover, in the middle of the earth—if there is a place there—is the ultimate separation from light and likewise the ultimate of density and grossness. Nor is it possible to imagine a body more gross than earth or more resistant to light. Hence, if the throne of the prince of darkness is in this world, it is necessary that it be there. Hence, as earth is the dregs of all bodies and that place is more foul and vile, so the inhabitants of that place are like the dregs of all spiritual substances, if their place is there, and he himself resides in lowest part of that place as the most vile of dregs.

Moreover, it is necessary that all the vices come from this prince of the evil, just as all the virtues come from the prince of the good. Just as, then, a person is more acceptable to the prince of the good to the extent that he is more virtuous, so one is more pleasing to the prince of the evil to the extent that he is more vicious.

Moreover, in accord with this, those things which are vices in the kingdom of the prince of the good will be virtues in the contrary kingdom, and the other way around. Hence, nothing will be virtue or vice unqualifiedly, but in a certain respect or in a certain place; so too, nothing will be good or evil without qualification.

Moreover, as the prince of the good is worshiped by virtues, so the prince of the evil is and must be worshiped by vices. What reward, then, is there before him for such a worship of vices? For since the reward of the virtues which exist in this life is the beauty of the virtues which are in the next life, will not the reward of the vices which exist here be likewise the deformity and perversity of the vices which exist in the next life? The reward of the vices will be greater than here to the extent that the future glory of souls will be greater than their beauty here. But this is not reward or happiness, but damnation and unhappiness than which a greater cannot be thought.

Moreover, it has already been explained to you that vices and virtues naturally have their coming to be with regard to the same subject, as do all contraries. According to this error, however, vices do not have their coming to be except in the nation of darkness, the whole of which was created by the prince of evil. Hence, it is obvious that they are not contraries according to them. For who is there who does not see that men become virtuous from vicious and evil from good, and the other way around?

Moreover, the reward by which the prince of evil rewards his worshipers is either happiness or misery. If it is misery, it is, therefore, not a reward, but a punishment. But if it is happiness, it is evident that happiness cannot come from vices nor exist with vices, since each of them is misery, and the greater misery to the extent that it is greater. After all, who has any doubt that avarice is a hunger or thirst for money and possessions? And no one doubts that a hunger, whether it is bodily or spiritual, is misery. So too, lechery is a hunger and thirst for bodily pleasure. Who does not see that anger, envy, and hatred are torments of human souls and spiritual fires in them? It is, therefore, evident that true happiness cannot exist with vices or even with a vice. If, then, the prince of evil rewards his worshipers with true happiness, it is necessary that he strip them of vices and purify them. Hence, he necessarily has to destroy their merits rather than give them a reward. It is also evident from this that as a result such worshipers are further from such reward to the extent that they are more vicious. But if you recall the glory of souls and their true happiness, it is certain for you that the state to which such (601a) happiness is owed is a certain very thin likeness and a shadow, so to speak, of it. But the vicious state is not only unlike the state of happiness, but also contrary to it. It is evident, then, that in the realm of the prince of the evil there is no reward of happiness for worship shown him, but rather damnation and misery, since it is impossible that the vices cease in his realm. In fact, it is necessary that they be greater to the extent that they are closer to him. And on this account it is necessary that the misery be greater and the torments more severe.

Moreover, what worship will be his? what rites? what sacrifices? what praises and prayers? For, as the prince of the good is worshiped by giving to and helping others, this one will be worshiped by defrauding others, robbing and stealing from them. He will then repay those who do this with reward or punishment. With regard to reward we have already said that he cannot offer happiness, nor can there in any sense be happiness in his realm. But if he repays them with punishment, he will, then, be good and just, since a good person punishes evils and since a just person repays evildoers with what is just. But what rites and sacrifices will they offer him but the abominations of all sins and vices? All these rites and sacrifices do not make one consecrated or holy, but are rather abominations and defilements of those who do them. Hence, all these things are not divine worship, but just the opposite.

Moreover, what praises will be offered to him by his subjects? And what will they praise in him and on account of what will they praise him? For he cannot be praised because he is good or because he does something good. What, then, will those who praise him proclaim of him? For if they proclaim of him that he is evil and that he does everything that he does in an evil manner, this is not praise, but reproach and denunciation. But if they proclaim that he is good and does everything he does well, this is not so much false adulation as mockery and derision, just as if someone wishing to praise a crow proclaims its whiteness, and so too, with a swan, if someone says that it is black, no one has any doubt that he is mocking both of them. But what prayers or petitions will they direct to him? For they cannot ask for good things from him, since he cannot bestow them. Therefore, they can only ask of him that he produce bad things for his petitioners and avert good things from them. But these are the petitions of madmen. For those who ask such things do not seek recompense or reward, but damnation and torment. Besides, if his worshipers are asked why they worship him, they could not answer anything else but that we worship him on this account, namely, that he may do evil to us and avert all good from us.

Moreover, according to these wrongheaded persons what will be said of all evildoers but that by doing evil they worship the prince of the evil, just as those who do good worship the prince of the good? According to this, it will be said that all fornicators, all thieves, all robbers are worshipers of such a prince; from this it follows that all brothels and dens of thieves are his temples since in those places such worship is practiced. But if they say that they do not worship him by doing this, since they do not do these things out of love or honor for him, but that, if someone does such things out of love or honor for him, that one honors and worships him in this way, I say: If this were the case, namely, that such things pleased him, he would be most hostile to his worshipers, since the dishonoring of their souls would please him and he would require this of them. It also follows from this that his worshipers should not only not flee from him, but should also attack him with all their energy and strength, because their worst evils are pleasing to him and he leads them to them by commands and laws and requires those evils of them. The worst evils of souls, after all, are the vices and sins, like their diseases and wounds and like a sort of (601b) death of them. One who does not see this is utterly crude and should not be judged worth of the name "human being." I have already satisfied you on this point, since I have destroyed the folly of the two principles by unsophisticated explanations that are easy to understand. This is the best known error of the Manichees which every law attacks. And as I have made clear to you, part of first philosophy destroys it in other ways, and besides those many ways [which] I here set forth for you, others can be produced for the destruction of this error which I suppress out of fear of wordiness. But I shall produce the arguments on behalf of this error which seem to have led these people into it, and I shall answer them when I find something worthy of a response.

Chapter Eight
The arguments or roots are produced
which seem to have led the Manichees into error.

The first of these is that from one of two contraries the other cannot arise. Evil, then, cannot come from good; it will, then, come from evil. Since this cannot go on to infinity, namely, so that this evil comes from that one and that one from a third and so on to infinity, it will be [necessary], then, to come to an evil which does not come from another and does not come from a good. Hence, that evil comes from nothing and is in that way a principle in itself and also the principle of evils, since the others come from it.

Moreover, either something is the first evil, namely, that prior to which there is no other, or nothing is the first evil. But if nothing is, this process, then, goes on to infinity. But the infinity of causes has already been destroyed, and I have explained their status in the treatise on the first principle[21] through the proofs and explanations by which its being is established and through the paths by which one comes to it. But if something is the first evil, since it cannot come from a good, it will of necessity be a principle in itself, as I said, and the cause of those other evils.

Moreover, everything which is evil is either evil from itself or from another. But if nothing is an evil from itself, everything which is evil will be evil from another, and either from another which is evil or from another which is good. But it cannot be from another which is good, because of the first root which I set forth. Hence, each thing which is evil will be evil from another which is evil, and in that way the process will go on to the previously mentioned infinity, or there will be a circle or turning back of causes so that, for example, A becomes evil from B and B becomes evil from A. But I have already destroyed this circular movement and turning back in the same treatise by a destruction which removed all doubt. But if something is evil essentially, it will have another principle from which it arises or it will not. If it will, that principle will be evil on the basis of the present root, and it will not be a lesser evil. Hence, it will be evil essentially, and in that way we come back to what I said earlier, namely, that there will be something that is essentially evil and the principle of evil. It is almost the same way in which one asks whether everything which is evil is evil according to substance or according to participation. Because if everything which is evil is evil according to participation, for example, if it were said that A is evil by having or participating in B and that B, again, is evil by having or participating in C, and so on to infinity, you recall that this error has been destroyed where an infinity of causes was destroyed. The same thing holds with a circular movement or a doubling back.

But this will be shown to be impossible in another way. For something evil will, in this meaning, be what has evil, and that evil will again have the same meaning, namely, what has another evil, and so on to infinity (602a). Hence, something evil will be nothing but something involving "having" in it an infinite number of times. For when you extract from something evil the whole "having" alone, there will be nothing left. For if there were something left, it will undoubtedly be something evil, but in every evil "having" and "something else" are understood. Hence, the "having" has not been totally removed from the evil since there is still in it what was left.

I shall make this more clear and say that, if an evil is something that has or participates in evil, evil will be by way of explanation its having evil, and the

---

[21] See *The Trinity, or The First Principle* (*De trinitate*), ch. 2: Switalski, pp. 20-24; Teske-Wade, pp. 69-71.

evil had will be a having of another evil, which will in the same way be a having of a third evil, and so on to infinity. Hence, when you have gathered all these explanations, evil will of necessity be found to be a having of a having of a having and so on to infinity so that one does not come to a having which is not a having of something else, and as often as one puts down "having," one understands the possessive case.

Hence, on this view, evil will be infinite and inexplicable and, therefore, unintelligible, and for this reason only someone who does not understand himself makes this claim. But you know from other sources that it is one of the principles of first philosophy that everything that is is intelligible being. You also know that philosophy does not concern itself with the errors of people who do not understand themselves or who assert what is unintelligible. I shall, therefore, return to where I was, and I shall say that it is impossible that everything which is evil be evil by way of participation. From this premise these wrongheaded people think that they have proved for themselves that something is evil essentially or according to its substance.

Chapter Nine
The destruction of the first root upon which the arguments of the Manichees rest most of all.

It is easy to resolve or rather dissolve all these points which have been proposed. I shall, therefore, begin from the root upon which their arguments rest most of all. But this root is the one I mentioned, namely, that from one of two contraries the other cannot come of itself. I say, then, that this root is false unless they understand it in this sense, namely, that from one of two contraries the other cannot arise of itself (*per se*). For it is evident that cold at times comes from heat accidentally, and the bodies of animals by accident cool through heat. For heat opens the pores in the bodies of animals and enlarges them, and for this reason heat leaves them and they later grow cold. So too, conversely, the pores of the same animals are contracted by cold, and increased warmth is retained within.

Moreover, drunkenness comes from wine. In that case it is evident that an evil comes from a good, unless one would say that wine is not good. In the same way, illness at times arises from medicine, however good and beneficial it may be, when one does not take it in the proper measure or in the proper way or at a proper time. But if someone says that neither medicine nor health are good, I will go on to other things. For one will not deny that knowledge is good or something good. After all, what is good if knowledge is not good? Nonetheless, the evil of pride and boasting clearly arises from it at times. But if one refuses to admit that knowledge is something good, one will not deny this of virtue, from which similar evils also arise at times. For many have fallen because of their sanctity into the evils of pride, boasting, and vainglory.

Moreover, the evil of envy at times arises from the good of another and ceases when that good ceases.

Moreover, if they grant that there is some good among visible things, they undoubtedly grant this concerning sunlight. But there is no doubt that from it there comes a darkening of vision and even blindness, namely, (602b) when it has been excessive in duration or strength.

But if they say that no visible thing is good and say the same thing of the things perceived by the other senses, they have already come to the point that they lack sense—not just for experience, but as senseless persons lack sense. For who does not perceive the benefits of food, clothing, and other such things? And even people this mad, whatever they might say as an account for others, perceive internally and in the mind that these things are useful and, for this reason, seek them. For example, on account of excessive cold whose harm they feel and fear even more, they seek warmth as useful and preventive of the harm of the cold. When these wrongheaded people, then, seek these things, not merely to their benefit, but also in a permissible and morally good way, they are witnesses against themselves that for someone suffering from excessive cold to seek salutary warmth is not only permissible, but even obligatory to the extent that one would be guilty of one's own death and would be the murderer of oneself, if one neglected to become warm in that situation. Since no one is obliged to seek anything but what is good, it is evident that such warmth is good, and it is likewise true with regard to cold.

Moreover, no one has any doubt that drunkenness comes from wine and the drunkenness is greater and easier in proportion to the goodness of the wine. Hence, it is obvious that an evil comes from a good. And conversely a good comes from an evil. For example, from ill health and whipping come correction and learning, and nature bears witness to this in each individual, because it suggests to us and teaches each one of us to whip little ones and fools and likewise to punish evil-doers so that either they or others are corrected. And the same holds for dogs and horses as well. This is the testimony of nature among all human beings and holds universally for all. But it is impossible that the universal testimony of nature be false; hence, it is evident that from such evils there comes the good of correction and learning. But who is there with a mind who can doubt that from the good of sanctity and the other virtues pride and contempt for others at times arise? Similarly, who can doubt that from the good of courage there at times arises hasty boldness and anger?

According to this position, they will either say that water and fire are good things or bad things. If they are good, since it is evident that many bad things come from them on occasion, for example, burns and the drowning of human beings and many other damages, it is evident that evils come from or arise from goods. But if they say that they are evil, it is likewise evident that many good things come from them, such as moderate warming, cleansing, cooking, illumination, and from water washing, nourishment of all sorts for fishes, fertilization of fields, and many benefits from water-driven mills. The same thing is true of the heavenly bodies, because both good things and bad things come from them to the lower bodies.

Moreover, who can fail to know that from the same human being there come good actions and also some bad ones? Otherwise, it would be necessary to say that one who is good cannot do anything evil or that one who is bad cannot do anything good. But this is the contrary of what each person experiences in oneself, and for this reason people regret having done many things and are even embarrassed when they are seen doing evil. And there is no one who in his heart or on his lips does not rebuke an evil-doer and who does not judge such a person worthy of punishment. Hence, each person believes that any evil-doer ought to act otherwise and also that one can. Otherwise, one would not judge that the evil-doer should be blamed or punished, just as one would not judge that a rock should be punished for moving downwards. Moreover, according to them, correction has no place with anyone, and it is also not possible.

Moreover, justice itself by which evil-doers are punished by public officials and magistrates would be most unfair and unjust. If, after all, evil persons were prevented by a natural impossibility (603a) from acting otherwise, one should not require it of them, nor should they be punished at all because they act wrongly. After all, you know that we do not require of heavy bodies that they move upwards, nor does anyone dare to become angry at them because they move downwards. Hence, if evil persons are pulled or bound to act wrongly by their own necessity, one should not be angry at them because they act badly, nor should one require of them [that they act otherwise] when they act in such a way.

Moreover, praise and blame will be completely incorrect, since the good and the bad act only naturally. But neither praise nor blame is owing to nature in itself for its activities, because it operates by necessity, not by freedom, in the manner of a servant who cannot do anything else than he is commanded, as you have learned elsewhere.[22] It remains, then, for misguided persons of this sort that they must concede that evil comes from good, and the other way around, though by accident, or that they admit that no sensible thing is good, since from each one of them evil comes.

Moreover, according to them, there is eternal war between the prince of light and the prince of darkness, either the prince of light harms him in some respect or he does not harm him. If he harms him, he causes him some evil, and that evil is obviously from the prince of light, since he causes it. Hence, not only does evil come from good, but even from the very best. But if he causes him no evil and for the same reason he cannot cause him any evil, he

---

[22]   The claim that nature operates in the manner of a servant is something that William derived from Avicenna and uses against him frequently. See Avicenna, *Metaphysics* IX, 2: Van Reit, p. 448, where Avicenna says, "A natural [cause] does not act through choice, but in the manner of one who serves . . . ." See also *The Trinity, or The First Principle* (*De trinitate*), ch. 11: Switalski, p.75; Teske-Wade, p. 112, where William says that the Aristotelians "have forgotten what they rightly said, namely, that nature does not operate according to choice and will, but in the manner of a servant."

knows this, since you, as foolish as you are, know this. Therefore, he fights against him, though he knows that he cannot cause him any evil and, for this reason, cannot harm him. Now I have destroyed for you the first root through which it could seem that those misguided people were led into this error.

Chapter Ten
The destruction of the second root of this error.

But there is a second root by which they ask whether something is the first evil or nothing is, and I determine this for you and resolve it through distinguishing the sense of "evil." For if evil is understood as "harmful," I have already told you that nothing is such without qualification, even if something is harmful or evil to you. In the same way, if something is healthy for someone, for example, a cauterizing or an incision or an amputation of a member, it is not for this reason healthy without qualification.

Besides, though it is true that something harms something else, it does not, for this reason, follow that it is also harmful to it, just as it does not follow that, if something kills something else, it is, for this reason, deadly for it or that, if something whitens something else, it is a whitener. The reason for this is that denominations of this sort are made according to natural power or aptitude. For only something that has the power or aptitude ordered toward and intending this is said to be percussive in the proper sense, just as something is called incisive only from the power it has for incising. And nothing is called penetrative or digestive unless it has a power that intends this. But there is nothing of the sort [i.e., harmful] in the whole universe of things. For although there are animals that hunt or plunder others by killing them or devouring them, their power does not intend the killing of them, but rather the benefit of its own subject, and it does this by feeding or nourishing or defending it and repelling harm which threatens it from another.

When a lion hunts and devours a wild ass, the lion does not intend to harm it, though it harms the ass very much, but intends to benefit itself by nourishing itself with its meat. The same thing holds for other things. Fire does not intend to destroy what it burns, but rather to increase its form in the matter which it overcomes (603b). But one who says that anger aims at harming another does not speak correctly; it aims rather at revenge or at victory, and the nature of animals regards both of these as good. It regards revenge as just, but regards victory as something magnificent, as can be seen in elephants who hold subject those they conquer and exercise over them the rights of slavery, as it were.

But if one takes evil as the harm itself, I answer that the first evil is a privation or lack of the first natural good, that is, of being. But the first gratuitous evil, that is, one opposite to grace, is the lack of first grace. What first grace is, however, I shall not further determine for you here, except that the orders of graces are in accord with the orders of recipients and in accord with the matters receptive of them. In the same way in human beings the first grace is gratuitous faith, because it must first be taught to and possessed by human beings, as the foundation and chief point of the true religion and of divine worship.

But in the angelic substances and other noble immaterial substances the first grace is that noble knowledge of God which is incomparable in every way to their natural knowledge and wisdom, and in this way the first evil, that is, harm, in intelligent substances is a turning away of thought or of knowledge from the creator. For from this evil there follows a defection or dereliction, which is undoubtedly a withdrawal from the fountain of goodness. And from this there follows the impoverishment and drying up and dying of those who withdraw. For it is necessary that those who are by their thought fixed upon the creator adhere to him with all the appropriate virtues. Thought is the cause by which the creator is, first of all, held in the intellect and, as a result of this, in the motive powers. Hence, if that thought is removed, the fountain of goodness dries up in a sense, and with respect to its noble gifts or goods which are far more excellent than natural ones, the outpouring of his generosity upon those who turn their thought away from him or direct it toward other things ceases. I mean those who turn it to other things with a lasting and permanent conversion or at the same time turn away, namely, in that way. But if one thinks something else or of something else for a moment or an hour, one does not on that account turn one's thought away from him. I shall investigate this question in more detail and at greater length, when I treat of the malice of the bad angels whom people commonly call devils.

With regard to this evil which we have said is a pure privation, it is not necessary that it come from something else, whether good or evil, since it does not exist at all. For it is impossible that what does not exist at all come from something else. One should not, nonetheless, deny that a negation is at times the cause of a negation. But if someone asks from what this comes or what the cause is on account of which one does not think of the creator, I answer that it is the privation of one of those things which make one think of him.

But if he understands evil in the third way, namely, as a vice or sin, though this belongs to another treatise, one can correctly answer that the occasion for the existence of either pride or envy is something good either of one's own or of another, and as I have already told you, this pertains to another treatise. In all these cases you see the feeblemindedness of such people. It is utterly evident that they do not know what it is that is called evil and that they make a confused use of the previously mentioned meanings.

But in none of these three meanings is it possible that the principle which they call the first evil should be called a god or a prince or king. For evil, as harmful, cannot be the prince of evil, as I have explained to you, since he bestows upon his own subjects, that is, all who are in his kingdom, so many and such great goods. But it is not right that the first evil, that is, the first harmful, should be called a principle or prince or king or god or source of something, since every harm is only (604a) a privation or near privation. For a harm is nothing but the removal of something good or useful or the application of something that brings about this removal. But nothing of the sort is worthy of the name "prince" or "principle." The same holds for vice or sin. For who would dare to think that something which is a vice or sin is a principle or prince or a god or a lord especially of so great a kingdom as they say the kingdom of darkness is? From this, therefore, you clearly see the great darkness of the ignorance in which those people are who do not even understand the meaning of "evil."

Moreover, I will ask them from what nation they themselves are and to whose kingdom they belong, namely, whether they are of the nation of darkness or of the nation of light. But if they come from the nation of darkness— as appears to be the case from the darkness of their ignorance—some of them perhaps attack—not without reason—the prince of light, since they are his enemies. Hence, their testimony against him is not appropriate.

Second, the nation of darkness is either entirely blind and thus sees nothing of the light or its kingdom, or it sees in the same way as animals which are called nocturnal, such as bats and owls and that sort. In either case they are not worthy to be believed about the light or its kingdom. For if they know nothing at all about it, they are not to be believed, since they speak about it like dreamers and people incapable of seeing anything of it. But if they know no more of the light than light-fleeing animals, it is evident, as I said, that their judgment about the light is not only false but perverse. Such animals think that the night is daylight and, conversely, that the sun is not light, but darkness. Hence, the whole kingdom of light is for them the kingdom of darkness, and vice versa.

Hence, when they believe that they are speaking of the god of darkness, they are speaking of the god of light, and vice versa, just like the animals we mentioned. Hence, they do not know for certain what they are speaking about, and they say what is false all the time, since they call the light darkness, and vice versa.

But if they say that they come from the kingdom of light and belong to the prince of light, these same people are intolerably injurious and contemptuous toward him, first of all, because they concede that he is only a half god. For power over both of the two contraries, that is, over good and evil, is perfect power, but power over only one of them is halved power, just as power over white and black human beings is complete power, while power over only the whites is half of that power.

So too, since they say that he should be adored and worshiped only by the nation of light and only by the good, they attribute to him only half a deity and take a half away from him. For it is evident that those who say that he ought to be worshiped and adored by all confess his full and entire deity. On the other hand, those say that he ought to be worshiped and adored only by a part attribute to him a part of the deity and, likewise, a part of the dominion, since they do not want to concede that he has dominion everywhere and over all. Just as that is not white without qualification which is not white in some part, so he is not lord without qualification who is not lord in some respect. For he is not said to be lord without qualification who lords it only over a particular house or city.

Moreover, a person does not truly and fully have possession who has possession in court or in battle. Hence, such a person does not truly or fully have lordship.

Moreover, one is not omnipotent or perfectly powerful whose power is opposed in the universe so that he faces war from the other side on an equal basis.

Moreover, since he could not produce and is unable to do whatever he wills, he admits his impotence, since he is able to do less than he wills.

Moreover, as that is not most white in comparison to which something else is equally white, and that is not best in comparison to which something else is equally good, so that is not first (604b) in comparison to which something else is coeval. But these people maintain two firsts, just as they maintain two principles.

You ought here to notice that, since evil, according to their dreams, means the same thing as pestilential, and since they maintain that it is evil first of all and universally, just as the principle and prince of the good is first of all and universally good, they must maintain that it is pestilential first of all and universally. Hence, it attacks and rages against everything it can and, for this reason, against its whole kingdom, since outside of it it can do nothing by the right of its power, since it is prevented by the limitation and boundaries of its kingdom. Hence, it rages and attacks everything of its own, like a plague, like corruption and death. But nothing of this sort can be a genuine principle or cause or source or prince or god or lord, since each of these which we have mentioned is not only not pestilential toward some of those things which come from or are under it, but is [a source] of great and abounding goodness and benefit to each of those things which comes from it. Hence, it can be called a principle or source only in the sense in which destruction or death are or in the sense in which what is destructive and deadly through intention and will is. But if it is only pestilential or destructive of other things contrary to it, that is, those which come from the contrary kingdom, then it is evident that it is not evil except by way of accident, namely, through the contrariety which it has to them. So too, heat in itself is at peace, but fights against cold when it confronts it, and the other way around, though it is not part of its natural intention to fight against the cold. Hence, it is evident that the principle of evil is not evil except accidentally or to some particular thing, and this meaning fits the principle of good just as well.

Chapter Eleven
The second treatise: It is shown that all things are a unity, and that there is only one universe, and that the world is one, and in what way.

I have now finished with the unity of the first principle, to the extent that was appropriate for the present treatise, and satisfied you concerning it with a collection of proofs and explanations that are quite easy to understand and vulgar ones which come after the sublime proofs and explanations which you learned in the first treatise of the first teaching on God in the mode of wisdom. There follows, as I promised you, the investigation of the unity of the universe and the explanation that it is one and that the world is one and how it is one. I state, then, that every whole is one, and this is seen from its name and meaning, for "whole" and "part" are used relatively to each other, and a whole in its truest definition or explanation is something unified or assembled from parts. But assembling or unification is merely the uniting or joining of part with part or of parts with parts, and this uniting or joining is nothing but the unity of the whole.

[The remainder of this chapter is omitted from the translation.]

(606a)

Chapter Twelve
The opinion of certain philosophers
concerning the unity of the world is presented.

Those of the philosophers who said that the world is the house or city, that is, the dwelling of gods and human beings, have said this with good reason, except that they have misused the name of the deity, as I explained to you in the previous treatise.[23] For the venerable name of deity does not truly and properly belong to anything but the one and true First. For this reason I explained to you in the same place that it does not have a plural unless it has be distorted and extended through abuse. But those who have said this made no mention of the dwelling of the animals, and they did this for two reasons, I suspect. The first is that they understood that the world was given to gods and human beings as their possession both to dwell in it and to use its goods with which God filled it. But he gave to the animals no right or possession in the world; rather, he gave them to human beings so that they would use them for their own benefit.

The second reason is that the animals were created on account of human beings, and their use is proof of this. For human beings use animals, as if they were created for them, as Aristotle himself says.[24] We use all of them as if they existed on account of us. We usually do not say: He built a home for his own habitation and that of his animals and cattle, and the reason is that animals do not associate with the lord of the house, because they are not his companions, but rather assist and serve him. There is, then, another union of creatures in the whole world or universe because of which it is called one house and one city. You know that those inhabiting a city or the citizens of one city are called one people on account of the unity of the place which they inhabit.

---

[23] See *The Trinity, or the First Principle* (*De trinitate*), ch. 5 and 44: Switalski, pp.34-35 and 230- 231; Teske-Wade, pp. 79-80 and 244-245.

[24] See Aristotle, *Politics* I, ch. 8, 1256b15-22.

But if there are divisions in that people, inasmuch as some are men, others women, some servants, others masters, some freemen, others philosophers, some merchants, others gardeners or practitioners of the other trades, regardless of the great variety, the city or the people is not divided on this account so that it is many cities or they are many peoples. So in the world of the gods and men, though there is (606b) great difference in conditions and offices, there is one people of the city which is the world, but the place is the one world, as you generally understand "place," as well as "dwelling."

[The remainder of this chapter is omitted from the translation.]

(607a)

Chapter Thirteen
*Other opinions concerning the plurality of worlds and
concerning the vacuum are stated and destroyed.*

But among ordinary people the idea of a plurality or diversity of worlds or ages is prevalent, and among philosophers another age is at times mentioned, and people customarily make mention of the present world and another world to which human souls are transferred through the death of their bodies. And they suppose that this world has a region that is most pleasant with grasses and flowers and the shade of the most noble and green trees, where they imagine the Elysian Fields after the description of the poets. The Saracens maintain in their madness that not only things like this are there, but also, on the basis of their law, all the shamefulness of carnal pleasures, and they hope that they will obtain them. Those previously mentioned wrongheaded people about whom I have said many things in order to establish the unity of the first principle maintain that the bodily world is contrary to it in every respect. Hence, it is appropriate that after what has preceded I go after those errors and destroy them. And first I will undertake to destroy that view that outside this world there is another world. For, if beyond the orbit of the last sphere, that is, of the ultimate heaven, there were another sphere like it or a body of any other form, it would either touch this sphere which I said was the ultimate of this world or it would not. If it did not, there would be some intervening body between those two spheres. Hence, it would be outside of both of them. It would, then, either surround each of the two spheres totally (607b), and then neither of those spheres would be the ultimate in its world. But this was what was asserted. If, however, it surrounded them only in part, that body would be outside both worlds, and this cannot be said except foolishly, since no usefulness can be imagined for such a body. Besides, after they maintain two or three worlds or however many they want, they have to admit that there is neither a body nor anything else outside of them, just as those who maintain only one world claim that there is no body outside it. Otherwise, they would not truly and intelligently maintain that it is a world. And in that way those who maintain many worlds, whether finite or infinite, are forced by necessity to maintain nothing outside them. The world, after all, necessarily contains either the whole universe without qualification or the universe appropriate to it. But it is impossible to imagine a body which belongs neither to this world nor to another. It remains, then, that there is no body between these worlds. Hence, such spheres touch each other not only at a point, as is explained by geometers, but also by their whole external arcs and also by means of their whole external surface. For it is necessary that all those two bodies be together by all their limits in that part by which they touch each other, unless some body separates them in that place. For only a body can produce a distance between bodies.

Chapter Fourteen
It is impossible that there be a vacuum or empty space
between the two worlds which they maintain.

But if someone said that there is a vacuum or void between them, you have already learned elsewhere that a vacuum or void is not possible. If you perhaps do not remember or that explanation which you learned is not enough for you, pay attention to these explanations which I am proposing here. I say, then, that a void can either be cut or divided or it cannot. If it cannot, it is impossible that motion come about in it or through it, just as if air and water were utterly indivisible and uncutable, it would be impossible that there be motion through one of them, since every body that moves through another cuts a path for itself by such a division in it or through it. But those who maintain a vacuum or a void say that all motion takes place in it or through it.

Moreover, on this view, the void or vacuum will be the most solid and strong of all bodies, since it will be neither penetrable nor divisible or cutable in any way, and it could not yield to any other body. How then will it be a void or vacuum?

[The remainder of this chapter is omitted from the translation.]

(610a)

Chapter Fifteen
The questions of these misguided people are resolved.

But I must first answer certain questions which trouble some people, and I must explain to you how much they misuse the name "universe."

[The remainder of this chapter is omitted from the translation.]

(611b)

Chapter Sixteen
He responds to another question on this point.

Now I shall reply to a question by which they seem to pressure misguided and feeble-minded persons like themselves. They speak in this way, if they at least have knowledge and understanding to this extent. Since God created this world out of his gratuitous goodness alone, he could have created many worlds with the same ease. He, therefore, created them, since he had the same reason in him for the creation of many as for the creation of this world, namely, his goodness.

Moreover, his goodness is not lessened, his generosity is not lessened, and his wealth is not lessened. Why then did he not create many worlds?

Moreover, since there is no end of his generosity or of his goodness, how will there be an end of his effect, that is, of his gifts and presents? For this world is finite. Why are his gifts and presents finite? Why is his generosity limited and restricted in this respect?

Moreover, why does one not give in accord with his generosity when one finds worthy recipients? Why is this but because of a defect or lessening of wealth? But this has no place in him, nor does he seem to have given in accord with his goodness or generosity, since both of these are infinite and what he has given is only finite. You see, then, that an argument of this sort seems to be brought not only against the creation of one world, but also against the creation of infinite worlds which, even if they were created, would not match equally the divine goodness and generosity since outside of him nothing finite is comparable to him, not to mention equal to him. I say, then, that he could not create and still cannot create many worlds, whether they would be finite or infinite, and this does not come from a defect that is in him or on his part, but rather on the part of the worlds which cannot be many, as I explained to you in the preceding sections. In the same way, the fact that someone cannot invite someone greater than himself to a dinner or cannot attend to someone greater than himself at a dinner does not come from one's greed or a lack of food which one suffers, but rather from the lack of such a person, that is, because such a person cannot be found, that is, a guest greater than the host is. So too, that someone does not know that the diameter is commensurate to a side does not stem from a lack of the knowledge he has but from the lack of the object itself which is not able to be known.

Chapter Seventeen
The third treatise: How the universe proceeded from the First, and what sort of things are created or made in some other way by him, and how some have erred about this.

After I have explained to you the oneness of the first principle and the oneness of the universe and have destroyed for you the errors of those who held views contrary to the truth on these matters, to the extent that was appropriate for the present treatise, I shall next begin to explain to you how the universe proceeded from the first and how those things which are created and generated (612a) or are produced by him in some other way proceed from him even today. I shall, first of all, set forth for you the opinions of those who have not spoken about this with sufficient care and of those who have erred on this. For errors of this sort are not lacking in hatred for the creator as well as in the aversion of our souls from their end, namely, that on account of which they exist. Know, then, that there have been people who said that everything proceeded from the creator in the manner of emanation from a fountain. They held that the creator was a fountain and that created things were, in accord with their largeness or smallness, rivers or streams or drops flowing from him. The error of these people is clearly destroyed in this way, because that which emanates from a fountain in this way was, before it emanated, in the fountain as a part of it because it was in it. Since, then, in the fountain which is the creator there is nothing besides him, it follows of necessity that everything created was either the whole creator or parts of him. But the impossibility of each of these is evident, since it has been shown that the creator is without parts in the ultimate degree of partlessness. In the way we stated, it is evident to you, then, that the creator cannot properly be said to be the fountain of the universe. Hence, he is said to be the fountain of the universe through an unlikeness, though a very remote one.

Others have said that the universe proceeds from the creator as the form of a viewer in the mirror proceeds from the viewer, and these too, though there was truth in their meaning, have still not spoken it with clear and proper language, since the universe is not in something else as in a mirror that receives it, unless perhaps one says that the possibility by which the universe is possible is in itself the recipient of the form or formed character of the whole universe. But this presents doubts and questions, namely, what is the position of the creator in relation to that possibility and his looking at it. For it is impossible to understand any bodily opposition between the creator and it, since the creator is incorporeal in the ultimate degree of incorporeality, and the universe was nothing before it was created.

Moreover, since the creator existed in himself from eternity in every respect and this possibility was likewise in itself in every respect, as it was in the creation of the universe and after, how is the creation of the world understood to have taken place? For it can seem on this view to have existed in every respect from eternity and in no respect to have begun.

Others have said that the universe proceeded from the creator in the manner of a shadow from a body. But these people do not explain the manner of its procession. Moreover, they speak with less care, since a shadow is not something that proceeds from a shady body, as light is something proceeding from a luminous body. Overshadowing or what is called "casting a shadow" is nothing other than the prevention of light which a shady body makes by its being placed between a luminous body and that upon which it casts a shadow. And each shady body makes this prevention of light according to its form or shape and the form or shape of the luminous body to which it is opposed. The situation is similar in accord with the size of these, as was explained in the book on shadows.[25] The shady body does not itself cast something, but rather

---

[25] See as probable source al-Kindi's *De aspectibus*, ed. Axel Björnbo and Seb. Vogl, in *Alkindi Tideus und Pseudo-Euklid: Drei optische Werke* (Leipzig-Berlin: B. G. Teubner,

prevents the luminous opposing body from casting light upon what is behind the shady body.

Others have said that the universe proceeds from the creator in the manner of a footprint from one who impresses it or from a walker,[26] and the same questions follow these people. After all, how are they to understand the creator as walking, and upon what? So too, how are they to understand his impressing that footprint and upon what, since apart from the universe there is nothing?

Others also said that the universe proceeded from the creator in the manner of an odor from a perfume so that the whole universe is, according to them, merely the tenuous odor of the goodness of the creator.

There was a sixth kind of person, and they still exist, who say that the universe proceeded from the creator as (612b) an artifact proceeds from a worker or as any product from its maker. These people seem to come close to the truth, though they do not state it clearly and plainly. For their language is clumsy and incomplete, since they do not explain the manner of the divine making or activity.

Chapter Eighteen
That the previous comparisons do not solve the question posed.

The statements of the foregoing people in no way solve the question, though they do really state useful comparisons for imagining the supereminence of the creator over the universe and over individual things in it and for raising up the human intellect and for contemplating to some extent the magnificence of the glory of the creator. For when the universe is said to be like a shadow of the creator, they who are able to understand something understand that the supereminence of the creator to the universe is that of a body to its shadow. It is accepted that a shadow is the most empty outline of a body in no way comparable to a body in strength or goodness, and the universe stands in this way in relation to the creator. This will be more evident if you compare to the creator individual things of the universe which seem great and marvelous in it. For example, if you say that every potency and power of the universe and of each part of it is a slight shadow of the potency of the creator, and likewise of his wisdom, goodness, beauty, life, sweetness, and greatness, you will speak the clear truth. And these comparisons will raise you up and help you no small amount to imagine in some way the supereminent majesty of the creator.

The same thing holds for the image of the one who looks into a mirror and the likeness from the one who looks into it. But they differ on this point that at times the image reflected in a mirror is seen to have almost the same beauty

---

1912). Al-Kindi's work was translated by Gerard of Cremona. The incipits of several manuscripts include "de umbris," and the content of al-Kindi's work fits will what William says.

[26] See Augustine, *The City of God* (*De ciuitate Dei*) X, 21 as a possible source.

as the person looking into it or as his face. But the universe is far from the creator and from his beauty by an unlikeness of incomparable distance. But as you see that the beauty of the one looking into the mirrors is reflected more or less in accord with the difference of mirrors, so the likeness of the beauty of the creator is reflected in the diversity of creatures, in some more, in others less, and this is in accord with their receptivity and their nearness to him. In this regard Plato spoke the truth, namely, that he is the best and that from the best envy is excluded.[27] Therefore, he wanted to make all things like to himself to the extent that the nature of each could be receptive of beatitude, that is, of goodness. Nor can intelligent people doubt that there are greater and more noble likenesses of God reflected in the separate substances than in human souls, and in human souls than in brute animals, and so with others things in order. It is the same way with other dispositions, namely, power, wisdom, life, and goodness. For whatever is found in the universe is a slight shadow in comparison to the first life, first power, first wisdom, first goodness, and first beauty which is that of the creator. Avicebron seems to have understood this in his statement in which he said that creatures raised themselves up to the creator and made a shadow for him.[28] But this raising up is nothing but the reception of some likeness of him. Perhaps he might have expressed this more clearly and made them a shadow of him, and perhaps there is another interpretation of this statement, but I pass it over here.

Those who said that the universe was a footprint of the creator (613a) have likewise made us understand his most remote distance from the universe and have given us the opportunity to imagine to some extent his greatness that incomparably surpasses the greatness of the universe and the smallness of the universe in comparison to his immensity. They have also made us understand that the universe and the individual things of the universe are certain signs or paths leading us to the creator, just as footprints of wild animals lead hunters to their hiding places and in general the footprints of all animals direct their seekers and help them to find them. They, therefore, made us to understand by this statement how much God wanted to be found and with what great helps he wanted to help those who seek him, for he left so many and such great footprints and signs by which he could to some extent be found. With

[27] See *Timaeus* 29E where Plato says of the Demiurge, "He was good, and one who is good never has any envy toward anything; and being without envy he wanted all things to be like himself as far as possible." William knew the *Timaeus* through the translation of Chalcidius. See *Plato: Timaeus: A Calcidio Translatus Commentarioque Instructus*; edited by J. H. Waszink (London: Warburg Institute and E. J. Brill, 1975).

[28] In the *Font of Life* (*Fons uitae*) III, 55, ed. Clemens Baeumker, in *Beiträge zur Geschichte des Philosophie des Mittelalters* (Münster, 1892-95), I, p. 201, ll. 6-8, Solomon Ibn Gabirol, or Avicebron, says, "It is not possible that the divine power be weakened, but out of a desire for it the powers raised themselves up and made a shadow on lower things." William refers to Avicebron as Avicembron and to his work as the *Font of Wisdom*.

regard to smell and scent you must work and understand carefully how all the sweetness, all the usefulness of the universe is a scent of the divine goodness and sweetness, and by this comparison your intellect is raised up to contemplate the immensity of the divine sweetness, and from this same comparison there has been shown the smallness of the hearts which are not only filled or inebriated with this slight scent, but also submerged in it and absorbed by it. Since the human heart was created for this font of sweetness, it is evident that it has been incomparably diminished from its due greatness. This comparison makes us know how shameful and how distant from the nobility of human souls it is to cling to these slight scents and to seek them out with such zeal and to inhale them with such ardor of desire while the fontal and profound sweetness is either neglected or completely ignored.

Chapter Nineteen
Whether the universe proceeded from the First, as an artifact from an artisan, and how it proceeded through a word.

Since it is evident that the universe is like an edifice or artifact or some product of God and a most noble and beautiful work, it is evident that the statement of those persons is true who said that the universe proceeded from the creator as an artifact from an artisan. But that part of the universe which was created first does not seem to have proceeded in the manner of an artifact from an artisan in this respect, namely, that it does not seem to have been made by instruments. And it is evident with regard to the spiritual part of the universe that he used nothing external, since he needed no matter nor any instrument for its formation. Hence, he created it through himself without using anything external. For it is necessary that everything that was created or established or made by him in any way proceeded from the creator in one of two ways, namely, either through some means or without any means. For if he created nothing without a means, there would come between him and every creature an infinite number of means. For since whatever there is besides the creator is created, as you have learned elsewhere, every means, then, through which something else is created by him, since it is something other than him, will be created by him and only through a means. But every means of any creation is the cause of that which is created through it. An infinite number of causes of it, therefore, precedes each thing created. Certitude, however, has already been produced for you concerning the situation of [an infinite number of] causes and their impossibility.[29] Hence, it remains that something has been created by the creator without any means. But whether it is only one or there are many remains a question among certain philosophers.[30] With regard to that one or those many creatures, if they are many, we must

---

[29] See *The Trinity, or The First Principle* (*De trinitate*) ch. 2: Switalski, pp. 21-23; Teske-Wade, pp. 69-71.

[30] William is perhaps thinking of Avicenna who held that from the First there immediately proceeded only one intelligence, the first intelligence from which there

investigate in this chapter how they proceeded (613b) from the creator without any means. I mean: without any external means. And since the Hebrew people rightly believe their prophecy and their scripture in which God said, "Let there be light, and light was made" (Gn 1:3), and many other such statements, it is appropriate to examine this idea, since, induced by such testimony, the Hebrew people believe that the creator created the first creatures by speaking or through a word. Another of their prophets, speaking of the creator, clearly said, "He spoke, and they were made; he commanded, and they were created" (Ps 32:9). Again, he says, "By the word of God the heavens were made firm" (Ps 32:6). The creator should not be supposed or thought to have spoken an external, that is, an audible word, since there was not any air which could be formed into a sound. And only an animal could possibly speak in that way, and there was also no one to whom God might speak in that way, since there was as yet no hearer with the sense of hearing, that is, one who could hear an audible word. He spoke, then, in a spiritual way and commanded by a spiritual command.

Moreover, it is impossible that a word of this sort, that is, one perceptible by hearing, help an artisan who acts through himself alone, though such a word could help an artisan who works through other servants and workmen either for instructing them or for moving them to action. Hence, such a word would be useless in every way in terms of the action by which the creator created those creatures, since he created them through himself and not by means of servants.

Chapter Twenty
That 'word' is said in three meanings.

You ought, then, to recall these points, namely, how 'word' is said in accord with three meanings. According to the first meaning it is the intellectual word, which they usually call the word in the mind, and this is nothing but the image or likeness of the thing understood or thought of actually reflected in the mirror of the mind, and this is thinking in actuality. The second meaning is the written marking or writing made by a visible shape or shapes, and it is usually called the word in writing. In the third meaning it is the audible word which is usually called the word on the lips, and it is evident to you that neither of these two latter meanings helps an artisan who works [through himself], and by neither of them does he produce something except in the way we said. For an artisan who works only through himself it is impossible to act through something that is outside of himself, and to finish this explanation in a few words, I say that it is necessary that every artisan who works by an art or through an art work through a word. A first explanation of this is that the word which I here intend, namely, the spiritual or intellectual word is

---

proceeded the second, and so on. See *De universo* Ia-IIae, ch. 9 and following where William undertakes the refutation of this error.

nothing but art in actuality, that is, in the act of thinking. Hence, the art by which the creator, the artisan of all things, produced the first creatures is nothing but his intellectual word. But this word is in God an act in the ultimate degree of actuality, for with him nothing is in potency of these things which belong to him and are in him, since he is being necessary through himself in every aspect of himself. On this account he does not admit and does not tolerate in himself the defect of potentiality. Hence, his art is not like the vision or thought of one asleep or resting, but like that of one awake and always existing in act. But this vision or thought is the intellectual or spiritual word in his mind. I have already made it evident to you in this way that the blessed creator created such creatures through his inmost word, because he did so through his art which is necessarily his word.

Moreover, look at all the artisans who work through their arts, and you will see clearly that none of them produces anything except by speaking spiritually (614a), that is, by thinking it and through their thought, that is, through their spiritual and inmost word. And when you write or speak, you do neither of these actions except by speaking in your heart with an intellectual speech which is nothing other than your thought by which you think what you write and how it should be written and the act of writing itself. For this reason if the writing has something less correct, you immediately correct it or set it aside for correction. Since, then, the arts among us and the products produced by them and the artisans themselves are likenesses of the first and universal art and of the products produced through it, it is necessary that they be here, that is, among us the same way they are there, insofar as it is possible to find a likeness, though one very unlike, in things so far apart.

But you ought to notice that, as the arts in the artisans in this world are composed of many parts and conclusions, so they go from potency to act one part after another, that is, by parts. For it is not possible for the human soul in the lowered state which it endures in the body to think in act all the particular artifacts or products which are produced by one art. I mean: to think them in act at one time. Rather, as it produces one part after another and one product after another, so it thinks them in actuality, or rather, just the opposite. After all, activities follow upon thoughts, and not the other way around, since they come from thoughts. But in the creator just the opposite is the case, since his art is simple in the ultimate degree of simplicity and in act, as I have already said to you, and in the ultimate of actuality.

Moreover, of all activities the first is undoubtedly thought, and this is intellectual speech, and this is the first in every artisan among us. For every artisan among us who produces something externally through art first produces within himself and in himself an image of the same product, or an exemplar, thinking out and planning beforehand within himself the product which he is going to fashion, and on this account, lest an exemplar of something in himself escape from his heart through forgetfulness, a painter meanwhile makes a sketch of it externally with markings and figures, and he has recourse to this as often as he sees that he has forgotten one of those things which he had thought of beforehand. Because, then, it is evident that external products do not proceed from the artisan, unless exemplars of them begotten in him have first proceeded from him in the manner I have stated, it ought to be evident to you that the generation of the exemplar which is in the artisan himself precedes every external work, and this generation is nothing but the generation of the word which I mentioned to you. And this is speech or the pre-speaking of the product and thought of it and art in actuality.

I have already, then, explained to you that by speaking with a speech most appropriate to himself, that is, which is most perfect and noble in every way, and through his word the high creator created whatever he created without any external means, and I have shown to you examples and likenesses which raise you up and help you to understand this until your intellect rests in these. And I have brought you to know the profundity of the statement by which it was said: "God said, Let there be light, and light was made" (Gn 1:3), although it might seem quite ordinary and easy to understand. From this, consequently, it has been shown to you that the principle of all things that can be caused is the word, and if it were permissible that an operation be said to be found within the creator, the saints and wise men who have spoken of the creator in accord with the truth and have taught others to speak of him would have extended to that point the name of operation and its meaning. And it would undoubtedly be most true and certain that the first operation of the creator is speech, that is, the bringing forth or generation of the Word. But their statements ought to be examples for all, even limits and a rule for speaking about the creator (614b), and one ought not to depart either in meaning or in speech from those to whom the creator first revealed himself to the extent that he taught concerning himself. And as you see in this statement philosophical depth, so I intend to show you in certain other statements of the prophets, where I shall make you know concerning many of their reports that they are the conclusions of certain sciences, just as you see concerning this same statement that it is a conclusion of the first part of first philosophy.[31]

Chapter Twenty-One
Whether through the eternal word things were made freely and from eternity.

Do not let the eternity or eternal actuality of the first-born disturb you, as if you were forced in this way to concede that the first creatures were created from eternity. Suppose someone were to argue: "God spoke, and they were made," and because he spoke from eternity, they were made from eternity. On these and similar points I shall respond to you in following parts, namely, in the destruction of the antiquity or eternity of the world and in the establishment of its newness.[32] In this chapter I shall also show you some things on these points.

[31] William is perhaps referring to his own *The Trinity, or the First Principle* (*De trinitate*) ch. 16: Switalski, pp. 98-100; Teske-Wade, pp. 132-134.

[32] William takes up the question of the eternity as opposed to the newness of the world in *De universo* IIa-Iae, ch. 8 and following.

The first and the root of these is the most free and powerful will of the creator; many have erred in not understanding this freedom. And they imposed not only necessity, but natural servitude upon the creator, supposing that he operates in the manner of nature. This manner, as I have often told you, is the manner of one who serves and is a servile manner.[33] For they thought that the universe proceeds from the creator like brightness from the sun or like heat from fire. In that way [they thought that] from his goodness there proceeded the goodness of the universe, and from his life the life which is in the universe, and so on in the same way with other things. And for this reason they were brought of necessity to that awkward point that they were forced to suppose that the creator could not have made something else or acted otherwise than we find in the previous examples of the sun and of fire. For the sun does not have its light in its power, nor does fire have its heat in its power, so that its operation proceeds or does not proceed according to its will. But the creator has his goodness and his power and his wisdom in such a way that there proceeds from it only what he wills and when he wills, and this is the nobility and sublimity of his power and freedom.

Moreover, the abundance and strength of the wisdom of the creator is such that whatever he can do he can do of himself and by himself, and he does nothing from something else or through something else; rather, other things have everything that they can do from him and through him. But when he does something through other things, he himself or his potency is not helped by those means, but those things which are created by those means are helped. The fact that some things cannot be produced immediately by the creator, such as animals which are generated by other animals, is not due to a defect or diminishment of the power of the creator, but rather to the distance of them from it. On this account they cannot receive being from the creator apart from some means, and for this same reason the being which they receive from him is less and more feeble, and it is like that with all the other things which descend upon them from the fontal goodness of the creator. Because, then, the creator can do everything both of himself and by himself in the creation of the first creatures which he undoubtedly creates without any means, it is evident that he creates them only by speaking and willing. I mean: by speaking as I explained above.

And if to create is something in him, it is only his speaking by such speech or his willing. For he does not move something external in such creation, as human artisans move their members when they work and move by the motion of their members (615a) tools, such as an ax or plane, and again by the motion of the tools they move the materials in which and on which they work. They move them, I mean, to the forms and acts which they intend to impress upon them. For this reason I said that, if to create is something in the creator, it is only his thinking or his willing in such creation. An example of this is found in the human soul or in another noble substance. If there is any cause that produces something through itself alone, its working within itself

[33] See above note 22 to the translation.

and in itself is nothing but its thinking and willing through which it produces that effect. And the situation is the same with each noble substance, and the reason is that in the operations which they perform through themselves, they have nothing within themselves by which they work except thinking and willing.

But whether they can produce something in other things which are not joined to them involves a question that is difficult to resolve, like that which Aristotle and his followers raised concerning the creation or generation of the ten intelligences, and they also held the same view concerning the creation of our souls. They said that the first intelligence which they call the mover of the first heaven created the second and that the second created the third until one gets to the tenth, and they claimed that these creations take place in ways which I shall state in the following parts.[34] But concerning our souls which are joined to bodies, it is evident that by their thinking and their willing, which are their first operations, they make impressions on their bodies, such as local motion and many other changes, and through these they act upon other bodies as you see in the example of the artifacts which I recently mentioned. You see that they make many impressions on other bodies that are not joined to them, such as the operation of an evil spell by which children are made ill and the operation of a basilisk which kills human beings by its mere look, and many such operations which are drawn from the secrets of natural science. I plan to tell you about many of them and to explain their causes in the proper place.

To this extent, then, it has been determined for you that each of the noble substances produces those things that it produces with wisdom or with knowledge through its thinking and its willing alone, and it produces them in the likeness of the operations of the creator to the extent that it is possible that they be like him. Whatever happens, however, with regard to them, you ought to know that the word of the creator of which we were speaking is one word that through itself pours forth from itself being and life over everything which is pleasing to his speaking or to itself. It is the same way with the will or the willing of the creator. When you want to understand this clearly, think of the strength of the imaginative power from whose operation there follows of necessity an external operation, as a certain philosopher said of a person who imagined a camel's fall and immediately a camel fell. Understand that strength of the imaginative power in someone such that whatever he imagines immediately takes place. If he imagines a home being built, it is immediately by that very fact built, and if he imagines that it falls down, it immediately falls down. Such is the strength and power of the first and first-born word. Hence, it is not so much art and wisdom as strength and life and effectiveness flowing abundantly into everything receptive; nonetheless, it is so through the ultimate degree of freedom, as I said above. For this reason it is art that is living and powerful in the ultimate degree of power and overflowing in the ultimate degree of abundance, and the same thing holds for the will of the creator.

---

[34] William deals with the Avicennian doctrine of the emanation of the intelligences from the creator in *De universo* Ia-IIae, ch. 2 and following.

But in our souls the arts are feeble and with so slight a flow that they are almost dry. On this account they have influence upon the crafts of this world only through much work and with many helps, and in this way our wills are feeble and weak. But the first art and the first will have equal influence and power over those things (615b) which exist and over those which do not exist, that is, equally over the possible in every respect. And they have the same facility of influence over those things which are not as over those things which are. This is what the holy and wise man said in his statement, "He calls those things which are not as those which are" (Rom 4:17), that is, he brings them into being. And this calling or bringing is nothing but his thinking and his willing, which we mentioned above.

But there is a question as to whether he could create other things or create them otherwise, and what I mentioned above provides the reason for this question or difficulty, namely, that all things proceed from the creator through his word or his art. Since, after all, his art and word can in no respect be changed in any way, but he necessarily works in accord with it, every operation of his must, then, follow his word and art. Hence, he is not able and never will be able to do anything else or otherwise than it is in his art or than he says or has said. But in that way there is in his art and word only the way in which he has acted or will act, and only those things are in his art and word which he has produced or will produce. Hence, he could never either produce other things or produce them in another way than he did. Nothing, therefore, could change from the course or order of the ages or from things or from arts. A very clear example of this is seen to be this: while you write, if you could not think of anything else than what you write or in another way than you write, your writing and your manner of writing of necessity will follow your thought and your manner of thinking, and you will not be able to write something else than what you write nor in another manner than you write.

Moreover, if in the art of an artisan there was only one house, it is evident that he could from that art only build one house, and if there were only one way of building in the exemplar within the architect, it would not be possible that another way of production should proceed from him. Hence, if only those things which have been created or are to be created were in the word or art of the creator, he could not create other things, and likewise, he could not create them in another way, unless one says that the art is universal and the exemplar also. It is evident, then, that, as many impressions are produced in the same wax or in many pieces of wax, so from one art of building countless structures come and from one art of writing many documents. But this answer amounts to this awkward point that one concedes that the divine art is narrowed and limited to those things which have been created or will be created and things like them. The end of the answer, then, is this, and the meaning is this: the creator could and can and will be able through his art and word to create many other things than he has created or will create, but not things dissimilar or other species or other kinds of things. These people, therefore, seem to make finite the art and wisdom of the creator which they limit to the kinds and species which now exist, which are undoubtedly finite in number, just as the individuals are perhaps finite. But they claim that it is infinite with regard to individuals which are undoubtedly infinite by reason of the potency of the creator. As they claim, a limit has not been set for the creator so that he can only create a certain number of them. But I have already told you elsewhere that the creator is in every way above the finite and above the infinite and above the complete and above the diminished.

Moreover, I have elsewhere explained to you that the power of the creator extends over the possible without qualification, not only over some possible or over a certain part of the possibles.[35] Because, then, the possible without qualification is something, in fact an infinite number of things which neither are nor will be nor things like them, it is evident that the power of the creator comprehends and contains under itself all things. Who, after all, would doubt that it was and is possible for the creator (616a) to give continuous brightness to the moon which he created or to another which he did not create? Or who would doubt that it is possible for the creator to create as many heavens of the stars as he might will, though it is beyond doubt that he only created one of them. For he adorned with a multitude of stars only the eighth heaven, which the astrologers call the heaven of the fixed stars. But to none of the lower heavens did he give more than one star alone.

Moreover, who doubts that the creator could have created a heaven whose motion would be contrary to the motion of the aforementioned heaven, namely, from west to east, and also a heaven whose motion would be from south to north and another whose motion would be from north to south? But these heavens would undoubtedly be very unlike the heavens already created. This will become evident, when you imagine the heavens already created in their possibility and apart from the act of existing. For then you will see that they are such heavens as I mentioned to you, namely, with motions contrary to the motions of the existing heavens. You will see, I mean, that they are that way in potency, and you will not find some more worthy than others so that being should be given to them rather than to the others, insofar as they are considered in themselves. Nothing, after all, which was outside the creator induced him to give being to these rather than to those. For that would then have been a cause of existing for the heavens prior to the creator himself and also more a cause because it would make the creator a cause in actuality, as you learned in the *Hearing* of Aristotle, that the end is more a cause than the efficient cause, because it makes the efficient cause to be efficient in actuality.[36]

---

[35] See *The Trinity, or the First Principle (De trinitate)*, ch. 10: Switalski, pp. 69-71; Teske-Wade, pp. 108-109.

[36] Despite the apparent reference to Aristotle's *Physics*, William seems, rather, to be referring to Avicenna, *Metaphysics* IX, 5: Van Reit, *passim*, but especially p. 337: "But the final cause insofar as it is a cause, is the cause that the other causes are causes in act. The causality of the final cause, then, is the cause of the being of the others."

Hence, it is evident that, if the first cause, which is the blessed and sublime creator, were such a cause, it would not be the first or the chief cause. The fact that being was given to these rather than to those is rather due to the most free choice and goodness of the creator alone, not swayed or induced by something external, that is, by something outside him in any way. You see, then, that many things are possible in themselves, that is, not prevented from existing by a natural impossibility, and the creator himself does not will them to exist or to draw them from the potentiality of existing into act, either because those things which have already been created do not permit them to exist along with them, as I showed you where I spoke about the unity of the universe.[37] There I explained to you that the one world does not admit the existence of another. But the creator limits other things in smallness or fewness on account of other things, as he does with serpents and dragons and other things which are called harmful. For such animals by their greatness or multitude would destroy or interfere with others and injure them intolerably

But someone might say: In immaterial things,[38] as Aristotle says, there is no distance between potency and act, and again that potency and act are the same,[39] or what is more true in the case of the creator, none of those things which belong to him of themselves are as potency; in fact, each of them is in the ultimate degree of actuality; therefore, whatever he can speak or say by that speaking or saying, he always says and thinks in act. Likewise, whatever he can will he wills. If, then, within him or in him his creating or making is nothing other than this, he creates and makes whatever he can make or create. In fact, he has created and made it from eternity.

Pay careful attention to these things which I shall tell you about this question in this place, though it pertains more to the first treatise of this teaching.[40] I say, then, that our audible utterances are made many by us out of necessity, that is, because our intelligible utterances which come to our intellective power from things are likewise many. But the reason for this is that such utterances follow upon the things from which they come, like images and shadows in their multitude and fewness and in their unity and diversity. But the utterance of the creator is not like that; likewise, his thought (616b) and wisdom or art are not like that. The reason is that he is not derived from things, but things are derived from him. For this reason things follow upon him insofar as is possible, but he precedes them according to the excellency of his nobility.

---

[37] William argued above in chapter 11 and following, most of which I have omitted, that a plurality of worlds is impossible in itself and, hence, could not be created even by an omnipotent God.

[38] Though the Latin has *materialibus*, I have read *immaterialibus*, since in *De universo* IIa-IIae, ch. 22: I, 865bA, William appeals to Aristotle as having said that "in spiritual and immaterial things there is no difference between act and potency."

[39] See as a possible source Aristotle's *Physics* III, ch. 4, 203b30.

[40] See *The Trinity, or the First Principle* (*De trinitate*), ch. 9: Switalski, pp. 66-73; Teske-Wade, pp. 106-111.

Notice something else here as well: though the utterance of the creator is one in the ultimate degree of oneness, so multiple and so countless a diversity of things is said through it by the creator—and said without mixture and without confusion in every way. Individual things which are and which can be are spoken through it with the clearest and most distinct expression, though they are spoken at once, as though each one of them were spoken alone. But with us things are just the opposite, because by one utterance we say only one thing, and it is not possible for us to say many things individually and clearly and distinctly by one utterance.

Moreover, by that same utterance by which the creator says that something will be when it is future, he would say that the same thing will not be, if it would not be, and the situation is the same with his thought. With us, however, it is just the opposite, since we say contrary things only by contrary utterances. Our arts and crafts then are determined to certain kinds of works and can do nothing beyond them. In that way the art of building is determined to houses, and can do nothing toward some other kind of work. But the divine art is just the opposite, since it is not more ordered to one kind of product than to others, whether they are contraries or utterly unlike or unconnected. But the cause of this is that our arts and sciences which exist separately in our souls come from the things themselves like certain shadows and appearances reflected in the mirrors of our intelligences from them. And for this reason they follow upon those things and are terminated and limited by them. The divine art, however, is not derived from things, but things are derived from it. And therefore, things follow upon it, and not the other way around. Nor do they come from it by a natural operation, but by the most free choice and most imperious will. For if they were from the divine art by a natural operation, as imprints from seals or impressions, it would be of necessity ordered to the things imprinted and impressed through it, and it would not be capable of other products, just as a seal or mold is not capable of images of another kind than that by which it is engraved or impressed. The reason is that it does not imprint as it wills and it does not command the matter to receive its likeness, but impresses the image to the extent it has it and of the sort it has.

But if someone should say that the divine art imprints in a similar way or gives forms of the sort it has to things and in the way it has them, I say that this is not true without qualification. In fact, it imprints and gives them as it wills and imprints and gives the sort of forms it wills. But it is true with qualification that it does imprint the images it has, though it has them through a most remote likeness and a distance that is incomparably supereminent. For from the same form or seal it imprints one form on one matter and on another a contrary form or a form of another kind. This is due to his most lofty amplitude by which it is not only possible for him, but equally easy for him to give one form or any other form to any receiver whatever, just as a power which extends over both contraries, that is, over both doing and not doing, is free to do both of them, that is, both of the contraries, and is not confined to one, though it is itself one, but turns itself to what it wills through choice. So it is with the divine art in terms of its freedom and amplitude.

But carefully consider the likeness which I proposed for you concerning the word. For, though the word of God, that is, his art is one in every way and not divisible into parts in the ultimate degree of partlessness, by it or through it God himself spoke himself and all things with a spiritual speaking perfect in every way. The great multitude (617a) of utterances we need on account of the multitude of things we can speak is obvious to you. But the relation of that word to our utterances is the same as the relation of his art to our arts. You see in the case of our utterances that none of them perfectly says among us but one thing, and this is due to the narrowness of our thoughts upon which our utterances follow. And if we gather a multitude under one name, we shall say through it that multitude, but only collectively, not individually. But by the first word they are said collectively and individually, and the first speaker said all things from eternity in the ultimate degree of clarity and sharpness in every respect, as I explained to you in the first part of this teaching.[41]

And if the things to come would have been other than they were and of other kinds, if that were possible, they would all have been said by the same word equally and similarly in every respect. It has already been explained to you by this that, just as other things would have been said by the same word, if he had willed to make other things, so too, by the same art other things would have been made, and the word would not have been changed in any way. And this is what had to be explained to you on the forgoing question. For if that art were like the arts in our world or the thought or thinking of the creator were like ours, he truly could not have made nor could he make in the future products of other kinds. An obvious example is found in a potency free with respect to both opposites or over many kinds of products. With regard to it there is no doubt that it is the same in every way, no matter what product proceeds from it. It is the same way with the art or word or thought of the creator.

In my opinion a quite appropriate example is found in the sound of a trumpet in an army of whatever magnitude. Though that sound is but one or single, so many and so manifold and varied ranks in the army go forth as a result of this sound. At the single sound of the trumpet some run to erect machines; some run to weapons of defense; other to weapons of attack. Some hasten or prepare to dig under walls; others to fill trenches; some to positions of fighting or crafts. Thus, by one sign given to the soldiers by the leader such diverse activity is found in the soldiers and other warriors. In the same way, when the creator speaks once and emits, as it were, the single ineffable spiritual sound of his speech, the universe of natural products goes forth in the world, as if the universe of creatures hears his word. For if by the one will or intention of the one king or prince who intends to take or storm some castle

---

[41] See *The Trinity, or the First Principle* (*De trinitate*), ch. 17: Switalski, pp. 102-107; Teske-Wade, pp. 135-140.

or city, so great a multitude of effects and instruments goes forth in the army or in the siege of that castle, or if this happens by one word by which he commands his army to storm that castle, why is it surprising if by the word of the omnipotent creator, though it is one in every way, the countless variety of effects goes forth in the world?

Chapter Twenty-Two
Whether all things were created through the word at once.

If someone asks how all things were not created at once with the utterance of this word, since all things were made by the word and through the word as an efficient and sufficient cause, I reply that all things could not be produced at once; in fact, though they were truly said [at once], they could not all be made at once. After all, you and your father and mother were not able to be produced at the same time; so too, the chicken and the egg from which it is to be hatched cannot be produced at the same time. The same holds for a seed and that which is to be generated from the seed (617b), and in the examples which I set forth this is evident. For, even if by one word the storming of a city were commanded and, on this account, all the things which they do for its storming, all those things cannot be done at the same time. You ought also to know that the blessed creator did not say that things should be produced otherwise than they were produced. In fact, he said that each thing should be produced in its time, order, and place, just as you do not suppose that all things which you write are written at the same time, but you write each thing in order. You also think of writing a book as a whole, but you do not think that you will write the whole book at once, but by parts and in order. The same thing holds of each thing made through craftsmanship. For much better reason, then, the most wise creator did not say by his omnipotent word, nor did he think by his ineffable thought that all things are made at the same time, but rather that they are and come to be in the order and at the time suited to them.

Chapter Twenty-Three
Whether the creator could create better things than he did create.

But someone might ask whether he could make or create better things than he made or created. But if he could, then what cause restrained the generosity of his goodness and limited it to the measure of goodness in which things were created? But if he could not, this is far more awkward, for this is to assert that his goodness and his power are finite. For if the greatest gift which can flow from the generosity of a person is finite, it seems that his generosity is finite; and his effect stands to his power in the same way. This, then, means that the divine generosity poured the whole of itself out in giving what it gave to creatures, since it could give nothing greater or better. You ought, there-fore, to know that, from the side of the amplitude and abundance of his power, he was able to create some things greater and better than he did create them, but they were not able to receive greater goodness or could not be created better. In that way he could not create the moon as light-giving, just as he could not create such an earth. For it would not be the earth if it were light-giving, nor would the moon be the moon, if it were created as light-giving. Nor would it be an ass, if God created that animal rational, nor would a flea be a flea if the creator had given it the size of a whale or of an elephant.

Moreover, the things themselves could not sustain such changes and increases. For if he had made a human being as large as the sun, the whole earth would not have sufficed for his dwelling, nor would all the grains and fruits of it have sufficed for his nourishment. Nor would all the wool and linen have sufficed for his garments, and in that way it is easy for you to see in the case of the other animals that they could in no way be compatible with one another. For if he had made snakes like elephants and whales, the other animals would not endure them. Likewise, if he had made flies the size of eagles, the living space of the air which is allotted to the birds would be occupied and filled by flies alone. It is, then, evident to you from these considerations that the most wise and most good creator so tempered everything, that is, the world or universe, and that it is so balanced by kinds and species that their large and small sizes are not only mutually compatible, but help one another, and they can survive and be preserved at the same time, that is, in the whole or the world.

But if someone says that it was not fitting that the infinite power of the creator and his infinite goodness and the immense riches of his goodness created everything which he created so small—even the heavens and the world itself—but that it was more fitting that he create an incomparably larger world and also incomparably larger heavens (618a) and that he create for its magnitude large human beings and other animals in the world. Here then you ought to recall that bodies and animals could neither be created infinite nor be infinite. For you have elsewhere learned that a body and something bodily is of necessity finite. Because, then, it was of necessity proper that they be created and be finite, this question would be the same if the creator had created all things much larger than they are. They would still be finite, and for this reason one could always ask why he had not created them larger. This measure, then, of the largeness and of other things in creatures did not exist as a result of a lack of either power or goodness in the creator; rather, the things themselves, as I showed you by a few examples, required this measure, though it could be said with complete truth that they were created in these measures and dispositions through the choice and providence of the most wise giver. But the heaven and other heavens were created as great as was fitting and as the usefulness of their creation required, and that usefulness is truly multiple as well as inexplicable even by the wisest of men. But with regard to the sun know for the present that for its heaven there perhaps neither ought to have been nor could have been a larger sun or another sun, just as you see in the body of one animal that there cannot be without a disturbance to it or perhaps a destruction of it a larger heart or another heart, for two hearts perhaps could not exist in the body of one animal. But if there could be two, as some people believe of hares of a certain region, there still could not be twenty or one hundred hearts in some animal. The same thing holds for the liver and spleen and many other parts.

I am not saying these things so that you hold it as certain and proven that the sun is in its heaven or in the superlunary world or even in the whole world like its heart, but I said these things about the parts of animals for the sake of example. The truth on these points will perhaps be explained to you in what follows, if God is willing. I shall likewise speak to you here about the fixed stars and their heaven. For perhaps, just as the human body by the necessity of its nature could not be content with only one or with only one other member, so the heaven of the stars could not be content with only one star. Do not understand me to decide that the stars are in it like bones in its body. For this involves a quite difficult question, and you should not expect or look for its resolution here. But it could perhaps seem to someone that the question is the same as if someone were to ask concerning the tail of a peacock why it is decorated with such beauty and variety of colors and why its whole body is clothed with such attractive and beautiful plumage, while the swan is content with its one white color and the crow with only black. Here it is evident to those who understand a little that this variety and beauty of colors is natural to a peacock, just as we say on account of the others[42] that singleness of color belongs to the swan and to the crow of their very nature. Why then is it surprising if the heaven, which in the opinion of the philosophers is the most noble of all bodies, has a variety and multitude of stars of its very nature? These things have been said with regard to the question of beauty and order so that your intellect may be aroused to think something about the heavenly bodies and the heavens themselves.

You ought also to know along with what has gone before that, as the speaking or word of the creator by which he spoke himself and all things was not such that all things would be or come to be at one time, so his will or willing was not such that all things would be or come to be at the same time, and though it seems strange, he can will something that he does not will. But if he had willed it, his will would have in no way been changed, and it would be true that he had willed that from eternity, and by the same (618b) willing by which he wills one thing, he can will its contrary or can not will it without any kind of change taking place within him or his will.

I have, however, already acquitted myself on these topics in the part of this teaching which precedes this, and I have explained to you what knowing and willing means in the creator.[43] And though they are one in subject and essence, since they, nonetheless, differ in definition or relation or respect, nei-

---

[42] I have read *alios* instead of *albos*.

[43] See *The Trinity, or the First Principle (De trinitate)*, ch. 9: Switalski, pp. 54-66; Teske-Wade, pp. 97-106.

ther of them is predicated of the one. In the same way you see that to know and to be known signify only one reality, that is, knowledge, but they do so in a different respect, and for this reason to know is not also said of everything of which to be known is said. The situation is the same with "to be loved" and "to love," and in general this holds of everything which signifies apprehension or passions of the soul or external actions which come from these, such as, "to say" and "to be said," "to signify" and "to be signified."

Concerning this error it has there been explained to you in the chapter on the predicaments and predications which are made in divine realties that creation does not signify something in the creator, but something from him,[44] nor does illumination signify something in the sun, but rather something from it. For creation is merely the newness of existing or of being from the will of the creator without any means. That is alone and properly created which comes from the creator without any means, that is, a means that generates or produces or even is a tool.

Chapter Twenty-Four
The error of Aristotle and other philosophers who follow him concerning the creation of the first intelligence and the heavenly bodies and elements.

It has, then, been explained to you in general terms how his first creatures, if they were many, or first creature, if it was only one, have proceeded from the creator. And it has been shown to you that [they proceeded] through his word, which is his speaking, because [they proceeded] by his speaking with a single spiritual utterance perfect in every respect. And I gave you examples and comparisons for these points. But because the philosophers, especially the Peripatetics, that is, the followers of Aristotle and those who were best known from the nation of the Arabs in the doctrines of Aristotle, maintained that the first creature was of necessity single and said that it was the first most noble intelligence and that from it there came, in the manner which I shall state, the first heaven and its movement, it is fitting that I produce here some reflection on these points.

The root, then, of their opinion was this. They thought that from what is one in so far as it is one there cannot in any way come anything but what is one.[45] A multitude, after all, in the effect or effects, as they supposed, would not have a cause, if from what is one in the way it is one there were many, and the reason is that unity cannot be the cause of multiplicity on account of the

---

[44] See *The Trinity, or the First Principle* (*De trinitate*), ch. 32: Switalski, pp. 178-184; Teske-Wade, pp. 198-203.

[45] In his *Metaphysics* IX, 4: Van Riet, p. 481, lines 50-51, Avicenna states this principle in almost the exact words which William used: "ex uno, secundum quod est unum, non est nisi unum." See my article, "William of Auvergne's Use of Avicenna's Principle: 'Ex Uno, Secundum Quod Unum, Non Nisi Unum,'" *The Modern Schoolman* 71 (1993), 1-15, where I examined William's use of the principle, but had failed to locate the above passage as William's obvious source.

contrariety between them. For from neither one of two contraries can the other arise. From where, then, will the multiplicity in the effect or effects come, since the cause is one and it causes in the way in which it is only one? In that way, after all, they thought that it cannot be the cause of many or of a multiplicity. Hence, since the creator is one and one reality in every way and did not cause his first effect otherwise than through himself, he did not cause it save in the way in which he is one reality. Hence, from what is one only what is one arises, and from what is single only what is single. Hence, they went further and thought that they explained the manner of this causation. They said that the creator did not cause his first effect through any external means, and (619a) this has been explained for you by me in what preceded. Otherwise, there would not be a first creature, since it is necessary for the means of that creation to have been created first. They thought, however, that no manner was suited to this causation except for understanding <and will-ing>.[46] Though the creator did not use anything—so to speak—except him-self in causing it and did not use anything external to himself, they still did not think that the creator would use himself in some other way in causing it than by understanding himself. For he does nothing outside of himself, since he does not produce the motion of an instrument or the motion of matter, but does within himself everything by which he caused it. But within himself what could he do but cause it by understanding himself?

But if someone said that it is more appropriate that he cause it by under-standing it than by understanding himself, they answered that he did not understand it or anything else outside himself except by understanding him-self as the exemplar and most brilliant and most clear mirror of all things and of individual things, and for this reason he first of all and most of all under-stands himself and eternally understood himself and for this reason all else besides. It was more appropriate, then, that he created it by understanding himself than by understanding other things. Therefore, the first intelligence proceeded from the creator through his intellect by which he understood himself, and since the creator could understand in himself only himself and could do this only in a way that is one, that is, without any manner of diver-sity, there proceeded from him in this way only one thing, the first and most noble of all the creatures. But this is, as they judged, the first intelligence.

Chapter Twenty-Five
How according to the philosopher a multitude proceeded from the first intelligence.

But since the first intelligence in itself and in its act of understanding and in what it understands has a multitude and a multiple diversity and could not operate save spiritually and intelligibly, that is, in the likeness of the creator

---

[46] There is some good reason to take the bracketed words as an interpolation, since William elsewhere accuses the Aristotelians of failing to see the role of the divine will. See below chapter 27 where he points to their failure in this respect.

and to the extent that it was possible for it to be like him, four things necessarily proceeded from it through its act of understanding and through its intellect. For, in understanding the first creator in his magnificence and glory, as though irradiated and filled with great light, it emitted, like a brightness, a second intelligence from itself. But in understanding its own potentiality, it cast from itself, like a shadow, the matter of the first heaven. But in understanding itself in its perfection, it emitted from itself a second brightness, and there proceeded from it, like a ray of a lesser and second light, the form of the first heaven, and in that way the first heaven is completed through its intellect and its act of understanding. And they wanted to understand this form of heaven as the bodily form of the same. Fourthly, in understanding its spiritual being, by which this intelligence is an intelligence, it shed from itself a third ray, that is, the soul of the first heaven which is a power that moves it only in place. And they understood this to be the form and perfection in the proper sense of the heaven.[47] They, of course, maintained that the heaven was an animal composed of the body moved, as its matter, and of such a soul that moves it in this way, as its form. And in this way they said that the lower intelligences, the matters of the lower heavens, and their bodily forms and souls proceeded from higher intelligences until they came to the tenth intelligence which they maintained was the intelligible sun of our souls. They maintained that from it there begins the production of many and multiple things and that nothing more noble than our souls can come from them (619b), as if their light were dimmed to that point and their power diminished through being distanced from the first and universal font.

Chapter Twenty-Six
The destruction of the previous error of Aristotle and of others.

With these points set forth, then, in accord with the opinion of those people, I shall begin to examine whether the truth is that way. For those who make this claim seem to detract much from the glory and magnificence of the creator and to attribute more than is fitting of might and power to the previously mentioned substances. First of all, then, they seem to have erred about the tenth intelligence which they call the agent intelligence. For either it is

---

[47] See Avicenna, *Metaphysics* IX, 4: Van Reit, p. 483, where Avicenna says, "But under each intelligence there is a heaven along with its matter and its form, which is a soul, and the intelligence below it. Beneath every intelligence, then, there are three things in being; hence, it is necessary that the possibility of there being these three come from that first intelligence in creation on account of the trinity which is mentioned in it, and what is noble follows from the more noble in many ways. Therefore, from the first intelligence insofar as it understands the first there follows the being of another intelligence inferior to it, and insofar as it understands itself, there follows from it the form of the ultimate heaven and its perfection, and this is a soul. . . ." Though Avicenna mentions only three things which follow upon the first intelligence, William counts four.

possible for it to use its intellect and its act of understanding, as the higher intelligences use theirs, or it is not possible for it. But if they say that it is not possible, then it is not possible for it to understand itself. Hence, it is not possible for it to understand something else. For if it cannot understand the truth of its own essence which it has most present through the presence of the same, how much less will it be able to understand things which are external to it? Therefore, they gave it the name "intelligence" to no point and in vain. But if it can use its intellect and its act of understanding in that way, another intelligence and another heaven ought to come from it in that manner. And in this way there will be no end of heavens and of intelligences.

Moreover, by understanding itself alone, namely, by understanding its potentiality, this tenth intelligence causes the matters of generable and corruptible things. But by understanding its actuality, that is, the perfection contrary to its potentiality, it causes the bodily forms of those same things. In understanding itself in its spirituality by which it is such an intelligence, it causes human souls or whatever else by understanding.[48] But in understanding itself in that way, it is only one, and it does not operate save as one; hence, there will come from it in this way only what is one. All human souls, then, will be but one soul according to their essence and truth. But you ought to know that they were brought even to this error, namely, that all human souls stripped of their bodies do not differ in any way except by the differences of their bodies, but are all one in truth and essence. I have not undertaken to destroy this error here, but it will be destroyed for you beyond all question in the treatise on the spiritual substances devoid [of matter].[49]

Moreover, the intellect or act of understanding by which the creator understands himself in himself and through himself alone does not regard one creature more than another, and in general whatever the creator is in himself, that is, without any comparison or relation to something else or to some other things, he is equally with respect to all of them. For example, the fact that he is and that he is wise in himself does not have more to do with one than another. He is not more wise about one thing than another, nor does he see or know one thing more than another, because he is seeing or knowing in himself and of himself. The fact that he understands himself and does so through himself does not, then, pertain to one thing more than to another. Hence, for this reason there does not come from him one thing rather than another, just as Socrates insofar as he is Socrates is equally related to all artifacts. Likewise, from the fact that one is an architect or a builder, this house will not proceed from him rather than another, nor from the fact that one is an artisan will there proceed from him one artifact rather than another. But by reason of the fact one is a builder, there will rather proceed from him a building or edifice

[48] The phrase, *vel intelligendo aliud quodcunque*, may be an interpolation.
[49] William refutes this doctrine which he takes to be an inference from Avicenna's views in *De universo* Ia-IIae, ch. 9. See my "William of Auvergne on the Individuation of Human Souls," *Traditio* 49 (1994): 77-93.

rather than some other product. Hence, it is evident that from the creator insofar as he understands himself, there will not proceed from him the first intelligence rather than something else. In this respect, after all (620a), it has no proximity or order or any relation to the creator rather than any other things. Hence, it is not more worthy that it should proceed from him rather than some other effect or that it should proceed first.

Moreover, in understanding all things through himself, the creator understands them equally. For if he should understand one more than another, this would come to him either from the side of things or from himself. But it cannot come from himself, since all things which he has from himself he has equally and in one way without any manner of diversity, just as, because he is wise and good from himself, he is equally wise and good. Hence, since he has from himself alone his knowledge of all things, he of necessity knows them equally. This inequality by which he knows one thing more than another cannot come from the side of things, since it is clearly impossible that things can add or take away anything from his knowledge. Therefore, in understanding himself, he understands all things equally in every way. Hence, neither by reason of the fact that he understands himself nor by reason of the fact that he understands all things, is the first intelligence more worthy to proceed from him rather than something else or to proceed prior to something else. There remains, then, for the creator his freedom and choice because of which there proceeded from him the first creature, whether one or many, which he willed and to the extent that he willed.

Moreover, if he did not operate in creation by his choice and supereminent freedom, but in accord with the order which these people suppose, he would undoubtedly have operated in the manner of nature. But this manner, as you have learned, is the manner of a servant and of one not choosing with ultimate freedom both his manner of operation and his operation.[50]

Moreover, if the first intelligence stopped or ceased from its understanding and knowing, none of the other things would be created, that is, neither the heavens nor those things which belong to them. Where, then, would the wisdom of the creator be in this area if he had placed the whole being and whole non-being of the universe in the power of one substance?

Moreover, either the first intelligence could cease from such understanding and knowing, or it could not. If it could, it applied itself, therefore, through will and choice to these objects of knowledge and to such understanding and knowing, and hence to the totality which followed from them as an effect. Through its freedom and choice, then, it caused all its effects. For how much better reasons is it fitting for the creator to cause in that way.

Moreover, in the order of nature its potentiality was prior to its actuality. But it understood things in an orderly fashion in the order in which they existed. Therefore, it understood its potentiality before its act or the perfection opposed to it. But the order of causes and effects is the same. Hence, the

---

[50] See above note 22 to the translation.

matter of the heaven, on this view, existed before the form of the same, and this is false. It is not prior in time, for then matter would exist in act deprived of its form. It is not prior in order of nature, since the act is the cause on account of which there is potentiality, and matter exists on account of form, not the other way around. For the body is for the sake of the soul, not the soul for the sake of the body. If it could not cease from that understanding and such knowing, but it was necessary for it to understand those things and in that way and order, that necessity was either due to a violence pressing down upon it on the part of something stronger, or it came to it from the perfection of its goodness. In that way the creator is said to produce good of necessity and not to be able to do otherwise, that is, to produce evil. But if that necessity of the intelligence were due to violence, then nothing of the being of the other effects should be attributed to it. For it suffered violence from that which coerced it, that is, which inflicted the violence, rather than did something. After all, a sword which is violently shaken at someone does nothing in the proper sense, but rather undergoes the action of another. But if from the perfection of its goodness it had this act of understanding, as I said, it surely understood in this way because it willed to cause the previously mentioned causes which it knew ought to exist through its intellect (620b) and act of understanding. And in that way we come back to the freedom and choice which I mentioned to you.

Moreover, on this view its will seems to have been the cause rather than the intellect or its act of understanding. For since it willed its effects to exist and knew that they could not exist otherwise than through its intellect and its act of understanding, it willed to understand in this way so that they would exist. Hence, the will was present there as the first mover and first agent. How then are they going to maintain that the bare intellect alone, or the act of understanding, of the first intelligence is the cause of those four things which I mentioned and remain utterly silent about the will of the same?[51]

Moreover, let them grant one of these two: either that it willed its effects to exist, because, as was said, it understood them in that way, or it understood them in that way because it willed them to exist. For, if because it willed that they exist, it understood them in that way, then the first and chief cause of subsequent things existing was undoubtedly its will. But if because it understood that they ought to exist through its act of understanding, it therefore willed to understand them in that way, namely, in order that they would exist, it is as if its understanding persuaded it to will that they exist, because through that it knew that it is good that they should exist. And this is found to be far different in other cases. For though sight shows to an animal at a distance the danger to its life or the safety in which it is or some other advantage, the animal's motion is not on this account called visual or said to be due to sight;

---

[51] See above chapter 25 where William explains how, according to the Aristotelians, the first intelligence emanates the second intelligence, the matter of the first heaven, the form of the first heaven, and the soul of the first heaven.

rather, it is called voluntary or from the will. Since, then, the intellect was within it, like interior or spiritual vision, one should not attribute to it one of the effects which were produced by it through the will. Why then do they attribute those things to its bare intellect alone, making no mention at all of its will?

Moreover, in the heaven of the stars which, according to some, is the first heaven and, according to others, is at least the second, there is found so great a multitude of stars and of things natural to them and of powers and of figures, and there is no diversity or multitude in each of the lower heavens comparable to this. Since, then, the higher the intelligences are, the more they are one, and the further they are removed from multiplicity, it is necessary according to the position of these people that the effects be more one and more removed from multiplicity than the lower ones. But we clearly see the opposite.

Moreover, if the intellect or the act of understanding of the creator by which he understood himself and, by understanding himself, caused the first intelligence did not go out to the intelligence, that is, if by it or through it he did not understand the first intelligence, he would not have caused it through it, and the situation is the same with every worker who works through an art or through an intellect that is a cause. For if the architect or builder did not understand or imagine the home which he builds or plans to build, he would in no sense build it through the intellect or imagination. For this would be as though a writer saw something other than the writing which he writes, or as though a painter saw something other than the painting he paints, for by looking at himself alone neither the writer nor the painter writes or paints something external to him in an artistic and fitting way. Likewise, he does not do so by thinking of or imagining himself alone. The situation is the same if one only thinks of or imagines something other than himself, whether a painting or a writing. For how could an artisan who is thinking of something other than his art produce it, if his art in no sense produces it? This could not come about except by chance, since it would not be possible except by chance that someone who is thinking of building something should write or paint something at that time. But everything that comes about by chance is not produced by art or by intellect or (621a) imagination.

With argumentation drawn from all these points, it is clear that through an intellect that is turned back upon itself alone and does not go out or is not extended to things in any way, the creator did not create or in some other way cause anything. That is, through the intellect or act of understanding by which he understood himself alone, he did not create or otherwise cause anything at all. Hence, he did not create the first intelligence or anything else. It was necessary, then, that the intellect of the creator went out and was extended beyond himself, that is, that he understood everything which he created. Hence, he of necessity understood the first intelligence, if he created it through his intellect and his act of understanding. Either, then, he understood it [alone] when he was causing it, or he understood it rather than some other thing. But if he understood it alone, you see the feeble-mindedness of such men and the impossibility of this statement. First, because they place limits on the intellect of the creator, limiting him to understand a single thing alone—at least at a single moment. Then, they imply in this statement of theirs that the intellect of the creator is so occupied at that time that he is then prevented from understanding other things. They clearly do not understand that the amplitude and freedom of his understanding and wisdom exist in the ultimate degree of amplitude and freedom, just as everything else which he has through himself and according to himself. For all such things are first and greatest, and they are present in him first of all and in the greatest way. But it is not possible that such amplitude and freedom be restrained or prevented in any way; otherwise, they would not exist in the ultimate degree of complete perfection, since they would not be in the ultimate degree of separation from their contraries. For something which either in potency or in act can approach its contrary does not exist in this ultimate degree.

But I shall add to these a demonstrative proof and state that with the creator who is first act by absolutely correct title there is in no sense a place for potentiality. That is to say that the whole of whatever belongs to him is act or in act and in the ultimate degree of actuality. But if at one time he understood the first intelligence alone, he would at that time understand in act it alone. He would, then, either understand something else in potency or not. If he did, then there is a place for potentiality in him. Hence, he is not perfect in all his respects, since he can be made perfect through the understanding of that thing or of those things which he then understood only in potency, since [his understanding] can be reduced from such potency to its act. But if he did not understand something else in potency or in act at that time, then his intellect is the most narrow and wretched of all, since every other intellect is not confined to one thing and understands very many things at least in potency. The blessed creator will also be ignorant of all other things, for he knows only what he understands. But he understands or can understand, according to this error, only the first intelligence alone. But you see by yourself what problems follow upon this error. For, it follows, first of all, that the creator is most unwise; second, that he does not know his worshipers, all the things which are in the world and countless other things with which I need not occupy myself or you.

Moreover, whatever the creator has from himself he has as equal and equally. Hence, understanding this and understanding that, no matter which two things are referred to, he has as equal and equally, since he has understanding this and understanding that only from himself. He did not, therefore, understand the first intelligence more than anything else at any time or moment. In the same way and for the same reason he did not understand it better, since he did not understand it at any time or moment better than any other thing, and the reason is that, (621b) on account of what I said, he could not have this from himself or from the side of the intelligence, since, as you know, the intellect of the creator or his act of understanding derives nothing from the side of things. Since, then, he both caused and causes all his effects exclusively through his intellect and his act of understanding and his intellect is related equally to all things in every way, he therefore causes and caused everything equally and simply and exclusively. He did not, therefore, cause only the first intelligence, as they claim, and this is certainly true. But know that this intellect is the intellect born of him, as has been explained to you elsewhere,[52] and only the Christian people boasts of the revelation and knowledge of such generation. And according to their laws and their other scriptures, they call this intellect that has been born: wisdom that has been born and the art and the word of God.[53]

This is the very great profundity which the Hebrew people have not attained, save perhaps in a few of their saints and wise men, that is, in their prophets and others perhaps who have received this from the prophets. But the Arab people have not yet known this in accord with their community; in fact, according to the error by which they have been led astray, they say in opposition that this is impossible. The theologian Avicebron, however, an Arab in name and pen, as it seems, clearly grasped this, since he expressly makes mention of this in the book which he calls *Font of Wisdom* and wrote a separate book on the word of God which does everything.[54] For this reason I think that he was a Christian, since it is clear from the accounts in histories that the whole kingdom of the Arabs had not long ago been subject to the Christian religion. But some of the ancient philosophers, such as Plato and Mercurius, seem to have seen these ideas, especially Mercurius who wrote a whole book on the perfect word which he for this reason called *The Perfect Word*.[55]

You ought to know that the intellect and the act of understanding, as I taught you in the treatise on predications which are made of the divine realities, are understood according to two modes and meanings.[56] One mode is that by which understanding adds nothing beyond being, save according to some respect or relation. And on this view the creator's act of understanding is his being, and his intellect is nothing other than his essence so that, when

---

[52] See *The Trinity, or the First Principle* (*De trinitate*), ch. 16: Switalski, pp. 98-100; Teske-Wade, pp. 132-134.

[53] See Sirach 24, Wisdom 7:22-30, and John 1:1.

[54] William takes the Jewish philosopher, Solomon Ibn Gabirol (Avicebron), to be a Christian because of his doctrine on the role of God's word in creation. See Kevin Caster, "William of Auvergne's Adaptation of Ibn Gabirol's Doctrine of the Divine Will," *Modern Schoolman* 74 (1996): pp. 31-42, for an account of William's use of Avicebron's doctrine of will to introduce a radical contingency into his Avicennian metaphysics of the created world.

[55] William refers to the work of Hermes Trismegistus, *Logion Teleion* (*De verbo perfecto*). See "Asclepius" in *Hermetica: The Ancient Greek and Latin Writings Which Contain Religious or Philosophic Teachings Ascribed to Hermes Trismegistus*, ed. Walter Scott (Oxford: Clarendon Press, 1924), I, pp. 286- 377.

[56] See *The Trinity, or the First Principle* (*De trinitate*), ch. 16: Switalski, pp. 98-99; Teske-Wade, pp. 132-133.

one is dealing with his intellect, that is, when one is speaking of his intellect or act of understanding, one is speaking of his essence or his being. In the second meaning and mode, his intellect is his spiritual or intelligible word, and his act of understanding is his spiritually or intelligibly speaking. Just as an audible word is a word that is born or brought forth, so a spiritual word or intelligible intellect is spiritually born or brought forth. People in error and opponents of the truth have forced holy and wise men, who have gone deep into divine realities, to make these distinctions as well as many others. For it was necessary that men be taught by the words by which they could be taught concerning things so remote from the intelligence of the ordinary person.

Understand, then, the magnificence of the word of God to the extent that he grants this. For the word of God, as I have taught you elsewhere,[57] is in no way less—as the word of God— than he whose word it is. Hence, it is necessarily God himself; I mean, one God with him from whom it is. And from this it follows of necessity that it is an utterance living in the ultimate degree of life and vitality and that it is an outpouring and overflowing in the ultimate degree of outpouring and overflow. It is the efficacious art and producer of all the works of the creator, and it is not like one of our arts or our spiritual words, like a lamp only showing what one should do and how. In fact, it is necessarily (622a) a most potent power that produces all things. It is not only like a seal or signature, but also like a stamp stamping all things with an impression of its likeness and decorating all things, and it does this by its most free choice and most imperious will. Hence, it is not only the art making known all things, but also the power productive of all things. For an utterance of another sort could not be the first utterance, that is, of the first speaker. It is, after all, necessary that the first utterance be equal in all respects to the speaker or generator, as I have explained to you in the first treatise.

This word or utterance of God is, therefore, like the brightness proceeding from its begetter, illuminating all things according to their capacity or receptivity and decorating all things as far as is fitting by the likenesses of its beauty, just like the brightness of the visible sun. And it is like a face of the ultimate beauty of the same begetter of it, pouring out likenesses of its beauty into the universe, as into a mirror of countless surfaces, so that the beauties of creatures are only reflections of it. On this account the holy prophets frequently call it the face of God, and he himself in them and speaking through them calls himself that.[58]

Pay close attention to what I tell you about mirrors so that you consider carefully the diversity and variety of them on account of which some receive the likenesses of such beauty and such a face more and others receive them less. And this variety and diversity is the greatest beauty of the universe, for if any of the species were lacking, the beauty of the universe would be less as a

---

[57] See *The Trinity, or the First Principle* (*De trinitate*), ch. 17: Switalski, pp. 100-101; Teske-Wade, pp. 134-135.

[58] See, for example, Psalm 41:3 and Exodus 33:20.23.

result of this lack. This variety also adds not a little to the well-being and conservation of the universe, as I have already shown you. It has already been explained to you through these points that the creator and the intellect born of him are equally the cause of all things. I mean: equally as far as concerns him, but certain things need other means, just as a human being needs soul and body. Likewise, what is fabricated needs material to be worked on and the tools of fabrication and fire and a carpenter. But God is the cause of all these, and he could produce without those means what is fabricated, but he could not produce a human being without soul and body, because it would not be a human being if it did not have them, for a human being is nothing but those two things taken together or one of them in the other in some relation or manner.

You already understand, therefore, from these things which I have said that the creator causes all things equally as far as pertains to him. But he causes some things through means, means which he himself causes; he causes things through means, when he wills, and without means, when he wills. For example, he caused the first human being without a father and a mother and by their union caused the rest through parents as means, either both parents or one of them. Nor does he for this reason cause them less equally if he causes them through one or through more means, just as if someone builds a house through one or through many workmen, he does not cause it more if he does it through many, or the other way around. In the same way, if he causes it through no means or through some means, he does not cause it more or less when he causes it through no means than through some means.

Hence, it is true without qualification that the creator causes all things equally, insofar as they are from him, and also causes them without qualification, since a means or several means do not add or take anything away from the causing. For I have already explained to you in the first treatise that the creator alone properly and truly is worthy of the title "cause," but other things are merely messengers and bearers of the last things received as if sent from the creator.[59] But an example of this sort is apparent to you in the air which is a medium of the illuminations which are produced on earth and in water and in the eyes of animals and in other things that can be illumined by the sun. From this it is clear that it is like a bearer (622b) or a messenger of such illuminations, and no one says that it is their cause truly and properly, though it offers much help so that these illuminations are accomplished. But they commonly call the sun the true and proper cause of them. It is the same way with fire and the mediate sources of heat. It is the same with any face and the reflections of it in mirrors.

But one should carefully consider that the sun and fire and whatever is like them in this respect have nothing that they have not received from the creator and that they are vessels of the outpouring and overflowing of the first font.

---

[59] See *The Trinity, or the First Principle* (*De trinitate*), ch. 11 and 12: Switalski, pp. 73-79; Teske- Wade, pp. 111-17.

They are such, as if under this agreement and condition that they are first filled and then pour out and spill what is beyond their capacity into other receptacles. In the same way, when riverbeds and other low spots are filled by outpourings of springs and by other means, they pass on what is beyond their capacity to other places. In that way all these things which are called causes, having been filled by the outpouring of the first and universal spring, carry or pass on what is beyond their capacity to other things. And this is what Avicebron says in his book on the *Font of Wisdom*; it is, he says, a proof of the generosity and goodness of the giver and of the obedience of all things to him that each thing is forced to give itself,[60] and he understood by this to give a likeness of itself. This is evident in natural outpourings, for in that way the creator banished greed from creatures, insofar as it is due to a law of nature, that none of them can claim as its own or keep for itself any of its natural goodness so that it does not share it with and bestow it upon others as much as is possible for it. Or do you suppose that the sun can keep for itself even the very least of its rays? And if it were to keep it, what do you think the creator would do? For he would rightly take it and all others from it. Therefore, gather all these examples and likenesses, and you will clearly see that the creator is the cause of all things equally and without qualification, as he knows and understands all things equally.

Moreover, if what they claim were true and in the sense they claim it, to create, that is, to make out of nothing would not be a work proper to the creator and to the creator alone, but would be common to all the intelligences. Hence, he would not properly and solely be the creator. For each of them would make out of nothing the immediately following intelligence and the soul of its heaven and also its heaven, since it would make out of nothing both its matter and its form.

Moreover, since the potentiality of the new intelligence would be greater than the potentiality of the first intelligence, it is apparent on the basis of contraries that the actuality and perfection of the first is far greater than the actuality and perfection of the new one. This is clear from its closeness to the most perfect, that is, to the creator, and from its nobility by which it is by far more noble than the new intelligence. Since, according to those people, through its potentiality, that is, by understanding it, each one of them causes the matter of its heaven, the matter of the heaven of the moon ought of necessity to be greater than the matter of the first heaven. Therefore, the heaven of the moon ought to be greater than the first heaven, for quantity is due to matter.

Moreover, according to this error, there will be only the ten spiritual substances that are observed from nature, and for this reason belief in the angels

---

60 Avicebron, *Font of Life* (*Fons vitae*) III, 46, in *Beiträge zur Geschichte der Philosophie des Mittelalters*, p. 184, where the teacher says, "You have contemplated all things obeying the divine command, and you saw that goodness is what moves all things." See also *The Trinity, or the First Principle* (*De trinitate*), ch. 12: Switalski, p. 78; Teske-Wade, pp. 115-16, where William attributes a similar view to Avicebron.

and in all the heavenly hosts which is found in every law and confirmed by the opinion of almost all human beings will be in vain. But this belief will be established for you by many demonstrative proofs in its proper place.[61]

Moreover, they pay less honor to the creator than to any of the kings or princes, since according to this error they do not maintain a multitude of those who stand before and minister to him. For in the proper sense only those who see him face to face—if one may say this—stand before him or are in his presence (623a), and according to them this is possible for only the ten intelligences or for some of them. Hence, they leave him quite alone and without royal honor, for the ten are not a multitude worthy of royal magnificence and ought not to appear alone in the royal palace.

Moreover, we see that the sun is greater in magnitude and splendor than all the other planets and stars, and on this account its heaven is seen to be more noble than the heavens of the other planets, since it is more adorned with light or brightness and the whole sublunar region is illumined by its brightness and it alone suffices to produce the day and put to flight the night. Because, then, the order of causes is the same as the order of effects, and causes and effects are always proportional, it is necessary that the intelligence of the solar heaven be more noble not only than the lesser intelligences, but also than the higher intelligences, that is, those of the higher heavens which are the heavens of the other planets. You clearly see, then, that there is not the same order of nobility in the heavens as in the intelligences. In the same way the star of Jupiter, which is much greater than the star of Saturn, also goes against this order. Likewise, the star of Mercury, which is the smallest of all the planets, [goes against this order], since its heaven is not the lowest of all the heavens of the planets, but rather according to everyone either the third or the fourth.

Moreover, if the nine intelligences in this way caused their heavens by understanding themselves or other things, they of necessity caused all the perfections of them; hence, they also caused those planets which are certain perfections of them or at least parts of their perfections. For the planets naturally add much beauty and ornament to their heavens. Hence, they are either perfections of them or parts of their perfections and, for this reason, effects of these intelligences. Their order, then, in nobility and other perfections ought to be the same as that of the intelligences themselves. Hence, Saturn will, on this view, be the greatest, most brilliant, and most powerful of the planets, and in this way each of the others will have these perfections according to its order and according to the greatness of its separation either from Saturn or from its heaven and in accord with the relations of the intelligences that cause them. But from the senses the opposite is evident to you and to all who see, even if they are little trained in these matters.

[61] William argues against the Avicennian view that there are only ten intelligences in *De universo* Ia-IIae, ch. 3 and following.

Moreover, if the intelligences caused those planets, they surely caused them by way of the causation by which they also caused their own heavens. Hence, they caused the matters of them by understanding their own possibilities, and by understanding their own perfections or actualities they caused the forms of them. I say, therefore, that on this view the planets of necessity were made not only equal to their heavens, but even the same, since the causes are the same in every respect. For example, the intellect by which the intelligence of the heaven of Saturn understood its own potentiality in causing the matter of its heaven and the matter of the star Saturn is either one and the same in number—not repeated—or it is not. But if it is one, it is numerically one. Therefore, the effect is one and the same, not merely equal. Hence, the matter of the star Saturn and the matter of its heaven will be one and the same numerically. In the same way it is possible to show that the form of them is also the same numerically. Hence, the heaven of Saturn will be numerically one with the star of the same, and the one is not merely equal to the other. But if it is not one and the same numerically, but was repeated, the intellect, nonetheless, by which it first understood its potentiality when it caused the matter of its heaven was of necessity equal to the intellect by which it understood, whether at the same hour or at another, the same potentiality by which it caused the matter of its star. For neither tiredness nor some darkening nor cause of diminishment was produced about it, since such changes do not affect the intelligences. Since, then, from equal (623b) causes that are equal in every respect the effects are necessarily equal, it is evident that their matters are of necessity equal in every way. And in the same way it is possible to show that the equality of the forms. The heaven of Saturn, then, will necessarily be equal to its star or planet, and in this way the situation must be the same with the other heavens and their planets, and about this there is no need for me or someone else to argue.

Moreover, where was that countless multitude of intellects which the intelligence of the starry heaven understood when it caused its form? It is evident, after all, that since it did not find so great a multitude within itself, it understood outside of itself the multitude, by understanding which it caused so great a variety of many forms in the form of that heaven. But this could not be unless the multitude which is found is still in the form of the heaven or in another after it. But another which would be after it could not be the cause of that one, since the cause cannot be subsequent to the effect. But if multitude so understood was the cause of a multitude afterward existing in act in the form of the heaven, that is, if it caused it by understanding, how will this be denied to the creator, namely, that by understanding a multitude in this way he does not cause the multitude of the universe or whatever multitude he pleases? In fact, this is the more extensively and more firmly belongs to the creator to the extent his intellect and act of understanding is beyond all comparison; indeed, it surpasses the thought of the intellects of all others. It ought, then, to be evident to you from these considerations that those claims they made about the generations of the intelligences and the heavens were stated with more subtlety and cleverness than truth.

Chapter Twenty-Seven
On the three causes which seem to have led Aristotle and others into this aforementioned error.

The chief causes of this error seem to have been three. The first of these was their ignorance as a result of which they did not understand the word of the creator or the power of this word. For it is not merely a word that states something, so to speak, but also a word that commands with strong imperiousness in the ultimate degree of strength. For this reason not only those things which are, but also those which are not obey his command, not only in doing and not doing what he commands or forbids, but also in being and not being, in coming to be and not coming to be. And for this reason one of the prophets of the Hebrews says, "He calls those things which are not as those which are."[62]

But an example of this is that, if it were the pleasure of the creator to speak to a dead person through that word of his or give the command, "Arise," the dead person would get up or arise with the same ease in every respect with which a living and healthy person who is lying down or sitting would obey him, if he ordered him to arise. For since he has the most imperious power from himself alone and through himself alone, they of necessity obey him both in death and in life with equal ease.

Notice also that by our words we ourselves not merely make statements, either affirming or denying, but also command that there be done whatever we will. In that way by his single word the creator not only said that all things are done which he willed to be done, but also commanded or ordered that they be done. This was one part of their ignorance, because if they perhaps knew or thought anything [about the will], they did not know that it had the power of command with that imperiousness which I mentioned, and this is his omnipotent power.

The second cause was the ignorance of the freedom of the creator by which he acts without being able to be prevented in any way from that which (624a) he wills or forced to that which he does not will. They, however, have tried to hold, as I have told you, that he works in the manner of nature and in accord with its order, though he works through choice and a perfectly free will. Their statement, then, that from what is one insofar as it is one and through that which is one in every way, and so on, does not apply to the creator in these causations and creations. For the creator does not produce or cause these effects through that which is one or insofar as it is one, but through his will and insofar as he wills, just as a potter does not shape clay vessels through his oneness, but through his will. And for this reason the potter makes them as

---

[62] Romans 4:17.

he wills and of the sort he wills. In the same way God makes things through his word which is not merely a word that states something, but a word that commands with most strong command. And his command and will is not something other than him. I gave you some likenesses and examples of this word here. For this word is not merely the image or expression of the creator; it is also the perfectly lucid and clear expression of the will of the creator for those who are allowed to hear and see it.

The third cause is their erroneous opinion because of which they thought that distance could be something for the creator, and they has supposed that the creator could be remote from some things and close to others and that, for this reason, he does not operate through himself or does so to a lesser degree. They have not understood, then, the supereminence of the creator and the amplitude and strength of his power by which he stretches from the height of the universe to the bottom and from the first creature to the last, containing, holding, retaining all things as he wills and as long as he wills. Otherwise, they would fall back into non-being from which they have been drawn by him and through him. He is, therefore, within all things; he is under all things, sustaining and supporting them as a foundation or pedestal; he is over all things, not only as king and emperor dominating all, but even as a spring most overflowing from which there unceasingly descend rivers and streams of his goodness upon his creatures, that is, upon all the ages and upon individual ages and within all things and in all things, nourishing, propagating, moderating, and ruling all things. For this reason he produces all things in all things,[63] as I shall explain. For, as I already told you, anything good, anything in any way salutary that comes from things has this from his presence, just as life proceeds from the soul, and the reason is that in the soul itself the very source of life is present. It is the same way in every other thing, just as light's proceeding from the sun is due to the presence of the universal and most overflowing source. It is the same way with all other natural operations or rather outpourings. For this reason the holy and wise men in the law of the Hebrews and in the law of the Christians said that the creator produces all things in all things, meaning and understanding all things of nature and of grace.

Chapter Twenty-Eight
On the origin of the heavens.

But I showed you that the word of the creator is not only the art and wisdom born from him eternally and within him and the word by which he not only said that all things either are being made or will be made, but also the word by which he also commanded or ordered this. For this reason I called it his command. I showed you this by a likeness with our words which are not only statements, that is, affirmations and negations, but also commands, that

---

[63] See 1 Corinthians 12:6.

is, orders and prohibitions. The holy and wise man clearly testified to this in his work, when he said, "God said: Let there be light" (Gn 1:3) and subsequently (624b) many other things like that: "Let the firmament be made" (Gn 1:6) They all express his command. For the words, "Let there be," are an order or command somehow conveying to those who understand that the word of the creator is also his order or command by which he commanded the light to be made. He added, "And light was made" (Gn 1:3), as if to say that the light which did not exist obeyed the omnipotent command of the creator and came from non-being into being, as if called by the same word, just as if a dead person were called to life. By the same word, then, and by that single word by which he said all things that either would be made or were being made, he ordered or commanded that they be made. In us, however, it is not possible that it be so, because of the imperfection of our words. For by one word and one expression we state something, that is, affirm it or deny it, and by another we order or command it. But notice the multiple diversity which exists in the heavens on the part of the motions of their poles and regions, and notice that their motion is declining and oblique to the motion of the first heaven which alone among them is straight, and their poles are different from it. For its poles are the poles of the world, and for this reason the philosophers called it "fixed," that is, without wandering, because its motion is always one, equal, not different, and not oblique over the poles of the equator of the day or the equinoctial circle. When you consider all these things, I say, all of them will be a proof for you by which it will be evident to you concerning the intelligences and the souls of the heavens and the heavens themselves, as they maintain them. The reason is that the intelligences and souls of the heavens and the heavens themselves would of necessity be alike in every respect, except for the relations which exist in terms of earlier and later and more or less in power and nobility and other things of this sort. Otherwise, from what would such a great diversity come? For it is impossible that like causes insofar as they are like have unlike effects. It has already been explained to you that the universe went forth from the creator through his word and command or order, that is, as he said by his eternal speaking and word and as he commanded by his same most omnipotent and most imperious word.

Chapter Twenty-Nine
On the generation of the heavens and of the elements: Whether they entered into being at once and suddenly or by succession and generation.

There still remain other questions to be settled, of which the first is whether all things have proceeded from him at once, I mean, all things which do not come to be through generation and corruption. For those things which are generated through the corruption of others are necessarily posterior to those from which they are generated through their corruption, since it is impossible that something generated be corrupted except after it has been generated.

With regard to these the order in which they proceeded or proceed from the creator is clear to you. But with regard to the noble substances that are separated from and devoid of matter it is not appropriate that I consider them here, since their procession from the creator has not yet been established and their being has not been explained, and it is necessary to do both of these things before it can appropriately be asked how they have proceeded from the creator. I shall, then, consider the heavens and the earth and the other elements, the stars, luminaries, and perhaps the animals and plants, if some such were first. I say this on account of those who maintained the antiquity or eternity of the world, for such people necessarily had to maintain that there was always the generation of animals and plants without any beginning (625a) and in general an eternal generation and corruption.

First, then, we must investigate with regard to the heavens and the elements whether they proceeded simultaneously and whether it was sudden or through continuous generation. And we must investigate whether among these any one of them proceeded first or many of them proceeded first. Here I shall also try to establish what the holy and wise prophet of the Hebrews said in his first statement to which the Christian people also assents, "In the beginning God created heaven and earth" (Gn 1:1). Here I shall set down first this root: The order of nature is the order of creation, and its meaning is that those things which are prior by nature should be understood to be prior in creation or first created.

[The rest of the chapter is omitted from this translation.]

(625b)

Chapter Thirty
That the creator alone gives being to created things, and from this the fourth conclusion is confirmed.

Though this has been explained to you in the first part of this teaching,[64] I shall, nonetheless, recall to mind here this explanation. I say, therefore, that if there were no light but the light of the sun, it would not be possible that there be light or a reflection in something else except from it or through it. In the same way, since there is no essential or primordial being except the creator, being will not be received or given except by him and through him. Pay careful attention to this comparison, since being is the first and greatest, that is, the most ample of all those things which proceed from the creator and which each thing receives from him. For it is clearly impossible that something be received or flow over anything whatsoever before being. For only what has already received and has being is able to receive any influence. Being, then, is like light shed by the light of the creator over the breadth and depth of the universe and like an outpouring filling the depth and capacity of the same. In that way, then, picture the creator of the universe as a most radiant light, and

---

[64] See *The Trinity, or the First Principle* (*De trinitate*), ch. 5: Switalski, pp. 34-35; Teske-Wade, pp. 79-80

likewise picture the being of the universe as his circumfulgence and radiantness and brightness spread upon all things and through all things. Just as, then, those things which are bright would owe their brightness only to it, if there was only the sunlight, so those things which exist owe their being to the creator alone, and they owe it incomparably more than bright things could owe their being bright to the light of the sun.

One reason for this is that the light of the sun necessarily has a bodily or local distance and nearness to the things which it can illumine. But the creator is next to and most present to each of his creatures; in fact, he is most interior to each of them. And this can be seen by you through the subtraction or stripping away of all the accidental and substantial conditions and forms. For when you subtract from each of the creatures all these, last of all there is found being or entity, and on this account its giver. For example, when you strip from Socrates his singular form by which he is Socrates and his specific form by which he is a human being and his generic forms by which he is a living bodily substance, there will still remain a being; hence, his being and entity will remain for him like his most intimate garment or undershirt by which the creator clothed him. And when you remove from him his being and entity, all causes of and helps toward being will be withdrawn from him, except the creator. Hence, it is evident that of all the helps and aids for existing, the creator is the first and the most intimate. I have, however, written all these things here for you so that they raise you up somehow to imagine the sublimity of the creator. Complete knowledge of him is the beatitude and glory of our intellective power. I have, therefore, already led you by the paths of proofs and explanations so that it is certain for you that among bodies and bodily things heaven and earth were created first. And [I have led you to know] that it is a prophetic narrative by which the holy and wise man said in his writing, "In the beginning God created heaven and earth" (Gn 1:1). It is a conclusion gathered from three or four conclusions explained and demonstrated in the divine and natural sciences, and I have led you to recall certain of such explanations that were needed and were fitting to be produced here.

[The remaining chapters of this part are omitted from this translation.]

The Universe of Creatures

The Second Part of the First Principal Part

Preface

After what has gone before, there follows an investigation about whether the universe is new or old, that is to say, whether it is temporal or eternal or something eternal.[65] Second, we should investigate the care and governance by which many say that it is governed and cared for by the creator, though many deny this.[66] Third, we should investigate whether this state, that is, the state in which it is, is its permanent state or whether it will have an end and what end or transformation it will have, (683a) whether for the better or for worse, and concerning its newness or the state it will have, whether it will be everlasting for it or it too will have an end. We must also ask whether this must go on without end, as some have thought. We must also ask about what state the human race will have both in terms of their souls and in terms of their bodies. And since the investigation about eternity precedes all these matters, I shall inquire about it first of all. Likewise, I shall ask about the age or the ages and about the ages of ages and the age of ages.

Chapter One
Concerning eternity, and against those who make time a part of eternity.

Know then that certain people have thought that eternity is not something other than time in its essence. For this reason they defined time as a part of the complete eternity, and these people were the Italians.[67] According to them, eternity does not, then, differ from time, except as a whole from its part or as a greater time from a lesser time. According to them, eternity also does not precede time; in fact, if time is really a part of eternity, it by nature precedes eternity. For every part is prior to its whole, since it is a cause of it.

Moreover, as nothing existed or could exist before eternity, so nothing existed or could exist before the whole of time.

Moreover, no one ever claimed that eternity was anything but endless; hence, nothing existed before eternity. For if something existed before it, it preceded it either by some interval or by none. For you know that today precedes to-

---

[65] William uses *aeternale* and *aeternum*, both of which mean "eternal" without any difference in meaning.

[66] William takes up the question of divine providence in *De universo* IIIa-Iae.

[67] See my article, "The Identity of the *Italici* in William of Auvergne's Discussion of the Eternity of the World," *Proceedings of the PMR Conference* 15 (1990): 191-203, where I suggest that William was mostly likely referring to Cicero.

morrow and the whole night which is the interval between these two days [also precedes tomorrow]. Hence, if it preceded it by some interval, eternity was in a sense contiguous with that interval. Hence, it was ended or was terminated at it. On this view, then, eternity will be finite and have a limit, that is, an end, namely, the end of that interval, just as tomorrow has an initial limit in the preceding night. But if it preceded it without an interval, then eternity will of necessity have a limit at it, just as tomorrow has a limit at the preceding night. Hence, in every way it follows from such a claim that eternity is finite. But it is evident that all people define the eternal as what has neither beginning or end, and beginning and end is understood as a beginning and end of duration or lastingness. Likewise, people commonly say that the eternal is what neither begins to be nor ceases to be. Hence, eternity is infinite according to the common understanding of human beings. I state, moreover, that eternity is not divisible into parts in terms of before and after, for the being of eternity is lasting. In fact, eternity is lastingness that is interminable and infinite in both directions. But lastingness and flux are contraries. Therefore, in eternity there is no flux, nothing that flows. Hence, there is neither before nor after in it.

Moreover, what is time but being that flows and that in no sense lasts, that is, that has nothing of itself that lasts in act or in potency? For if some time did last, it would not be time or a part of time, since the being of time is nothing but flowing in its totality—flowing, I mean, without any retention or stability. Hence, the being of eternity is to last without any flux.

Moreover, unceasingness belongs to the definition of eternity; for the eternal is, according to the understanding of all, as I have said, what neither begins nor ceases. Cessation is, however, essential to time, just as flowing is. For to flow in time is nothing but to fall into non-being, but to fall into non-being is nothing but to cease to be (683b). Hence, unceasingness is essential to eternity. Time and eternity, then, are essentially contraries; hence, just as it is proper and essential to time to flow or cease to be, so it is proper and essential to eternity to remain and stand still. But if someone says that to stand still is proper to eternity as a whole, but to flow is essential to the parts, this claim is destroyed in two ways. First, because eternity as a whole is homogenous, just as time is, and for this reason, if to flow or to cease to be is essential to some of its parts, it will also be essential to the whole. Hence, neither in act nor in potency will to flow or to cease to be be separated from the whole of eternity, just as it will not be separated from some of its parts. Hence, it is necessary that the whole of eternity continually ceases and falls into non-being. Notice that this position is equivalent to someone's claiming that a whole is white and a part of it is black, or the other way around.

The second way of destruction is taken from this root that nothing admits into itself what is contrary to its essence. But time is continual, unstoppable flowing, because its being is to flow continually and without stopping. Eternity, on the other hand, is continual, unflowing stability, because the eternal is the continuously stable without flow, that is to say, without ceasing to be.

The essence, then, of eternity is contrary to flowingness and cessation. It does not, then, admit it into itself or into its parts, since its essence cannot be different from the essence of the parts by contrariety.

It has already been explained to you in this way that time is not eternity or a part of eternity and that in eternity there can be neither before nor after in terms of succession or flux or ceasing to be. Hence, the being of eternity is whole at once;[68] I do not mean: at once by reason of temporal concomitance, but by the denial of priority and posteriority, just as if I should say that there is in it nothing before and nothing after. It has also been explained to you that it is endless and interminable in both directions, that is, it does not have either beginning or end. Likewise, it does not have a first or a last and, on this account, does not have a middle. For where there is a middle in duration, it is necessary that there be earlier and later and an order of succession. Hence, it is necessary that eternity be simple and indivisible into parts.

However, many questions follow upon this point. The first is that, since eternity is indivisible into parts, while time is infinitely divisible into parts, eternity stands in relation to time as the indivisible now to the whole of time. Hence, time is infinitely greater than eternity. But no one has ever doubted up to the present day that eternity is infinitely greater than time and that time is within eternity, for eternity precedes it and follows it. For if time ceased, there would be eternity after it, that is to say, if time ceased to be; likewise, if time began, there was eternity before it.

Notice, then, that the blessed creator is simple and indivisible into parts and is, nonetheless, infinite and immense in his amplitude and immensity, containing all things within himself and surrounding them. But with what sort of amplitude and circumscription does he surround and circumscribe and enclose all things within himself? It is evident that he does so with an incorporeal amplitude. Take another example: a species is indivisible into parts in itself in bodily terms, that is, in length and breadth and height, just like a line, but by the amplitude of generality (which is of course a potential ampli-tude), it contains an infinite number of individuals. Yet by bodily contain-ment it contains only its parts. In another way, however, [a line] contains the points which are in it, and it has to none of them a proportional relation in quantity, and for this reason it is most truly said to be infinitely (684a) greater than any of them, that is, beyond all proportion, since it is more than double, more than triple, in relation to each of them. It can, therefore, be said with complete truth on the basis of those things which I have already told you that an individual is in the amplitude of the species like a point in a line, and the reason is that the number of individuals is infinite. Hence, the amplitude of the species is potentially infinite with respect to individuals. For its amplitude does not contain in its power only individuals which are in act, but whatever

[68]   See my *Paradoxes of Time in Saint Augustine*. The Aquinas Lecture, 1996 (Mil-waukee: Marquette University Press, 1996), pp. 16-22, where I trace of concept of eternity as timelessness to Plotinus from whom, I argue, Augustine derived it.

individuals can exist and whichever individuals its definition can belong to. That is to say that this species "man" is not limited so that it can contain only individuals which exist or are coming to be or which will be in the future, as if its capacity and amplitude would have to be expanded if the creator decided to create more human beings than he had determined or that it would have to be narrowed if he decided to create fewer.

It is evident to every intelligent person that the species in itself remains utterly unchanged in amplitude. And for this reason, though the examples of Avicebron are praiseworthy and help the intellect, they are not, nonetheless, proper and suited to the matter with which we are dealing here. For the same philosopher said that the sensible or non-sensible world is in being in the universal, as if he would say in the height or amplitude of being, so that you would understand common and general being and the common being of all things. I mean: in that amplitude of this community the sensible world exists as a little boat in the middle of the sea or as a little bird in the middle of the air.[69] For one should have no doubt that the sea and the air are finite and that the finite cannot contain infinite things of the same quantity, that is, of the same quantity as it. On this account the sea, no matter how great it is, cannot accept an infinite number of little boats, however small they may be, and the air likewise cannot accept an infinite number of little birds. It was explained to you elsewhere that no finite aggregate can be composed of an infinite number of things of the same kind; that is, no quantity can be composed of an infinite number of cubits or inches. Hence, it is evident that, when any little boat however small exists in the sea, there is taken from the amplitude of the sea as much as the capacity of the little boat, however small. Hence, it is evident that there is a certain and definite number beyond which it cannot admit even one little boat or a half of one of these boats—I understand here a boat of equal quantity. It would, then, be necessary that the sea be expanded or that an addition be made to its amplitude, if a greater number of ships were to be sent into it. But concerning the amplitude of the species and genus, it has been explained to you elsewhere.

You ought also to know that quantities which are not of the same genus and which do not have one mode of measurement are not comparable proportionally, and on this account eternity and time are not comparable to each other. For this reason bodily amplitude and spiritual amplitude have no proportion to each other. A multitude of parts and their aggregation produces bodily amplitude, but unity and simplicity produces spiritual amplitude. This

[69]   Avicebron, *Font of Life* (*Fons vitae*) III, 57, in *Beiträge zur Geschichte der Philosophie des Mittelalters* I, p. 205, where the disciple says, "Now I have carried out what you commanded, and I have raised myself up through the levels of intelligible substances, and I have walked about in their flourishing beauty, and I have found that sensible bodies in comparison with them are in the ultimate degree of baseness and imperfection, and I saw the whole bodily world swimming in them, like a little ship in the sea or a little bird in the air."

is the reason why the most high and blessed creator is in the ultimate degree of amplitude, as he is in the ultimate degree of simplicity and indivisibility into parts. And the order of simplicity and indivisibility into parts is the same as the order of spiritual amplitude and capacity, as I shall bring you to know in the treatise following this one which will be about the spiritual and separate substances.[70] Because, then, stability produces amplitude or breadth or length in eternity, but flux and flowingness produces amplitude in time, it is impossible that eternity and time be comparable in terms of proportion. By reason of the fact that (684b) eternity stands still, unable to begin or to end, it does not have a first or a last and, therefore, it does not have before or after or a middle. On the other hand, time is constituted by the fact that it flows without being able to be stopped, and simplicity is the reason for this in eternity. Simplicity prevents it from having an aggregate of parts and an order of them; hence, it prevents it from having before and after and, consequently, a first and a last. In accord with this way you should know that time, place, and number are not proportional to one another. For it is not true to say that some number is greater than a time, or the other way around. Likewise, it is not true to say that a time is greater than a place, or a place than a time. And one should laugh at such expressions of the sophists and at the comparisons by which they say that an hour or a part of time is greater or less than or equal to a mile. I saw in my time teachers of grammar who said that those who speak that way do not speak grammatically.

You ought also to know that the verbs which are most appropriate to eternity include the verbs for being, standing, and likewise for remaining, and these in the present tense only. For to have been or to be going to be, to have stood or to be going to stand, or to have remained or to be going to remain do not properly pertain to it, and I have already told you the reasons for this, and in the books of the prophets when the prophets speak of the creator you will often find that they use "that which is" or "being" in reference to him or of him.[71] But only rarely do they use of him verbs of the other tenses, although they could also be reasonably said of him, but with the interpretations and explanations which you learned elsewhere.

Aristotle, however, said that a curved line and a straight line are incommensurable,[72] but the reason why he said these things is that they do not have the same mode of measuring, and the reason is that a straight line is measured according to the distance of its extremes from each other. A straight line whose

---

[70] William refers to the Second Principal Part of *De universo* in which he deals with the spiritual universe of intelligences and of good and bad angels.

[71] William is thinking especially of Exodus 3:14 where God spoke to Moses and said, "I am who am," and told him to tell the people of Israel, "He who is has sent me to you." See also William's *The Trinity, or the First Principle* (*De trinitate*), ch. 4: Switalski, p. 32; Teske-Wade, p. 78, where William also appeals to Wisdom 13:1 and Job 23:13.

[72] See Aristotle, *Physics* VII, ch. 4, 248b4-7 as a possible source; also *On the Heavens* I, ch. 12, 281b7-8.

extremes are more distant from each other is said to be longer than another. For there is not the same mode of measuring for a curved line; otherwise, every chord would be equal to its arc, and the other way around.

But I shall, nonetheless, return to eternity's indivisibility into parts, and I shall say that perpetuity seems to be a half of eternity, for it has a half of its definition. For, since the eternal is that which did not have a beginning and will not have an end, a half of this definition is the definition of perpetuity. In the same way, if you say, that the eternal is that which cannot begin to be or cease to be, the inability to cease to be is the same as perpetuity. Hence, it seems to be half of eternity.

Moreover, take the midpoint or half of eternal duration; perpetuity is half of this duration. For the duration which does not begin and ends in the present moment is as great as the duration which begins from the same moment and will never end. Hence, the present moment divides the whole duration which neither begins nor is going to end into two equal parts, and in each of them there is half of the whole. Know then that "duration" is said with two meanings. In one meaning it is said to be the time of the life or endurance or existence of some thing, and it is the measure of each of them, and the verb for duration according to this meaning fits only things that exist in time, that is, those things whose being or actions flow with time, as the being of motion flows with time. Likewise, the actions of the heavenly bodies; so too the passions and operations of natural things and the lives of many animals flow by with time. And that is the way it is with all things which begin in time or from time. All things of this sort are measured by time either in terms of their being or in terms of their actions and passions. All such things, then, are mobile and otherwise changeable. With regard to perennial things, that is, those whose being (685a) has no end, they too are measured from the time of their beginning which marks a term for them. Though their being is not ended in time, it is, nonetheless, measured by time, though by time without an end, if time is to be without an end. On this point, after all, there is a question of much difficulty, and there is no doubt that such an immensity is a certain temporal measure. For how does one measure a line if one says that it is finite in itself and infinite at a point, and for this reason perpetuity is a certain measure. And if some bodies were infinite or a line was infinite, but finite on the other end, such a measure would not inappropriately be said to be the measure of such a line, nor is there any clear reason why, if a finite measure measures what is finite, an infinite measure should not measure what it is infinite, if there is something infinite in some genus of quantity. For example, if someone should say that a finite number, namely, ten, enumerates ten points, and the number one thousand enumerates a thousand, and so on with other individual things that are enumerated; in the same way an infinite number enumerates infinite or countless points. And an authoritative and holy statement has it that the number of God's years is beyond estimation.[73] But since nothing at all of the being of such substances existed with time, but

73 See Job 36:26.

it is whole and entire and unaffected in every respect in any moment of time, their being is not properly said to be in time, just as what is whole in a point of a place is not properly said to be in the whole place. Likewise, what is in a part of a place is not properly said to be in the whole of the place, but rather to be there by accident. So too, a place is not said to be the place of something unless it contains it precisely, but a larger place is not said to be the place of that which does not fill the whole of it.

In that way human souls are in no sense of themselves said to be in time, because it is less or greater than their duration, and their being in bodies is undoubtedly temporal, that is, is measured by time, since it has a beginning and an end in time. Likewise, the actions which they do and passions they undergo in bodies and through bodies are measurable and are measured by time. But regarding its being in itself, that is, outside the body, there is no question that, if in that state it has some actions or passions, albeit spiritual ones, they are not measured by time or by a point of time. For if they were sudden and had no duration, it is evident that they are measured by a point of time. If, however, they last, but have an end, since it is certain that they begin, it is evident that they are measured by time. But if some of them do not have an end, they will be infinite in duration, but in the direction of the future, for in the other direction, they are finite, since they begin and have a beginning in time. For if time is infinite, since time is essentially a measure, it will be a measure of infinite things, such as, for example, those which begin in time and end in time. For it is evident that an increase, no matter how great it is, does not change the essence or the species of that in which it is, except in these things alone which have a determinate essence, such as numbers, each one of which has a determinate essence. And thus by addition and subtraction of a single unit they are different in species, but an hour does not seem, in the essence by which it is time, to be of another species than a day, though it could perhaps be said to be another species on account of the determination of the measure or quantity. In the same way a cubit and two cubits are different species of measure on account of the evident determination by which the one comes from the other. For the being of time, as I told you, is wholly to flow, and in this a day does not differ from an hour, or the other way around, but they really differ by these determinations, and this is what I mean here, and (685b) this determination is essential to quantity in the way in which it is quantity.

But there is a question among the wise about whether time is infinite or will have an end. For Aristotle thought that it did not have a beginning and will not have an end. And the investigation of this will be sufficient for you in the following parts toward which I am now moving. But with regard to what I was previously asking, namely, whether perpetuity is a half of eternity, I have already said to you that eternity is utterly indivisible into parts, but that, if time were, in accord with the opinion of Aristotle, without beginning and without end, perpetuity would really be a half of time without a limit in one direction. But this cannot be called "eternity" except equivocally. For I have already disclosed to you the evident contrariety between eternity and time, and from it you can see that one who said that time is part of eternity called the whole of time, namely, time without limit, eternity. For this reason, in his account or definition he did not speak of it, but of determinate parts of it, and so when he said, "Time is part of eternity," he added, "with a certain measurement of the year and the day measuring it."[74]

I shall return to eternity itself and say that it is the contrary of time, as I showed you before, and that it is indivisible into parts in terms of parts of a continuum and that it surrounds time and is greater than time and without a proportional relation. Next, I say that it is proper to the blessed and lofty creator. For everything else begins after it was not, and ceases, that is to say, [everything] else has being after non-being, and I shall make you know this in the following parts after a bit.[75] For only the being of the creator is necessary through itself in all its respects; every other being is possible through itself and is not necessary being. It is, in fact, being that ceases to be insofar as lies in it, and for this reason it falls back into and returns to non-being insofar as lies in it, unless it is retained by the creator, that is to say, through the being necessary through itself.

But we must determine and examine carefully regarding what is the being of eternity, namely, whether it is the being of the creator or something other than him or a privation. But if someone said that it is the being of the creator, how will it then be contrary to time? For the being of the creator has no contrary or opposite except non-being, as I have already made you know in other areas. But if he says that the being of eternity is other than the being of the creator, then eternity began to be. But because this has not yet been explained, I shall say that eternity stands in this way in relation to the lesser being of the possible in itself and, for this reason, [to the lesser being] of that which can end and cease to be insofar as lies in it. You have, however, passed over those points where it was said that nothing admits what is contrary to it or to its essence. For blackness cannot in any way be whitened, nor can cold be warmed, nor can unendingness be ended. But if he says that eternity is continuity of being, there will be the same question. And if someone says that it is the privation of beginning and of ceasing, since it is granted that a privation is nothing, it will follow that he grants that eternity is nothing and cannot even exist, something that is for far better reasons likely with regard to time, since the whole of past time is not now and the whole of future time is not yet, while in the meanwhile no particle of time exists. But if someone says

---

[74] In *On Discovery* (*De inventione*) I, 26, 39, Cicero says, "Time is, in the sense we are now employing— for it is difficult to define it in general—a part of eternity with the certain denotation of the space of a year, a month, a day, or a night." This definition of Cicero's was cited with some variations by William of Conches in his *Gloss on the Plato's Timaeus*; see my article on the identity of the "Italici," note 67 above.

[75] See below chapter 11, where William presents a series of arguments to show that the world began in time. He argues, for example, that everything that receives being from another at first did not exist and then existed.

that eternity is the state or stability of the creator by which he stands in his being without beginning and without end and without any flowing in any respect, he will not escape in this way. For the same questions arise with regard to that state and stability. I say, therefore, that eternity is only the being of the creator or the creator himself, but the name "eternity" says more than his being, namely, the privations of beginning and ending, as well as of flux (686a) and change, and this both in act and in potency, because many such privations really follow upon the being of the creator, and they convey to us his glory and magnificence.

But if he says that unendingness is not a pure privation, but is the strength and might of the being of the creator excluding from him ending and beginning in act and in potency, one should not say that this person is mistaken. But concerning such strength and might there remain the same questions which went before concerning eternity. Hence, he will not escape without returning to what I said, namely, that eternity and unendingness and the other things of this sort signify nothing but the being of the creator, but preserved from beginning and ending and flux and change.

But if you say that to be preserved in this way or to be with such preservations does not matter and that "eternal" and "eternity" do not differ, just as "God" and "deity" do not differ, and as no one with intelligence doubts that God is his deity and vice versa, so the eternal God and his eternity are one reality. Though the name "deity" seems abstract, it is not abstract in such a way that nothing is left of the signification of the concrete name which is "God." In fact, it signifies the whole which this name "God" signifies, though perhaps in another signification.

But if the name "eternity" abstracted only privations from what is signified by this name "eternal," then it would undoubtedly signify things which do not exist, which are only privations, and this sentence, "Eternity is nothing," would signify something true.

Chapter Two
On the eternal, the perpetual, and the temporal.

After this it is appropriate that I inquire about the common expressions by which people say that all things—past, present, and future—are present at once in eternity and are also seen in it as if they were present. I shall investigate what it means to be in eternity and the relation of eternity to time, where I shall set forth an example that can be imagined of the relation of these to each other.

First, then, I shall ask whether eternity has preceded [time] and by how much and in what manner. I say, then, that either eternity preceded time or it did not precede time. If it did not precede it, for the same reason time did not follow after it; hence, it begins together with time and will end together with it. It will be equal to it, and it will be finite, if time is finite, but if it is infinite, eternity will be no greater than time, since it was not before it and will not be after it.

But if it preceded time, either it preceded it by time or by a part of time or by a part of itself or by the whole of itself. It could not precede time by time, since there was no time before the whole of time. Eternity preceded time by either the whole of itself or by a part of itself. But is it evident that it did not precede it by some part of itself, because it does not have a part. Hence, it preceded it by the whole of itself. In the same way it is said that any line is greater than any point by the whole of itself. But if that is true, the whole of eternity was before time, and the whole of it preceded it. Hence, after it there was nothing of eternity and there will not be.

Moreover, if the whole of eternity preceded time, for the same reason the whole of it will follow time. Hence, the whole of it will be after it. Nothing of it, then, either is now or was before.

Moreover, the being of time began and had a first [moment] of its being. Therefore, its non-being before there was time was either perpetual or eternal. It cannot be said to have been eternal, since it was ended or was limited by the creation of the first instant of the whole of time. But it cannot be said (686b) to be perpetual, since it did not begin and because it ceases. We, therefore, lack a proper name for it. I say, then, that perpetuity stands as the opposite to the non-being of time, for the perpetual has a beginning without an end, but the non-being of time has an end without a beginning. For this reason it can be called "anti-perpetual," because it stands as its opposite. Eternity, however, preceded time by the whole of itself, and by the whole of itself it is after time. The reason for this is that, since eternity is always whole, nothing of it passed away, and nothing of it was at all. Hence, it does not follow that, if the whole of eternity was before time or preceded time, nothing of it will, on this account, be future. It is the same way as if one said that God is wholly in heaven and above the earth; therefore, nothing of God is on earth or below the earth. For his being in heaven and above the earth does not prevent his being on the earth or below the earth, since he is whole everywhere. In the same way eternity is whole always, and for this reason its being before time does not prevent its being after time. It is also evident to you from this that perpetuity and anti-perpetuity do not enclose an eternal duration or an eternity of duration. The reason is that something in between can intervene, as you see, because the perpetuity of a human soul which is created now and the anti-perpetuity of the non-being of heaven do not make up one eternal duration. For there is lacking from such "eternal" duration that whole duration of heaven from its creation up to the present moment.

Be careful with such comparisons. A line is said to be greater than its beginning point and than its end point by the whole of itself. But eternity cannot in that way be said to be greater than time by the whole of itself. In the same way the creator cannot be said to be greater than the world by the whole of himself, first, because greatness is not said of the creator and of the world in a univocal sense, and for this reason they are not comparable to each other, as you learned elsewhere. Moreover, since the beginning point or end point of a line are in the same location, as a point in the line or of the line, so the whole line is truly after the point, and if the point is removed from the line, no particle [of the line] will be removed on this account, and the line would not for this reason become smaller. But eternity and time are not related in that way. For eternity is not a point of time, nor are eternity and time, as it were, in the same location or same series.

Likewise, God and the soul are not related in that way, nor the human soul and its body. But if one asks whether eternity is in time, one must without a doubt distinguish, just as when one asks whether God is in time. For he is not in time in such a way as to be measured by it, as is often said, but as concomitant to it, so to speak. He is, then, when time is and whenever any part of time exists. But if anyone said that this concomitance alone made God to be in time, you could say to him in accord with this mode that he is in every house and in every city, because he is where every house and city is. You know on this point that being in time and being in place are not said with one meaning. For to be in a place is to be surrounded and contained by the place, but the motion which is in time is not surrounded in that way by time, that is, according to every dimension and part, but is applied to it, as if through the length of a succession, and for this reason only "long" and "short" among the names of the dimensions are said of time. "Wide" and "narrow" and "high" and "low" are never said of time. That motion, then, is properly said to be in a time which accompanies it precisely, namely, because the motion has nothing before the first or beginning and nothing after the last or end of it, and this concomitance is the temporal measurement which is far from the creator who preceded all time eternally and (687a) will be eternally after time. Time itself continually abandons him, since it flows each day and unstoppably, as it is said. But eternity stands immobile and without any flow in absolutely every respect. There is, then, such concomitance between the creator and time as can be imagined between what stands in the ultimate degree of stability and what flees in the ultimate degree of fleetingness.

With these related in this way, I shall take up the fact that some people say that all things are in eternity and are seen in it and seen in it simultaneously, and I shall investigate what it is properly and truly to be in eternity. I say, then, that to be properly and truly in time is to be measured by time according to the length of the succession of time and that to be properly and truly in eternity will be to be in the state and ultimate degree of stability. But this belongs to the most high and blessed creator alone.

Moreover, if the truly and properly temporal alone is truly and properly in time, the truly and properly eternal alone will be truly and properly in eternity. And I answer to this that this is correct, namely, that the creator alone is in eternity truly and properly. For the meaning of eternity is, as I told you, duration not having beginning or end—in fact, the state which I described for you, namely, in which there is neither flow, nor change, nor before, nor after, that is to say, a state in every respect without flux, without beginning, without end, without divisibility into parts. But those who say that everything is in eternity, if they understand correctly, have almost the same meaning in this statement as they have when they say that all things are in God. For in this statement they understand that the creator surrounds and embraces and, so to speak, encompasses within himself all things by the immensity of his amplitude. They also say in this way that time is in eternity and revolves or flows within the immensity of eternity, just as the whole movable world revolves and moves within the immensity of the creator, since the immensity of the creator surrounds it wholly. For he is above it as its most high lord, and within it as its supporter and sustainer so that it does not fall back into non-being, and around it as conserving it and protecting it.

Chapter Three
How all things are at once and present in eternity.

Concerning their statement that all things are present and at once in eternity, there is some question about how they understand this. For opposites cannot exist at once in the same thing. How then is it possible? Socrates is in eternity. Is he there at once as an old man and as a boy? As healthy and as sick? Or is there in eternity only his old age? Or only his boyhood? Only his health? Only the illness of Socrates? Both of them? Or neither of them? But if neither of them is in eternity, then all things are not in eternity. But if both of them are there, since in eternity there is no earlier and later or before and after, they will, therefore, be in eternity simultaneously. In eternity Socrates will be a boy and an old man, healthy and ill. And the same thing will hold for all the other contraries by which change takes place. And in general, how do they understand that those things are simultaneous in eternity which could never be simultaneous in time?

Moreover, either in eternity there are past things and future things according to their truth, or there are not. That is, they are there or they are not there insofar as they were or will be. If they are there according to their truth, then, since they were or will be according to before and after and in an order of succession, they will likewise be that way in eternity. There will, then, be in eternity earlier and later, before and after, and succession. But such names have already been excluded from (687b) eternity. If, however, they were not there according to their truth which I stated, since they do not have another mode of being than successive and ordered, as I said, they will, therefore, either not be there at all, or they will be there fraudulently or falsely. I, then, say to this that I have already set myself and you free on this point, for nothing temporal, as I already disclosed to you, can truly and properly be in eternity. But the language of such men has this sort of meaning: that all the things which eternity possesses are within it as always present, since nothing in it flows or passes, begins, or ceases. When, therefore, they universally understand about all things, namely, temporal and spiritual things, that they are all present in eternity, they undoubtedly understand that the eternal creator, who is the most brilliant or infallible viewer of all ages, has all things present to himself, that is, he sees and looks at them, because he does not see present things more than past or future things or absent things in some other way. For just as the presence or existence of things adds nothing to his most luminous knowledge, so their being past or future takes nothing away from his knowledge of them. The reason, however, for this is that the creator does not see things through something other than himself. For he is for himself the light by which he sees, and he himself is for himself the likeness or example or mirror in which he sees whatever he sees. In gazing upon himself, he sees all things; I shall produce a consideration of this point which should be sufficient for you in the treatise which follows this one.[76]

Chapter Four
The relation of eternity and time, and on each of these.

The imaginable example of the relation of eternity and time which I promised you is that you imagine eternity as an immense wheel and within it the wheel of time so that it touches it at one point only. For you learned elsewhere that it is necessary that a circle touch a circle or a sphere a sphere—whether this be on the inside or outside—at only one point. Because, then, the whole eternity stands still and, as you heard, is whole all at once, imagine that, as the wheel of time touches the wheel of eternity, there is contact only to the extent that point by point in its revolution a point touches it, and this is time, and on this account nothing of time is whole at the same time. It is similar, if you imagine eternity as a most brilliant wheel and its luminosity is the very being or entity of it, and from it its light flows over time insofar as time is receptive of it. And since it is not receptive of its being according to some totality, that is, neither according to its own totality nor according to the totality of one of its parts, the light of being from eternity does not flow over it except point by point, just as a wheel of this sort cannot be touched except point by point. For on account of its unstoppable flow it can be illumined only point by point. You will also be helped in this, if you imagine water coming out of some vessel drop by drop and unable to come out in some other way, for potentiality confined in that way is so strong that time cannot come forth from it into act except moment by moment, just as the narrowness of the hole in the previously mentioned vessel does not permit the water to go out except drop by drop. Of all created things time has a weaker being, but this is evident from the fact that its actuality is in the ultimate degree of smallness, while its potentiality is just the opposite. For time exists only according to its least part, that is, according to only a point, and it does not exist (688a) in terms of the most of itself, and I understand here this being as the ultimate of actuality, while I understand that non-being, that is, the non-being that belongs to time, as the most potentiality. It seems worthy of wonder that between the mighty being of eternity and the weakest being of time there is nothing in between, as it seems. If that middle something did

---

[76] See below *De Universo* Ia-IIae, ch. 8.

exist, it would either be wholly flowing like time, or it would be wholly permanent like eternity, and in neither of these two ways would it be something in between. Or it would be flowing in part and permanent in part, and this would not be one thing; in fact it would be an aggregate of eternity and time, if a part of it were truly lasting and another part of it were truly flowing,

But if someone says that the horizon of eternity and time which the philosophers maintain is what is in between, for it shares, it seems, in each of them, this horizon is nothing but perpetuity, and perpetuity seems to share with time a beginning and with eternity the lack of an end. For these two reasons the philosopher said that it is the horizon of eternity and of time and [that it is] after eternity and above time; I mean: after eternity on account of its beginning and above time on account of its lacking an end.[77] And they seem to hold that time is finite, that is, a finite duration, insofar as it is said to be above time. But he called perpetuity the horizon, for an horizon is the circle dividing two hemispheres, namely, that which is seen of the heaven above the earth, which is undoubtedly a half of it, and that which is not seen, which the earth prevents from being seen, which is necessarily the other half. For this reason it seems to him that in the very beginning of perpetuity there would be a division as by the halves of eternity, as I told you above.

But such eternity can be understood only as eternal time. "Horizon" is understood as the zone of what rises (*zona orientis*), and in common speech it is said to be the circle that limits our vision. Hence, we begin to see the sun and the moon and the stars when they rise by the motion of their revolution above our horizon. But we cease to see them when they descend beneath it. But one can rightly ask what the philosopher understands [in saying] that all being is before eternity or above it or is in eternity and with it or is above eternity and above time, as is the soul which is at the horizon of eternity. But nothing can be understood to be before eternity or beyond it except the blessed creator himself, and this anteriority or priority can be only that of causality by which every efficient cause is universally understood to be prior to its effect. For it is impossible that he precede eternity by eternity or by time. It is impossible that he precede eternity by time, because it would then be necessary that that time preceded eternity. Hence, eternity would be finite and brought to an end at that time.

Likewise, it is impossible that the creator precede eternity by eternity, for then it would be necessary that he precede it by the same eternity or by another eternity. If by the same eternity, the same eternity would be prior to itself. But if by another eternity, one eternity would be after another, and this cannot be except in one of two ways: Either it would be after it without any interval or with some interval. If without an interval, then it would have a limit at it, and it would begin from it, as a day has a limit at dawn or the night immediately preceding it. But if there were an interval between the two eternities, the later eternity would have a limit at it and would begin from it, and

---

[77] I have not been able to identify the author to whom William refers.

in that way the eternity would be limited in that direction. It is evident, then, that nothing is before eternity by duration, because it is not before it by either time or eternity, as I have already shown you. It is the same way in the other direction. Therefore, when the blessed creator (688b) is said to be before eternity, he is said to be before eternity in the manner of causal order, not by the order of duration or of succession.

Chapter Five
What sort of eternity there is according to Aristotle.

Know also that according to Aristotle this eternity does not exist, and according to the meaning of that philosopher this term means only eternal time, that is, duration that is infinite in both directions.[78] But I shall bring you to know and explain whether such duration is possible in some created things, because neither time nor some other continuum can be infinite in any way. In this continuity, then, and with it Aristotle posited the ten intelligences or more of them, if they were more than ten—for he did not settle this question in his metaphysics, but claimed that there were as many intelligences moving the heavenly bodies as there were heavenly motions, but he did not clarify the number of the heavenly motions in the treatise which came into my hands.[79] He was brought to locate the intelligences in eternity especially on account of the belief by which he supposed that they have nothing in potency and that for this reason nothing can be added to them, nothing can be taken away, and nothing acquired by them. Rather, they have in act the whole of what they naturally could have, and for this reason none of those things which they have could be in flux for them, and none of those things which they do not have could flow into them, and this is undoubtedly a certain approximation and closeness to eternity.

Chapter Six
Some difficulties from Scripture regarding eternity are explained.

What the prophetic language of the prophet of the Hebrews and of their lawgiver contains is strange and involves no small question. He says, "The Lord will reign for eternity and beyond" (Ex 15:18) . Another prophet of that

---

[78] Since the real Aristotle had no idea of eternity as timeless duration, William is probably referring to Avicenna here, as he often does when he talks about Aristotle and his followers.

[79] In *Metaphysics* IX, 3: Van Reit, p. 475, Avicenna says, "Hence, the number of the separate intelligences after the first principle will be according to the number of the motions. But if the cycles of the planets were such that the principle of the motion of the cycles of each of the planets is a power flowing from the planet, then it will not be far from their being distinguished according to the number of the planets, not according to the number of the cycles, and then the number will be ten."

nation says, "The Lord will reign for eternity and for age upon age" (Ps 9:37). Either, then, there is something beyond eternity and after it; I mean: something which is either time or eternity or perpetuity, or there is not. If there is, you know that this has already been excluded by what has already been said. For it would follow from this that eternity would come to an end at it, if it were immediately after eternity. But if there were an interval between it and eternity, eternity would of necessity be ended in that interval and at it. But if there is nothing of the sort after eternity, how, then, will God reign in it? Nor does it seem that it is something in eternity or in perpetuity or in time or in a moment of time. And for this reason it seemed to some that the meaning of that statement, "The Lord will reign for eternity and beyond," is this: "for a duration of whatever length and beyond," taken separately, as if he said, "for a thousand years and beyond" and "for a hundred thousand years and beyond," and so on to infinity. But how will they explain that other passage, "He will reign for eternity and for age upon age"? He seems to understand by "age upon age" the age which will be after the present age, that is, after the age which now exists, and in accord with this "for eternity" would be an concept referring only to the present age. But someone could understand that "age upon age" is an explanation of "for eternity," because he said, "for eternity," as if to say, "The Lord will reign for eternity, that is, for age upon age." For it has already been explained to you that, just as eternity (689a) precedes the present age and time, so it follows them, for they are within it, as you heard in the preceding part.

But if someone says that it was said in the figure which the Greeks call "hyperbole," do not be surprised that this manner of speaking is found in the books of the prophets which are undoubtedly the words and oracles of God. In this way cities are in them said to be walled to the heavens.[80] And by such a figure of speech which is called "excessive," he wanted to express the infinity of the creator. You ought, however, to recall that another prophet of the same nation said of the creator, "He made the earth in everlasting time."[81] How, then, did he understand "everlasting time"? Likewise, in the scriptures of the Christians one often reads that eternal life and eternal happiness will be given to God's elect and friends after this life. In this usage there is an extended sense and not the proper understanding of the name "eternal," for the happiness which will be given after this life necessarily begins then. Hence, it cannot on this account be called eternal. They say "eternal," then, in place of "perpetual." In that way they call time "everlasting" on account of its long duration. For if, as some have thought, the whole of time, that is, taken in its totality, namely, which begins from the creation of the world and will end on the day of the general judgment, is only seven thousand years, its duration is undoubtedly very long, and for this reason the prophet called it "everlasting."

---

[80] See Genesis 11:14.
[81] See Baruch 3:32: "Qui praeparavit terram in aeterno tempore" as a possible source for this citation.

Chapter Seven
The meaning of age, generation, family, lifetime, era, the ancient day,
and of the eternal years of the Lord which do not fail.

Having settled these points, I shall continue according to my promise to show that age is understood in two meanings, namely, for the things themselves, as the world is called the age. For this reason the heavenly paradise is called the next age. The present age is said to be this present state of instability and mutability in which we are, and these are the valid meanings of this term "age," and they are very commonly used.

[The rest of this chapter is omitted from this translation.]

Chapter Eight
Whether the world is eternal, and
concerning the error of Aristotle and Avicenna.

Having settled these points, I shall undertake the promised investigation and explanation concerning the newness and antiquity of the universe as a whole and concerning the temporality and eternity of it. My meaning in these statements is: Is the universe itself new or old, that is to say, temporal or eternal? Did it begin to be, and will it cease to be? But I said "as a whole" because it is not my intention to investigate the individual parts of the universe, that is, of the totality of creatures. For I do not intend to examine concerning individual creatures, for example, concerning Socrates and Plato, whether they began to exist, because such [an investigation] raises no doubt or question, but concerning the great parts of it [i.e., the universe], concerning species and genera of created things.

I shall, then, first of all set forth the opinion of Aristotle and the reasons which led him to his opinion and also others which could have moved him to this view. Whatever may be said and whoever may try to excuse Aristotle,[82] it was undoubtedly his opinion that the world is eternal and that it did not begin to be, and he held the same view concerning motion. Avicenna held this after him, and they added reasons and proofs for this. Likewise, other expositors of the same Aristotle held the same view and made it theirs.

Their first reason is that the creator either preceded the world or did not precede the world. If he did not precede the world, the creator did not exist without the world's also existing. The world, then, did not begin to exist, and this is what they intend: the creator did not exist before the beginning of the

---

[82] Maimonides and William of Conches tried to exonerate Aristotle; see Richard C. Dales, "Robert Grosseteste's Place in Medieval Discussions of the Eternity of the World," *Speculum* 61(1986): 544-563, especially 561, where Dales points out that Grosseteste "was very much concerned with the claim . . . that Aristotle's teaching on the eternity of the world was not contrary to the faith." In "William of Auvergne on the Eternity of the World," *Modern Schoolman* 67 (1990): 187-205, I argued that William of Auvergne shared Grosseteste's concern.

world, and for this reason he first existed when the world began to exist. Therefore, he began to exist with the world. But it is evident that this is impossible for even the promoters of such view do not accept it. But if the creator did precede the world (691a) and did not precede it, as Avicenna says, by time, he preceded it only as a cause precedes an effect.[83] But you have already heard that there is also another manner of preceding, and I explained to you in the foregoing parts that eternity precedes time and does this to infinity, because it is endless. Hence, since the creator is eternal and always was, so to speak, in the whole of eternity, the creator preceded the world by an infinite duration, and as I told you, the creator preceded the world by the whole of eternity.

Avicenna, then, must be helped in this argument. For he proceeds as if there were no other manner of preceding than those two which he mentioned. He could, therefore, have said in defense of his view: If the creator preceded the world, then the creator existed even when the world did not yet exist, or the creator existed without the world. Imagine, then, that some creature existed in eternity with the creator and pondered within itself about whether the world would exist or not, at least if it could be said in eternity that the world is going to exist, because it really could not be said in eternity that the world is. Otherwise, the world would be in eternity, and would be eternal. One of these, then, could truly be said: The world will exist, or the world will not exist. It could not truly be said: The world will not exist or is not going to exist. For from eternity it could truly be said of the future: The world will exist, or the world is going to exist. Therefore, the world is going to exist either without an interval or after an interval. If without an interval, then it is going to exist immediately. Hence, the instant of its beginning already was, and for this reason it existed simultaneously with the creator. For those beings between whose existence there is no interval are simultaneous.

But if someone says that the creator preceded the world by the whole of eternity; therefore, he preceded the world by an infinite duration. According, then, to such a statement, the being of the world followed after an infinite duration. For it would not be true to say that the world will be at a point infinitely after this speaking, unless the creation of the world were infinitely distant from this speaking of mine. Hence, one would for this reason never come to it. For the infinite cannot be traversed, as you learned elsewhere from Aristotle.[84] But suppose that he said this in the sense that the creator spoke in

83   See Avicenna, *Metaphysics* IX, 1: Van Reit, p. 443, where Avicenna asks, "Likewise, by what does the First precede those things which begin to be: through his essence or through time?"

84   Aristotle, *Posterior Analytics* I, 22, 83b6: "An infinite series cannot be traversed in thought." William uses—or perhaps misuses—Aristotle's principle against the Aristotelian position. See Herbert A. Davidson, "John Philoponus as a Source of Medieval Islamic and Jewish Proofs of Creation," *American Oriental Society Journal* 89 (1969), 357-91, especially 366, where he illustrates Saʿadia's use of the principle applied to time.

himself in his eternity and before time and spoke of the creation of the world and said, "I am creating the world" or "I have created it" or "I will create it," If he said, "I am creating or have created the world," since it is clearly impossible that he says or said what is false, it would have been true before time that he is creating or created the world. Hence, on this supposition, the world would have existed before time and, therefore, would have been eternal. But if the creator said before time, "I shall create the world," then he was going to create the world a short while after such a statement. How long is that while? For it is necessary that it be the whole of eternity or a part of eternity or time. If it is the whole of eternity, since it is impossible that it come to an end, it will be impossible to come to the creation of the world, as I said, since it is impossible that it come to an end. But if it is a part of eternity, I have already excluded this point in the preceding sections, namely, that eternity has a part.

But if he also concedes this point, namely, that eternity has a part, and that part preceded the creation of the world and occurred between that statement of the creator [and the creation of the world], this is destroyed in two ways. First, because the creator says nothing within himself that he did not say from eternity. Hence, it is impossible that only a part of eternity intervene between that statement and the creation of the world. In the second way, because that whole part of eternity shall of necessity have passed, when the world was created, or the whole of it did not pass, or nothing of it passed. If the whole of it passed, then it was finite and, moreover, flowing like time, and no difference will be found between it and time. On this view, then, time will not have a beginning, and this is what they intend. But if the whole of eternity had not passed or some part of it had not passed when the world was created, two problems result (691b): First, on this view the creation of the world occurred in it and along with it; hence, the world was created in a part of eternity, and for this reason in eternity, and second, on this view that part was not an interval between the creation of the world and the statement of the creator. Because, then, these are self-contradictory and impossible, it is necessary that that from which the self-contradictory follows is itself impossible. But that from which all these follow is the beginning of the world and the newness of creation. Hence, both of them are impossible.

The second argument of Avicenna on this is the following: A pure and true intellect, he says, bears witness that, if one essence is in all its respects as it was previously when nothing came from it, that is, when it was not doing anything and making anything, and then it does something or makes something, then it of necessity was producing and making it before.[85] Otherwise, he says, how would it now be producing rather than before? Hence, if it was not producing anything before, it is not producing anything now.

---

[85] William comes close to a direct quotation of Avicenna's argument; see *Metaphysics* IX, 1; Van Reit, p. 440, lines 23-25. William also appeals to this passage in Avicenna in *The Trinity, or First Principle* (*De trinitate*), ch. 10: Switalski, p. 69; Wade-Teske, p. 108.

And to help him, as I helped him before, I say that he could have said with the same error that he said this that this is universally the case in natural causes and in voluntary causes or operations, and I shall set forth examples of both. For if fire warms something now which it previously was not warming, it is necessary that in one of its respects it is not the way it was before. This is to say, that it is necessary that a change has been produced in the fire itself or in its dispositions or operations. For example, [a change was produced] in the fire, if there was not as great a quantity before so that it could warm it, but afterward it increased to the point that it could warm it. But [a change was produced] in dispositions and operations, if before there was perhaps something set in between that prevented the heating, or it was farther[86] from the thing to be heated or the thing to be heated had something on it which prevented or impeded its being heated, such as frozen hardness, or iron, or water poured over it. Or perhaps the object to be heated is taken away too quickly before the work of the fire can be completed on it. There may be other impediments and other relations and dispositions. In all of these it is clear that, when fire does its operation, it either has suffered a change in itself, or in terms of one of its dispositions and its relations to the object to be heated there has been a change in its being or non-being. Avicenna, therefore, concludes that fire will not now perform its activity if it did not previously do it, unless it is now different in one of these respects from how it was before.

The situation seems to be the same in voluntary relations and operations. For if an artisan who builds a house is exactly as he was before in every respect as when he was not building the house, then, if he was first not building the house, he is not building it now either, or if he is now building it, he was building it before too. But it is necessary that he receive a new disposition in himself such as the power of acting or the will, knowledge, and art of building, or that he is externally different in some respect from what he was. That is to say, he has acquired new resources which he previously did not have, or workers, or material without which the house could not be built, or some other impediment was removed, or new help was offered. And this is evident in every artisan and everyone who acts voluntarily. For if one is not different in power or knowledge or will from what one was before in any respect, and if one has the same helps and impediments to building as before, then, if one acts now, it is necessary that one acted before, and if one did not act before, one does not act now either. What reason or cause, he asks, could there be why one acts now rather than earlier?

Because the blessed creator was in every respect the same before he created the world or before the world came from him as he was in the moment of time in which he created (692a) it, since he did not create it before, he did not create it then, or if he created it then, he necessarily created it before. It is evident that the creator was from eternity in every respect just as when he

---

86 The Latin has "minus longe"—which seems to be just the opposite of the required sense.

created the world, since he is in the ultimate degree of immutability in every respect, and he has no external help or impediment in any way, since there was nothing before the creation of the universe that could either help or impede him. And in general, since there was nothing at all apart from it, it is impossible that the universe itself or the world be understood as either helping or impeding its own creation. Hence, it is necessary that the creator created the world as soon as he existed, that is to say, from eternity, since nothing new emerged in the creation of the world which would help its creation and nothing was lacking then which would have prevented or impeded its creation.

And so that this argument might be clearer and stronger, I add that no newness at all came to be in the power or knowing or willing of the creator or with regard to these or one of these. Nor is creation opposed to something else. With regard to it no one intended that its newness or existence brought it about that the world ought to be created at the point when it was created rather than not or that it should help toward the world's being. For then it would necessarily be a cause of itself. For everything that brings it about that a thing ought to be or that helps it toward being is a cause of it and a cause of its creation and making. But beginning is nothing but newness, and likewise creation is nothing else on the side of the creature than its newness of being or the new essence of the same.

Moreover, the fact that the cause and the effect are inseparably joined together so that, given the cause, it is necessary that the effect also be given, is brought about only by the sufficiency of the cause by which it is sufficient through itself alone, that is, without being helped in any way by something else, to cause or produce the being [of the effect]. But it is evident that the creator is such a cause with respect to the universe, for he created the universe by himself alone, unhelped in any way by something else. But understand "helped" generally so that you understand as a help: inducement and persuasion and counsel. It is obvious that he had none of them from someone else, for he did not create or cause the world with counsel or inducement or persuasion from someone else. It is evident, then, that by every sort of causal sufficiency the creator is through himself alone the most sufficient cause of the universe. Hence, he is a cause most closely joined to it. Hence, of necessity, if he exists, the universe exists. But such conjunction prevents a separation between cause and effect. The creator, then, was not separated either in eternity or in time from the universe, that is to say: without the universe.

I shall also set forth for you the third argument of Avicenna in which he speaks as follows: Before the world the creator either could create some body that would have a motion that lasts up to the creation of the world, or he could not.[87] It is, however, frivolous, as he says, to say of the creator that he could not have created such a body. But if he could create the body, since

---

[87] See Avicenna, *Metaphysics* XI, 1: Van Reit, p. 445, though William's argument only resembles in some general lines the argument that Avicenna presents.

from what is possible it is not possible that the impossible results,[88] given that he created such a body, the impossible will not result. Let us suppose that he created such a body. Since its motion is going to last until the creation of the world, and since all motion in time necessarily is with it, time will, then, be the measure of that motion lasting up to the creation of the world. The creation of the world, then, was not in the beginning of time, since that time preceded it.

One can proceed in the same way: If it was possible that the creator created many bodies of unequal motion before the creation of the world, then, of necessity it (692b) would follow that motion then existed as well as "before and after" on account of the inequality of the motions.[89] It is necessary that of those things which are moved unequally one of them passes through a larger space than the other in an equal time and that it passes through a smaller space more quickly than the other. And generally, in whatever quantity or in a space of whatever quantity that is to be traversed by both, it is necessary that the one whose motion is faster pass through it before that one whose motion is slower. It follows, then, that in such motions there is before and after according to time; hence, there is time, and for this reason it was possible that time existed before the creation of the world. It is not, therefore, necessary that time began with the creation of the world and that the world began in the beginning of time.

Chapter Nine
He resolves the arguments of Avicenna.

I shall reply, then, first of all to these arguments and proofs of Avicenna, and I shall say that with regard to what he says about the precedence of the creator a response has already been made in what I said to you, namely, that the creator precedes the world by his eternity which I described for you. And he was before the world by a priority, not of time, that is, by a past and flowing priority, but by a priority of eternity that stands forever in its presentness. You ought to know that the "before" of time and the "before" of eternity are not spoken of univocally or in a single meaning, just as is the case with the duration of time and the duration of eternity. And for this reason relations in accord with before and after have no place between eternity and time, nor between the eternal in the true sense and the temporal. Everything comparable is univocal, as Aristotle says.[90] Just as, then, one should not admit a comparison between a time and a number or a place so that one says that a time is greater than a number or a place, or the other way around, so one should not admit a comparison between eternity and time and between the

88 See Aristotle, *Physics* VIII, ch. 5, 256b10-12 for this principle to which William frequently appeals.

89 See Avicenna, *Metaphysics* XI, 1: Van Reit, pp. 445-446, where he seems to develop an argument similar to what William here presents.

90 See Aristotle, *Physics* VII, ch. 4, 248b7-12 as a possible source.

creator and the world or anything else that is temporal. Note too that "before" and "after" and likewise "earlier" and "later" and "was" and "will be" are concepts belonging to time, and for this reason they imply flux and succession and passing.

Bear in mind too that the expressions are similar when one says that something existed before the world and when one says that something is outside or beyond the world. Just as the world does not have an outside or a beyond, since it contains and embraces all things, so time which began with the creation of the world does not have a before or after, since it contains all times within itself as its parts. Bear in mind also that teachers of grammar have said that these ways of speaking are silly and not sufficiently grammatical. For if someone asks another whether, if he were in the highest of the heavens, he could extend his hand further, he would answer him that he was not saying anything and that his utterance was without sense. It is just as if he asked, Have you seen the man who is an ass? For, just as this implies something impossible, namely, that a man is an ass, the other implies something impossible when he says that there is a place which is not the world or in the world. But these statements that there was something or there was nothing before the world do not contradict each other in the meaning which I stated, just as those expressions: Either you saw the man who is an ass or you did not see him. And what is more, not only do they not say something contradictory to each other; they do not say anything at all. For if someone asks whether there was something before the beginning of time, since "before" is a meaning belonging to time, it is the same as if he asked whether in the time which preceded the beginning of time there was (693a) something. Likewise, if someone asks whether there is something outside or beyond the world, it is the same as if he asked whether there is something in a place which is outside the world. But no one with intelligence regards these expressions as true expressions or as worthy of response.

To the second argument upon which he especially relies and which he says is the testimony of a true and pure intellect, one must clearly reply that such testimony is not true and, for this reason, it is not the statement of a true and pure intellect. The explanation is as follows: Either it is impossible for the creator to create a substance, the creation of which does not need to be helped by one of those things which exist, or it is possible. But for this not to be possible for the creator is problematic, even for Avicenna. Hence, he necessarily has to admit this point. I shall, nonetheless, explain that it is true, and I shall say that the power of the creator does not extend only over a particular possible, but over the possible absolutely and, for this reason, over every possible or everything that in itself can be created. The reason for this is that the power of the creator would not be in the ultimate degree of amplitude since it would be restricted to certain possibles. For the possible in itself without qualification is far more ample than a particular possible.

Moreover, the influx and the receptacle are said relatively to each other. Hence, one of them is not more ample than the other. As the receptacle in the ultimate degree of amplitude stands in relation to all influences, that is to say, so that there is nothing else upon which an influence can fall, so the first and greatest source of influence is in the ultimate degree in relation to other influences so that neither in act nor in potency nor even in intelligence is there an influence that does not come from it or which could not be from it. For a river bed of receptivity ought not to be more ample for receiving than the source that is spoken of in relation to it is for pouring into it.

Moreover, I shall set an example for Avicenna himself in the first intelligence. He says that it is the most noble of all creatures and that it does not exist in a body or depend upon a body or upon one of those things which exist but upon the creator alone. It is clear, however, that it is not impossible for our intellect to imagine another similar intelligence and to contemplate these, insofar as they are in themselves, just as we do with two individuals of the human species, for example, Aristotle and Plato, about whom no one with intelligence doubts that, when they are considered in themselves, they are equally generable and were so before they were generated. So I say about the sun that it is possible for you to imagine another sun with it and that, when you consider them both in themselves, you will undoubtedly find them to be equally possible and equally generable and creatable, insofar as they are in themselves. I say the same thing about the first intelligence and about another intelligence similar to it which, nonetheless, does not exist. For when they are considered in themselves, that is, abstracted from their being and stripped of the same, you will find that they are equally near to being and, hence, equally possible, and for this reason, equally creatable insofar as they are in themselves. But nothing can be created except by the blessed creator; hence, you will find that the creator is equally powerful for creating something else or another intelligence.

Moreover, the power of the creator does not regard one intelligence or its possibility more than another or its possibility. Nor is there a reason in one of them why the power of the creator should regard it rather than the other insofar as it is considered in itself. The reason is that in this consideration, namely, by which it is considered in this abstraction and nakedness, the one is neither greater nor better in any way, nor is it closer to being than the other. Hence, it is evident that the creator has no more reason to create the one than the other. Suppose that he created the other one. Since (693b) given something possible, it is impossible that the impossible results,[91] the impossible will not result from that supposition. I say, therefore, that the creator who now creates this intelligence is now when he creates it in every respect as he was before when he did not create it, for in himself he is in the ultimate degree of immutability. But there are no dispositions or relations which help the creator so that he creates it or so that it is created now. For I have already stated for you that he in no way depends upon any of those things which exist; hence, it is helped by none of those things which are in order that it be

---

[91] See Aristotle, *Physics* VIII, ch. 5, 256b10-12.

created, except for the creator alone. This can be seen by you from the creation of another intelligence which is brought into being by the creator alone and through him alone. It is, then, evident to you from this example that, when he creates this intelligence, he is in every respect as he was before when he did not create it. Hence, the contrary of this is false, and for this reason it is not the testimony of a true and pure intellect. And this is the root from which he intended to draw the strongest proof of the eternity or antiquity of the world.

But I shall destroy for you in another way this root upon which Avicenna leans so heavily, and I shall say that either there is something new or there is not and all things are eternal. By "new," as I told you, I understand something that began. Hence, if there is nothing new among those things which are, all things will be eternal, that is, without a beginning of their existing. But it is so clear that this is problematic and impossible that one should not argue about it by reason, but rather attack it with fire and sword and wipe it out along with those who say this. It remains, then, that he admits that something really begins. For the sake of clearer understanding, let this cause be called A. Before A produced anything, it was in all respects as when it produced it, or it was not. If it was, this already contravenes that which he said was the testimony of a true and pure intellect. But if the cause A was not in every respect before A produced anything as it was afterwards when A had produced something, it was, therefore, changed in some respect. Let that new element produced in it or around it be called B. And since it is certain the B has a cause, the same question remains about the cause of B. Either before it produced B, the cause of B was in all its respects as it was after it produced B, or it was not. If it was, they already contradict that irrefragable testimony. But if he says that it was not, there will, therefore, be something new produced with regard to the cause of B. Let this something new, then, be in turn called C. Since C has a cause, the question remains. Either the process will go on to infinity, or there will turn up a cause which is contrary to the testimony of that true and pure intellect. If he says that the process goes on to infinity in that way, it will, then, be impossible that something come to be unless infinite things come to be with it.

But Aristotle already explained in his book which he called *Hearing* that this is impossible,[92] and another explanation of this impossibility is easy for you, because an infinite number of things cannot be done at the same time by one and the same agent, nor is it possible that an infinite number be acting at the same time, and on this account it is not possible that there be an infinite number of bodies or an infinite number of bodily agents at the same time. Hence, there cannot be an infinite number of things acted upon; likewise, one thing acted upon cannot receive an infinite number of actions upon it.

But if he says that, when something new is produced, it is not necessary that an infinite number of things be produced at the same time, but that it is

---

[92] See Aristotle, *Physics* VIII, ch. 5, 256a3-256b3.

necessary that certain things be produced which help the new thing toward
being, while others are destroyed which impede it, he falls back into the same
problem of infinity, and this is that it is no less a problem for an infinite
number to be destroyed or for an infinite number of destructions to take
place than for an infinite number of things to be produced (694a) or for an
infinite number of productions to take place. And it will follow from this that
it is impossible that something be produced, because in the production of
anything new it will be necessary that an infinite number of things be destroyed. Just as, however, it is impossible that an infinite number of things be
produced at the same time, so it is impossible that an infinite number of
things be destroyed at the same time. From these arguments it also turns out
for Avicenna that in every making or creation of anything new an infinite
number of innovations are produced. And you can argue if you wish over this
point in the same way more briefly and more clearly, it seems, as follows: You
may say that the cause of something new is new either according to itself or
according to something that is in it or according to one of the dispositions or
relations which are around it, and these are the things by which it is helped or
impeded, and this is what I mean by "something new" or by "newness" here.
It is evident, then, that the cause of everything new is new in this way. Therefore, because the new cause is something new, it is in this way necessary that
it too have a new cause in the same way, and in that way the argument will go
to infinity, or there will be a circle of causes. It has, however, already been
explained to you that it is impossible that there be an infinite ascent of causes
and likewise that there be a circle.[93]

But I added for you a proof and said that the sufficiency of a cause is the
cause which produces the inseparable conjunction between the cause and
effect. It is indeed probable, and its probability deceives many. To it I reply
that some causes work through necessity, and these are natural causes, and
they do not have power over their action or freedom or choice for both alter-
natives. For this reason Aristotle said that nature works in the manner of a
servant.[94] An example of this is fire; you know that it does not have power
over heating and not heating, nor freedom to choose both of them; in fact, it
must heat the material that comes into contact with it and is receptive of its
action. But other causes operate through will and choice, and among these
are some which operate by a will that can change to the contrary, that is, to
not willing. Likewise, some act by a will that is renewable by new counsel or
a new persuasion or by one of the passions, such as love and hatred, sorrow
and joy, hope and fear, anger and peace. For such a will is changed to the
opposite. Or something new is produced in the one who wills, and it is undoubtedly true in such wills that, when they produce something new that

[93] See William's *The Trinity, or First Principle (De trinitate)*, ch. 1: Switalski, p. 18;
Teske-Wade, p. 66.
[94] See above note 22 to the translation.

they were not producing before, an innovation is necessarily produced in the agents or in one of the dispositions or relations that we have often mentioned. You ought, nonetheless, to know that it is not necessary that everything which is destroyed or which perishes be destroyed by something new acting upon it. For some things are so feeble and weak in being that they fail of themselves, and you clearly see this in time and motion. For time flows into non-being with nothing pushing it along.

The creator, however, acts through a will that is most free and most dominant and immutable in every respect, and on this account his effects are joined to him when he wills and are separated from him when he wills. In natural causes, then, which act through necessity, as I told you, such sufficiency suffices for the previously mentioned conjunction. The same is true in those beings which act voluntarily among us, and the reason is that it is not in their power that they do not begin to act once the power, knowing, willing, and other dispositions concur. But in the creator on account of a will that is most free and most dominant and on account of his immutability, it is not necessary that he act or begin to act, except when he wills. And notice that it is possible that the creator now will something, but he could have not willed it without any change of his will. In us, however, just the opposite is necessarily (694b) the case, and you learned this elsewhere. On account of this Avicenna was mistaken on this point, and so too was Aristotle, for they did not see that the creator could will something and could not will it without any change of his will, just as is the case with his knowledge. For the creator knows that something will be, though it is possible that it will not be. But if it turned out that it will not be, then the creator in truth would not now know that it will be. Hence, the creator knows something, though it is possible that he not know it now, and this happens without any change which is produced in him or in his knowledge, and this is what they did not notice in the blessed creator.

Chapter Ten
Some difficulties are resolved.

After these arguments, however, I shall add some others before I come to the arguments of Aristotle, and I shall say that people erred about the newness of the world on account of the shortsightedness of their intellect and the difficulty of their imagination. For it is most difficult for them to imagine that every place either is[95] within the world or is beyond the world, since they cannot free themselves or release themselves from the meanings of these expressions "outside" or "beyond." Likewise, they cannot free themselves from the meanings of "before" and "after." I have, however, already freed myself and you from these. As a result of this error and this difficulty a certain phi-

---

[95] I have omitted the negative as the sense seems to require.

losopher from the Italians asked, inquiring why they slept or the creator had slept for countless ages, and afterwards, as if awakened, he created the world.[96] For such a man belonged to those who could not imagine a finite time containing all times, since he says that the creator slept for countless ages as if countless times had preceded time. But you have already been freed from these problems, and you will be set free even better in the next chapter against the error of Aristotle, namely, on the question: Did God create the world from eternity? For nothing else but his most pure and most generous goodness induced him to create it, and this is not decreased or increased or otherwise changed in any way. And he too was unchanged in every way, and he did not for the first time see benefits on account of which the world should be created, nor did he see that they were greater in the creation of the world than in his eternity. Nor did he see that creation was then easier for him than in his eternity. And so why did he create it then rather than in eternity?

To this I reply that the solution of this question is found in the doubt itself. For it is seen from this argument that it has been established that there was not an impediment preventing the world from being created from eternity or in eternity because of a defect or an impediment on the side of the creator. Hence, it is evident that this impediment comes from the side of the world whose nature was not able to be created from eternity or was not receptive of eternity. And this will be explained to you in the chapter just mentioned not only regarding the world, but regarding every possible, because its very nature which is possibility is excluded from eternity.

In the same path and in the same manner you will reply to all similar questions, such as, when one asks what the creator intended in the creation of the world. Either he intended his glory in the creation of the world, or the benefit of the world and of worldly things, or both. Whichever of these one says, it is evident that greater glory would have been caused from the creation of the world, if the world had been created from eternity and greater benefit for the world and for worldly things to the extent that eternity is greater than time. He, therefore, ought to have created it from eternity. (695a) But if he says that the creator intended none of these, but created it on account of himself alone or freely, for even greater reason he ought to have created it from eternity.

Know, however, that when he says "freely," he expresses the idea of a benefit for another. But with regard to the statement that the creator is said to do something for his own praise and glory, know that, when the praise and glory of the creator is examined more closely, it is totally and solely the benefit of others. For from this it follows that what is good for other things comes not only most of all, but also singly and solely from him, and whatever good they have they have from him. As for the statement that his glory would have been infinitely greater and the benefit for the world and worldly things would be

---

[96] See Cicero, *The Nature of the Gods* (*De natura deorum*) I, 9, 21, where Velleius says, "But I ask . . . why the builders of the world suddenly arose; they had slept for countless ages."

infinitely greater, this is true, but it does not follow that on this account he ought to have created the world from eternity, because it is impossible, as I told you, for the world to have been created from eternity. This statement is not like the statement by which one might say: If God created you incapable of suffering, greater glory would belong to God as a result of your creation, and greater benefit would belong to you. He ought, therefore, to have created you incapable of suffering. I say that he ought not to have created you such, because God ought not to have done something that could not be done—no matter what benefit might result from it. You, after all, could not become incapable of suffering naturally, and for this reason the creator ought not to have made you such.

But after this it is appropriate that I set forth here the arguments of Aristotle by which he was induced to believe in the eternity of the world. Here it is necessary that you recall those things which went before by which we sufficiently replied to those arguments by which he tries in the book called *Hearing* to defend the view that motion is eternal.[97] And on this account I shall not repeat for you those arguments and the responses I mentioned.

Aristotle says, then, in the book on *The Heavens and the World* that nature determined for some things that they always not exist, for example, impossible things which are prevented from being by a natural and proper possibility, as some monsters which the contrariety of natures does not permit to be, such as the chimera they imagine and many others.[98] Nature also determined that some things be at some time and not be at some time, as you see in animals and human beings and many other things. Hence, it is necessary that there be other things which nature determined always to be. Hence, the creator is not alone in always existing and being eternal. In fact there are many other things with him, and this argument is helped by what Avicenna says, namely, that if there is found one of two contraries in the universe of nature and something in the middle between them, it is necessary that there be found the other. He gives an example of vinegar, oxymel (a mixture of vinegar and honey), and honey, for since vinegar is found in the universe of nature and oxymel, which is the middle between vinegar and honey, is found there, it is necessary that there also be found in the universe of nature honey, since vinegar is one of the two contraries and honey the other according to him.

Moreover, this argument is helped by the fact that, if it were not so, two problems would seem to follow: First, that such contrariety would be incomplete, since one of the principal parts would be lacking to it, and this is not fitting for the creator nor fitting for nature, namely, to make something naturally incomplete, especially if it were susceptible of completion. The second problem is that in the universe there would be a vacuum in nature, just as if in

---

[97] See Aristotle, *Physics* VIII, ch. 1, 251a8-251b9. William argued against this in *The Trinity, or the First Principle*, ch. 8: Switalski, pp. 51-54; Teske-Wade, pp. 95-97.

[98] See Aristotle, *On the Heavens* I, ch. 12, 281a27ff.

the universe of the heavens there were lacking one of the extremes or a species of those in between. But nature does not tolerate such things, just as it does not tolerate a vacuum in place. Likewise, you see that in kinds of animals there is no vacuum in nature, that is, a lack of some species.

From all these it seems to be necessary that in the universe there are found these three kinds, namely, things that always exist, things that always do not exist, and things which exist at some time. But the things which always exist are eternal, (695b) and thus sempiternity is eternity in one meaning. But if there is found a multitude of things that always are or exist, there is found a multitude of eternal things, and the world or universe of them is eternal. In this way it is possible to reason concerning these three, namely, the necessary, the impossible, and the possible. Aristotle says that the necessary has the power to exist always and never not to exist. But the impossible has the power never to exist, and he gives the example of the diameter and the side,[99] because the diameter has the power never to be equal to the side, and this power cannot be understood except as an exclusion from being and a distance that is immobile and unapproachable.

Since Aristotle's discussion of this is lengthy, I say that being is not said of the creator and other things according to one meaning, nor is it said univocally. In the same way white is said of the color and of a surface equivocally. For the color is said to be white essentially and not according to participation. It is not, after all, said to be white because it has or participates in whiteness, but because it is whiteness itself. But a surface or wall is white in the opposite way. Thus the creator is not said to be being because he has being itself, but because he is his own being so that in every respect that which is and that by which he is is understood to be the same in him.[100] But in nothing else is it that way, for in everything else that which is is one thing, and that by which it is is another, and in general everything other than the creator is said to be being by participation. Hence, just as if someone says "white," he does not grasp in one meaning the colors and the colored things, so he who says "beings,"[101] does not grasp in one meaning the creator and created things, because he cannot use equivocally a single application of the one name.

That argument of Aristotle does not survive this refutation. His statement is that nature determined for some things that they would always not be, though this statement has much falsity both on account of the word "nature" and on account of the verb "determined," for neither of which did he deter-

---

[99] See *On the Heavens* I, ch. 12, 281b5-7.

[100] William alludes to Boethius' axiom, "Everything simple has its being and that which it is as one," in *De hebdomadibus*, ll. 45-46; see *Boethius: The Theological Treatises*, ed. H. F. Stewart and E. K. Rand (Cambridge: Harvard Univ. Press, 1946), pp. 40-41: a statement which William cites in *The Trinity, or the First Principle* (*De trinitate*), ch. 1: Switalski, p. 17; Teske-Wade, p. 66.

[101] William's Latin has "entes" and "entia"—the masculine or feminine and neuter genders.

mine his meaning or understanding. Nor does he explain what he calls "nature" there, and he does not disclose what he understands by "determine." I reply, nonetheless, that no nature determined anything for the creator, even if it were true that by its most noble nature it would always exist and that it would have no possibility at all of approaching non-being. But in created things it is impossible that such be the case, and I shall bring you to know this in what follows. It is not appropriate, and no necessity demands that, if there is a multitude of things which always are not or do not exist, there is on this account a multitude of things that always exist.[102] So too, it is not necessary that, if there is a multitude of cheap things, there is on this account a multitude of precious things. Nor is it necessary that, if there is a multitude of effects, there is a multitude of causes. It is the same way with streams and sources, with branches and roots, though there is a certain contrariety between them. For a multitude of streams does not necessarily imply a multitude of sources, nor does a multitude of branches imply a multitude of roots.

But you now have no doubt that the creator is the cause of all other beings and that they are his effects and that he stands in relation to them in some way as the source for them and they stand in relation to him as streams. Likewise, he is like a root in relation to them, and they are, just the other way around, like branches in relation to him, though not in a proper sense but by a likeness that is, if I may say so, quite unlike. Between created things, then, and the creator of all of them[103] such comparisons and likenesses which Aristotle uses have no place, since the creator is not somehow counted among them. Even if they may hold among creatures, it is not necessary that these comparisons be extended by likeness to the being of the creator, since the creator is (696a) distant from them by an immeasurable distance and is supereminent and stands above them in an unlikeness that is beyond thought.

Though Aristotle says that some things have the power always to exist and others have the power always not to exist,[104] you ought to know that this statement is not true on this point. For that "always to be" is proper to the creator alone, and no created things have the power always to be. Even if it were true that some of them always exist, it belongs to no one of them that it subsists by its own power. It has already been explained to you elsewhere that being is accidental to each thing except for the creator, to whom alone it is essential.[105] For he is by his own power, and he always is by the strength of his stability. Each of the other things, however, is as it is and as long as it is by his power and gift, and insofar as lies in itself, each would fall back into non-being if the power and goodness of the creator did not retain it and make it stable in being. But it is even more surprising that he said that some things

---

[102] I have omitted a negative here, since "things that always do not exist" seems to be wrong.

[103] I have read *universorum creatorem* instead of *universum creatum*.

[104] See, for example, *On the Heavens* I, ch. 12, 282a21-25.

[105] See *The Trinity, or the First Principle (De trinitate)*, ch. 1: Switalski, p. 18; Teske-Wade, pp. 66-67.

have the power always not to be or not to be always, as if not to be were the end of some power and as if nature gave it a beginning for this purpose, namely, for non-being, though it is evident that non-being is nothing and is never desired or sought by nature.

For even if a negation follows from an affirmation, an affirmation does not, nonetheless, exist for this or on account of this. After all, from something being white it follows that it is not black, but whiteness does not exist for this purpose, namely, for the sake of something not being black. And so, in the example he gives of the diameter and the side,[106] neither the diameter nor its length exists for the purpose of not being equal to the side, and the same thing holds of the side. It follows of necessity with regard to any two lines that, if they are related in the same square so that one of them is the diameter of that square and the other is the side, they are not equal, just as it follows with regard to any two bodies that, if they were related to the same whole so that one is its half and the other a quarter, they are not equal, though they are not there for this purpose and do not exist for this purpose without qualification.

No less erroneous is his statement by which he said that some things have the power not to exist at some time or to be corrupted at some time and to cease to be at some time,[107] since that, namely, to cease to be, cannot come from a power. For no one has any doubt that this comes from the weakness of the being and that failing and ceasing to be properly follows upon defectibility. But Aristotle himself and his commentators and the followers of his opinion say that the non-being itself comes from potentiality. But no one says the defectability or the ability to cease to be is a power; in fact, they give it the opposite name, calling it impotence and weakness.

Chapter Eleven
He proves the beginning of the world through histories and arguments.

After this it is appropriate that I bring forth arguments and proofs to establish the newness of the world and to destroy its eternity. After all, for complete certitude it is not enough to reply to the arguments of those who hold the opposite view and to resolve their questions and to refute their opinions, unless the truth is defended and explained by irrefragable proofs. The aim of one who philosophizes truly and correctly consists in these two.

I shall begin then from the testimonies of the world, and I shall say that there are found among all nations annals of history and chronicles in which the creation or building and foundations of great well-known cities are reported. Likewise, they report the beginnings of all kingdoms. From these (696b) it is evident that the world had a beginning in time. Since all these things which I mentioned had definite beginnings, if the world lasted before

---

[106] See *On the Heavens* I, ch. 12, 281b5-7.
[107] See *On the Heavens* I, ch. 12, 281a27-31.

them for an infinite stretch, it would have existed in an infinite amount of time without cities and kingdoms, and in that way it would have been idle and empty of the greater part of its usefulness. But concerning these beginnings there would be the same question which Aristotle and his followers posed concerning the beginning of the world. But to contradict so many great testimonies is a mark not only of foolishness, but also of intolerable madness. There remain the histories of the Hebrews and of the Christians that testify that Adam was the first human being. But the prophet of the Hebrews himself testifies to this in the beginning of the law of the Hebrews, and the creator himself bore witness to him by such magnificent signs and unheard of prodigies, since the nation of the Hebrews refused to believe the same prophet save on the basis of signs. But to contradict the testimony of so great a prophet to whom the creator bore the testimony of such great signs is to contradict the creator himself and make him a liar.

I shall, however, proceed further, and I shall say that for those who are able to hear it and understand the whole world itself confesses that it had a beginning from time. It confesses its potentiality and that it is impossible for it to exist through itself. Hence, it confesses that its potentiality or possibility of existing is natural to itself and comes from itself, but that it has received its actuality or act of existing from elsewhere or from something else. The reason is that the possible or the potential, insofar as it is such or by reason of the fact that it is such, does not come into the act of existing or into being. And it does not come to the act of existing or into being through something similar insofar as it is similar, that is, insofar as it is potential or possible. Rather, it remains in its potentiality or possibility insofar as lies in it. Hence, it remains in non-being according to act or in non-being actually. Because, then, potentiality is natural to it, non-being will also be natural to it. Hence, [non-being] will necessarily be before being. But what is natural to each thing of necessity is prior to what is adventitious. Likewise, what is essential (*per se*) to each thing is prior to what comes to it from elsewhere or from something else. Hence, from all these considerations, the world confesses that it received being after non-being.

Moreover, it is evident that the world has been made or created, but white is not made except from black, and hot is not made except from cold. Therefore, the world was not made being except from non-being. In every making that from which something is made is necessarily prior to that which is made. Hence, the world was non-being before it was made being. It was, then, once non-being, and for this reason it was not always being.

Moreover, since the world received being from the creator, because it both is and has being from him, it either received it when it was not existing or when it was already existing. The latter is impossible, since, when it was, it had being. For it is not possible that it receive what it had. If someone says that it received it when it had it, because it received it instantaneously and not part by part, then it received it when it first had it. Hence, at some point it first had being, and when it first had being, it undoubtedly began to be;

therefore, at some time it undoubtedly began to be. But if he says that it began to be, when it did not have it, then, at some point it did not have it; hence, at some point the world did not exist. Hence, it began to be. For everything that at another time was not and at another time was began to be.

Moreover, the world was drawn from its natural potentiality into the act of being. Hence, it was drawn either instantaneously or part by part or continuously. If it was drawn into being instantaneously, it was drawn into being in an instant or in a moment of time; hence, in that moment it was first in the act of existing or being, and this is what I was after. But if it went from potency to act part by part or continuously, this emergence is (697a) beyond all doubt generation. But the generation of something finite takes place in a finite time that has a limit in both directions. Something generated is not yet existing in the whole time of its generation, but first exists and begins to be at the term of its generation. Hence, the world began to be in the term of its generation, since it did not exist previously, just as is the case with other things generated. For nothing generated can exist or ever could exist before the completion of its generation.

Moreover, potentiality and actuality are contraries; likewise, potency and act are contraries, and they cannot exist in the same thing at the same time and they do not tolerate each other. Either, then, the potentiality of being preceded its act in the world, or it did not precede it. If he says that it preceded its act, then, such potentiality existed without the act. Hence, the world existed at some time in the potency of being and was not yet in act. The world, then, was being in act at some time; hence, it was not so always. But if potentiality never preceded act in the world, since it is evident that it is naturally prior to act, the order of nature was not preserved in the creation of the world. It is, therefore, contrary to the order of nature that the world always is in act.

Moreover, how was the world created by the creator? Either it was generated as the result of the corruption of something else or through the corruption of something else, or it was made from something without its being corrupted, as a house is at times made from wood and stones, or it was caused and made out of nothing, or it was otherwise created by the same creator. But whether it was generated or made, as I said, it received being after non-being. If it was created, that is, made out of nothing, either it was created instantly or continuously and part by part. If instantly, then it was created in some moment of time; hence, it began then. But if it was created part after part and continuously, in the endpoint of its creation, that is, at the point in which its creation was complete, it began to be, since it then first existed. In the same way one must proceed in whatever other manner he says that it was caused by the creator, because it is necessary that he say that its causation was instantaneous or produced instantly or that he say it was caused part after part.

Moreover, what will he say about the human race? Either he will say that it too is eternal and no human being was first, or he will not say that. If he says that it is eternal and no one of the human beings was the first, since the father is necessarily the cause of the son, and the grandfather the cause of the father, and so on to infinity, he necessarily has to admit that causes run back to infinity, that is, efficient causes. For the father is the efficient cause of the son in terms of the generation of the body, or both parents are, that is, the father and the mother. But the status of causes in every kind of cause has already been explained and established, and it has been shown that it is impossible that they go back to infinity. And this has been shown by Aristotle and his followers and the commentators on his books.[108]

I shall proceed in another way, and I shall say that being necessary through itself and being possible through itself are contraries. In the same way necessity through itself and possibility through itself. So too, antiquity and newness. For, just as necessity through itself is the cause of eternity or of antiquity, it will necessarily be the case that possibility through itself is the cause of newness. Hence, just as necessity through itself is found only in one being alone, which is the blessed creator, so eternity or antiquity is found only in the same.

Moreover, just as necessity through itself does not tolerate newness or temporality in that in which it is, so it is necessary that possibility through itself does not tolerate eternity in the same subject with itself. Hence, it is impossible that some creature be eternal, and in other dispositions it is the same way. For necessity through itself admits with itself neither creation nor temporal corruption or generation, nor a beginning of any sort. Hence, it is necessary that possibility through itself be just the opposite (697b), and this proof is based on this root, namely, that contraries are essential (*per se*) causes of their contraries, and upon this other root, that is, if one of the correlatives is present, so is the other, and upon this third root that those things which are correlative are necessarily and mutually correlative. Hence, as necessity through itself stands in relation to eternity and antiquity, so possibility through itself stands to newness and temporality. Hence, if necessity through itself is the cause of eternity or antiquity, possibility will be the cause through itself of temporality and newness. And if eternity or antiquity is an inseparable consequent or concomitant of necessity through itself, temporality or newness will be an inseparable consequent and concomitant of possibility through itself.

And since the arguments which have been set forth thus far are partly ethical or moral, such as those which are drawn from testimonies, but partly natural and metaphysical, I shall take up the metaphysical arguments of Aristotle on this opinion,[109] and I shall say first of all that it turns out for Aristotle that an hour of the whole of past time has not flowed by before a day or month or year and even not before a million years. But the proof is as follows: If someone says that an hour flowed by before a million years had

---

[108] See *Physics* VIII, ch. 5, 256a3-21.

[109] See my article, "William of Auvergne's Arguments for the Newness of the World," *Mediaevalia: Textos e Estudos* 7-8 (1995): 287-302. See also H. A. Davidson, "John Philoponus as a Source of Medieval Islamic and Jewish Proofs of Creation," *American Oriental Society Journal* 89 (1969): 357-91, for the use of Philoponus' arguments in Islamic and Jewish thinkers.

flowed by, either that hour preceded time by an infinite amount, or it did not precede time by an infinite amount. If it preceded time by an infinite amount, it is certain that the million years were a part of that infinite time, hence by that whole of it it preceded that hour we mentioned. That hour, then, did not flow by before a million years, and not only a million of years preceded that hour, but even infinite thousands, since infinite time of necessity contains infinite thousands. But if infinite time did not precede that hour, either finite time preceded it, or no time preceded it. If finite time preceded it, the beginning of it, then, was the beginning of the whole of time; hence, time had a beginning. But if no time preceded that hour, it is evident that the beginning of that hour was the beginning of the whole of time; hence, it is evident that according to this opinion of Aristotle an hour of the whole of time did not flow by before a million years, and it is not possible to show that infinite thousands of years did not precede it.[110]

Moreover, as he himself says, the infinite cannot be traversed,[111] and especially by a finite motion, but the whole of time which has passed is either infinite, as he said, or finite. If it is finite, it, therefore, has a beginning. Hence, motion does also, and this is opposed to him. But if it is infinite, how, then, has the whole of it already passed? For its flow does not have an infinite velocity, nor is its velocity greater than the motion of the heavens.[112] I shall, however, give you an example from water, and I shall say that, if you imagine an infinite amount of water and you make its flow finite, that is, so that it flows off through a finite pipe or a finite channel and at a finite velocity, it will never be possible that the whole of it has flowed off.

Moreover, the whole of the future is, according to Aristotle, infinite, and will never end. What is future of the whole of time is, then, not less than that of it which has passed. For the velocities are equal by which the whole past has flowed by or passed and by which the future will pass. But we have come to the end of the passing of that time which has already passed with such a great velocity, despite its infinity. We will, then, come to the end of the passing of the whole of time which is in the future, which will pass at a velocity equal to that by which past time has passed despite its infinity. Hence, it is necessary that it come to an end.

Moreover, in the whole of past (698a) time the heaven completed a finite number of revolutions or an infinite number of them. If a finite number, it is necessary that it completed them in a finite time, since it completed them in as many equal parts of time as there were, since all the revolutions of the

---

[110] The point of William's argument would seem to be that, if infinite time had to pass before any particular hour, day, month, or year could pass, none of these times could pass, as they obviously do.

[111] See Aristotle, *Posterior Analytics* I, 22, 83b6.

[112] The point of the argument is that, since an infinite cannot be traversed, if past time were infinite, the present could never have been reached. See Davidson's article, p. 366, for the occurrence of this argument in Philoponus and in Sa'adia.

heaven have a like velocity. The whole of past time which has passed up to the present moment, therefore, is finite. But if he says that the heaven completed an infinite number of revolutions in the whole of past time, I shall imagine — for this imagining is possible for the intellect — that the heaven moved in the whole of past time by a velocity that was less by half. Because, then, the proportion of the one motion to the other is the same as the proportion of amount traversed to the other amount traversed, it is necessarily the case that in the same time it completed only a half of the number of revolutions. The revolutions, then, which it completed in the whole of past time, necessarily have a half, and in the same way they have a quarter and an eighth and so on to infinity. But it is evident that the infinite does not have a half.[113]

Moreover, when the opposite is imagined, namely, that the motion of the whole heaven in the whole time that has passed is twice as fast, then, for the same reason the revolutions completed in the same time will be twice as many. But the heaven will not complete more revolutions than those which have passed and those which are in the future taken together, but it completed that number by having revolved at twice the speed; hence, it has completed its motion.

Moreover, there is no doubt that it would have completed twice as many revolutions if its velocity was doubled, and would have done so in the same time. Hence, the number of revolutions already completed had a double, and it is the half of some number. Such a number, therefore, is not infinite, since it has a half, as was said, and also a double.

Moreover, it is evident that the heaven of the sun or the sun itself completes one of its revolutions in a year in accord with its average and equal movement.[114] I shall imagine, then, for example, a year of this revolution of three hundred and sixty days so that one degree of the solar circle is ascribed to each day. By those things which you have heard, the proportion of the motion of this heaven to the motion of the sun will be three hundred and sixty to one. Hence, the revolutions of the heaven will have the same proportion to the revolutions of the sun. The revolutions of the sun and the years of its revolutions will stand to the revolution of the heaven and the years of its revolutions in a proportion of one to three hundred and sixty. Let it not disturb you that I said "years" in both cases, because it is the same as if I said "a day" in relation to the heaven. In the same way it is possible to consider the revolutions of Saturn which stand in relation to the revolutions of the sun in a proportion of

---

[113] William uses another of Philoponus' arguments; the point of the argument is that one infinite cannot be a fraction or a multiple of another infinite. See Davidson, "John Philoponus as a Source," p. 368.

[114] Here is another of John Philoponus' arguments. The argument runs as follows: Since the celestial bodies move at different speeds so that the faster ones perform more revolutions than the slower ones in the same time, one infinity would be a multiple of another, if time were infinite. See H. A. Davidson, "John Philoponus as a Source," p. 368

one to thirty. Likewise, one can consider the revolutions of Jupiter, since they are similarly in accord with the same measure in relation to the revolutions of the sun in a proportion of one to twelve. And in the same way one can consider the revolutions of Mars, Venus, Mercury, and the moon. You will find that their proportions in relation to the revolution of the heaven are most definite, and this means that the proportions of the furthest are taken from their proportion to the intermediate and the proportions of the intermediate to one another. You will find, then, that the revolutions of each of the planets will be according to astronomical calculation a definite part, that is, will have a definite proportion to all the revolutions of the heaven taken together, which are completed in the whole of time, which comes to an end in the present moment. It is impossible, however, that it be infinite since its parts are found to have a definite relation and proportion to it, etc.

[The remainder of the chapter and of the part is omitted from this translation.]

The Universe of Creatures

The First Part of the Second Principal Part

Preface.

May God honor you, because you honor him no small amount by loving and investigating the sciences by which our souls are illumined most of all and directed toward exalting him and toward understanding and contemplating his supereminence and glory. In doing this you also care for the excellent honor of your own soul, in seeking for it perfections so noble and so desirable. For these two reasons it is clear that you truly know the finest goals and most splendid blessedness of the sublime philosophy in the mode of wisdom; these are undoubtedly the exaltation of the creator and the perfection of our souls, which is nothing but the brilliance of such sciences and beauty of the virtues. From these two and in these two perfections consists the entirety of religion, which is a mark of full honor and is the whole honor of our souls. But when religion has been brought to its ultimate completion, it will be the glory of these same souls, as you learned through me from other sources. But the relation of the sciences to one another in nobility is according to the relation of their knowable objects.[115] For this reason it is necessary that the science of the spiritual universe is more noble than the science of the corporeal or bodily universe to the extent that the spiritual nature is recognized as more excellent than any bodily nature. From this it is evident that you should study it and I should hand it on with an examination that is that much more careful and that it should be received with an attention that is that much more eager, especially since almost nothing concerning it has come down to these times from those philosophers who have gone before us, apart from a few stories. It is not likely that there was any other reason for this except for its profundity, the shortsightedness of the human intellect, and the remoteness of those substances from our ordinary life. And for these three reasons this universe was neglected and left aside by those philosophers who preceded me. For it seems incredible that men who were completely dedicated to the pursuits of philosophy and who were most eager researchers of the sciences and who were most fervent with the love of philosophy held so noble a science in contempt and passed it over out of laziness or negligence.

---

[115] See Aristotle, *Metaphysics* I, ch. 2, 983a5-11 as a possible source, but also Avicenna, *Metaphysics* I, 1: Van Reit, p. 2, where he ranks the philosophical sciences according to their subject matters.

(807b)

Chapter One.
That according to the opinion of the ancients
there are three parts of the spiritual universe, and the aim of the treatise.

As I begin this treatise on the spiritual universe, know, first of all, that this universe is divided into three parts according to the opinion of the ancients. Of these the first and most noble deals with the intelligences that are pure and most separated from matter and its appendages, according to what Aristotle and his followers held. I intend to argue against their errors in this part and in the first chapter of this part. The second part deals with the substances which the Greeks call good demons (*kalodaemones*), but we call, according to the Christian law and teaching, good angels and holy angels. The third part deals with the substances which the Greeks call evil demons (*kakodaemones*), but we usually call bad angels or malign spirits and in ordinary language call devils.

You ought also to know that I pass over the determination of their specific character (*specialitas*) without examination and distinction, for it involves a question among the learned that is difficult to determine, namely, whether those which are called demons or angels are truly and purely spiritual or spirits in a body, and whether they have bodies, and whether all are incorporeal or only a part of them. And you will hear about this in the following chapters.[116] But they seem to behave in many respects in the manner of spirits, because they seem not to take nourishment and they are said to be untouchable or intangible and are said to be able neither to be cut or wounded. That they also enter and exit temples and houses when the doors and entrances are all carefully blocked and make themselves visible when they want and also invisible is quite well known among people. For these reasons they should be called spiritual until the truth has been revealed, as best I can, through the path of proofs.

It will belong to the present task to explain the species, degrees, differences, powers, and offices of all these and to assign their authentic and common names—I do not mean their individual names, but their common names. For whether they have individual names or can have them is open to dispute, as you will learn in the following chapters. I shall first try to deal with their essential or natural characteristics; then with those which come after these and which were produced in them and about them in time; thirdly, with those things which they are said to do to human beings or with regard to them. There I will examine the works of magicians and witches, divination,

---

[116] William takes up the question of the spirituality or immateriality of the separate substances in *De universo* IIa-IIae, ch. 1 and following. In the Prooemium he mentions a sect of the Hebrew people, probably the Sadducees, and Aristotle's view regarding evil demons. Even Christian thinkers, such as Augustine, thought that angels had bodies, though immortal ones. In fact, until William's time it was generally held that there was a matter-form composition in everything other than God.

responses, revelations, and other marvelous things which are done or are said to be done by both, that is, by the good and the bad spirits.[117] In this way you will attain certitude about all these matters, if God wills.

(808a)

Chapter Two
That Aristotle and others who posit the intelligences must necessarily hold that they are perfect with the perfection of the sciences and natural virtues.

In order that you may become more certain and clear about my discussion of the intelligences which were maintained by Aristotle who is followed by many of the Greek philosophers and by all the Arabs whose treatises have come down to us, recall those things which you heard about them in the first part of this treatise, and add them to these points which I shall mention.[118] Bear in mind that they will help you no small amount toward the knowledge of the truth concerning the intelligences.

Know, then, that Aristotle maintained that each noble substance of the intelligences is naturally fully perfect in all ways, that is, in the ways appropriate to them. I say this on account of the supereminence of the creator whose perfection stands out far above all number and measure and also above all comparison and surpasses all other perfections. But the intelligences are, according to this opinion, naturally perfect in terms of what is appropriate to their level and rank. Just as we say that human beings are perfect in wisdom or in the virtues or in both, as human beings, of course, that is, as befits their nature or state or office, so we say that the creator is perfect in terms of his sublimity. The perfection of each intelligence, therefore, is not merely the light or brilliance of innate knowledge, but also the beauty of all the natural virtues of which the intelligence is naturally capable. For if it did not have the beauty of the virtues, it would be intolerably deformed and shamefully mutilated.

Moreover, it would know good things with no benefit since it would not have the wherewithal to love them. So too with evils, since it could not hate them.

Moreover, it could be neither good nor evil, since it could will neither good nor evil. For by loving and willing the good we are good, or by loving and willing evil they become evil. The mere and bare knowledge of good and evil does not suffice to make good or bad the one who has it. For this reason Aristotle himself says that knowledge contributes little or nothing to virtue.[119]

---

[117] William turns to the topic of magic in *De universo* IIIa-IIae, ch. 22 and following.

[118] See *De universo* Ia-Iae, chs. 24 to 27, where William discusses the Avicennian account of the procession of the ten intelligences from the First.

[119] Aristotle, *Nicomachean Ethics* II, ch. 4, 1105b1-2. The translation of the *Ethica vetus* reads: "ad habendum autem virtutes scire quidem parum aut nihil potest." See Gabriel Jüssen, "Die Tugend und der gute Wille: Wilhelm von Auvergnes Auseinandersetzung mit der aristotelischen Ethik," *Les philosphies morales et politiques au Moyen Âge*, ed. B. Carlos Bazán et al., 3 vols. (New York: Legas, 1995), II, 709-22.

Moreover, on this view each of the intelligences would be merely an eye. But to see does not belong to an eye for its own sake, but for the sake of other operations, namely, for guiding the feet in walking or the hands in working and many other things.

Moreover, to see for its own sake does not make the seer good, because even seeing something good does not make one good. Hence, the wisdom and goodness of the creator would have created such substances neither wisely nor well.

Moreover, since the knowledge of the intelligences is so noble and so perfect, it is necessary that they know the creator more clearly and more perfectly than all other subjects and, for this reason, that they love him more. But love of the creator is the most noble of all the virtues. But this could not be, unless there was virtue in them, since it would be in them immobile and perfect according to the perfection of the cognition or knowledge by which they know the creator.

Moreover, either they are delighted by the knowledge of the creator or they are not. If they are, they love the creator. There is in them, then, love of the creator, the most noble, as I said, of the virtues, which, as you learned elsewhere, cannot exist alone.[120] But if they are not delighted at the sight or knowledge [of the creator], then they are not delighted at the sight or knowledge of any other things. For the creator is naturally most intelligible for their intellect and also for every intellect. Hence, the union (808b) of such an intellect and the creator is most natural; hence, it is most delightful. Delight, after all, is—as you learned elsewhere—the apprehension of something natural to the apprehending power.

Moreover, since the intellect is the most noble of all the apprehensive powers, it will of necessity be apprehensive of the most noble of all the things that can be apprehended, and it will be more suited to this insofar as the intellect is more noble. Hence, because the intellect of such substances is the most noble of all intellects, according to this view, its union with the most noble intelligible will be most fitting of all such unions and, hence, the most delightful, since, as you learned elsewhere, joy or delight is the suitable union of the suitable with the suitable.

Moreover, how did the most wise and most good creator give so excellent and so precious a gift, namely, a most noble intellect to a substance which does not either through it or on account of it love him and which cannot love and, therefore, cannot praise him or thank him for this?

Moreover, either such an intelligence loves its act of understanding or its knowing, or it does not. If it does, it is delighted; therefore, it necessarily loves in it its giver from whom it knows that it has received it. But if it does not love it, it does not care to make use of it rather than not to make use of it or to have it rather than not to have it. Therefore, it does not use it except perhaps

---

[120] See *De virtutibus*, ch. 9; I, 127aD-129aA for the love of God and ch. 22; I, 187aC-188bF for the interconnection of the virtues.

as the sun uses its light or as fire its heat. But this is as the result of necessity and in the manner of a servant.[121] But it is evident that such use has no utility or benefit for the intellect. For, even though the sun sheds light for the benefit of something else, not for its own benefit, one who understands cannot, none-theless, understand except for himself unless one might perhaps understand as a teacher in order to teach another or one might understand in advance as one who plans ahead. But this is not found in anyone except with the inten-tion and will to teach. These thinkers, however, remove from the intelligences all will and love and all other motive dispositions and virtues. From all these arguments, then, it has been made clear to you that whoever posit the intelli-gences must maintain that they are perfect with both perfections, namely, of natural knowledge and of the virtues. But they posit them as bare and sepa-rate from matter, as I told you, and yet they have to maintain that they are the more perfect in every mode of perfection suited to them to the extent that they locate them closer or nearer to the creator in the order of nobility.

Chapter Three
The reasons which lead Aristotle and others to posit the nine intelligences,
namely, the nine movements, and the destruction of their position.

The reasons which led Aristotle to maintain nine intelligences were the nine movements of the nine moveable heavens. For he posited for those heav-ens souls that move the heavens and for those souls living, immaterial intelligibles, namely, completely perfect intelligent substances. The [souls] constantly view the perfection of those substances and seek with a very strong love and most ardent desire to become like them and also to make the heav-ens like them in perfection. But he understood and said that this perfection is the complete actuality in them by which they have nothing in potency, but they have the totality which pertains to their perfection—as was possible for them—always in act. The state of glory of our souls can correctly be seen as such a state, when they will obtain in act as present the totality that pertains to their glory (809a), hoping for nothing and desiring nothing in the future that pertains to their glory. For this reason he maintained that the heavens are moved by their souls in a continuous revolution, and the reason is that he maintained that locations were certain perfections for parts of the heavens, just as for bodies that move by nature there are their natural places. Since then the parts of the heavens could not at the same time have all such loca-tions, because they cannot, for example, all at the same time be above this part of the earth, but each of them has the potentiality for each location, each soul of the heavens educes this potentiality for each part of its heaven with the speed that it can and in the way it is possible. And it supplies through succes-sion and perfects the potentiality for each part of its heaven by act after act,

---

[121] William again appeals to Avicenna's line about nature's working in the manner of a servant; see above note 22 to the translation.

since the acts of such potentialities cannot all be at the same time. For no part of the heaven can at the same time be directly above all the parts of the earth. And for this reason it acquires such location above each part through succession and renewal.

Pay attention and understand that this error is not only ridiculous in many ways, but also impossible. It is clear that no benefit comes to any part of the heavens from any of these locations and positionings overhead, nor would any benefit come from all of them if it had all of them at once. Therefore, such locations are sought by them without any benefit; hence, this motion is idle and useless.

Moreover, location insofar as it is location, that is, the positioning of one body over another, produces no benefit for the body positioned on top, unless this is intended for some other reason—as happens in fighters or warriors—for the position above enemies benefits the ones on top in many ways, for example, for seeing what the enemy down below are doing and for throwing at them rocks or spears or other things which could harm them. But no part of the heaven acquires something else by such location or positioning on top. In no respect, then, is it better off because of such a location; hence, it is acquired to no purpose.

But if someone says that it is better off in this respect as the result of such location, because the potentiality which it has for it is realized by it, I simply say that through such an act another act or perfection no less good is destroyed, because in acquiring this location it loses one equally good, and in that way it falls into a potentiality or imperfection that is equally bad. It is, then, as if nothing were acquired, when it loses as much as it gains. It is evident, then, that it is in no respect better off as a result of the gain of such a location than it was before.

Moreover, since by one revolution it acquires all the locations and also loses them, that revolution does not benefit it more than it harms it. It is, then, simply useless.

Moreover, if we claim that each part of each heaven has all such locations at the same time, the question is: What benefit is there from these parts of the heavens? Aristotle will say in fact that it is the perfection of the potentiality we mentioned. I ask Aristotle then: Why was it bad for one of such parts because of the lack of any of all those locations? For it is not bad for any of the lower bodies by reason of the fact that it is not in every place in which it is possible that it be. For then its nature would turn it away from every place and impel it toward every place, just as the souls of the heavens do, according to him, with their parts.

Moreover, nature turns aside its proper subject and makes it flee from every place in which it is bad for it and turns it from the evil of such potentiality, but inclines it and impels it to the place where it is good for it. But it makes it rest where it is good for it. It is, then, bad for each part (809b) of the heavens, in whatever location it might be, since each one has much more potentiality as a result of the lack of all those locations than actuality from the one.

Moreover, each of the natural bodies which are beneath the circle of the moon is contained under a single natural place, and the potentiality which such bodies have does not force them to flee from their natural places. How then will each part of each of the heavens not be contained by a single location so that the potentiality which it has for others does not force it to hasten with such great speed to them?

Moreover, motion from something and motion to it are contraries, like flight and pursuit. They do not, then, belong to one and the same thing at the same time. But according to this potency each part of each of the heavens moves to each such location and from it at the same time. And it pursues it and flees from it at the same time. The whole motion, then, of each of such revolutions is equally the pursuit of all those locations and the flight from them. Hence, the whole motion of each of the heavens is contrary to itself, and for this reason another will be contrary to itself.

Moreover, not every lack nor every potentiality is perfectible in act or habit so that there should be motion on its account. For even if you have the potentiality to hold or have one straw, it is not necessary that you move toward this either by spiritual motion, which is desire, or by local motion, which is the grasping of the straw or by the motion of your body to grasp it. The cause, however, is the usefulness or uselessness of the straw. But it would be a mark of greater stupidity to move toward it with either of the two motions we mentioned, if you are immediately forced to let it go or take your hand off of it. Because, then, the situation is obviously the same in such locations, since they claim no benefit for the parts of the heavens that acquire them, nor do they lessen the evil of potentiality, which ought to be one of the benefits of every motion. Moreover, since the locations acquired are immediately lost, it is most stupid to intend their acquisition, and it is ridiculous that those noble bodies labor in continually seeking and losing them. An example of this stupidity is perfectly evident in every miser who is wholly and most foolishly aflame with the love of riches and possessions,[122] but not so that he could be brought by the madness of greed to the point that he wants to acquire money which he would lose while acquiring it. And what is more amazing, the acquisition of it would be the loss of it. He would regard its acquisition as a mere illusion, just as if his money were put into a torn sack or if money put in his hands were taken away by being put there or if a city were given to someone so that he acquired it by running through it by a very rapid running and at the same time lost it by the same passage so that the acquisition was simultaneous with the loss. No one would be so foolish as not to regard such a gift as an illusion rather than an acquisition. Since you heard much on this in the first part of this treatise, I shall pass on to other things which I did not say there.

---

[122] I have read *possessionum* for *passionum*.

Chapter Four
The destruction of the errors of Aristotle and the others who posit souls that move the heavens because they love the higher intelligences and aim to become like them.

I say, therefore, that after Aristotle posited souls for the heavens which are able to love such most noble substances separated from matter and its appendages (810a) and conditions, he necessarily posited for them an intellect that is very noble. For with such an intellect those souls do not understand the intelligences universally, but rather singularly. For suppose that they understood them universally, as when you understand a man by the definition of the species, that is, as a man. In that case you do not really understand Socrates or Plato, and thus if you love man in that concept or consideration, you do not on this account love Socrates or Plato. Hence, if it were that way with these souls so that they understood and loved [those substances] through a universal or common mode, but not this one or that one, each of them would not have its own beloved, that is, its own intelligence, but there would be one beloved common to them all, namely, intelligence without qualification, not this one or that one. The nine heavens, then, would not have many motions that are different from one another, but all of them would have one and the same motion, because it would come from one and the same cause without any difference, namely from one universal knowledge and one universal love. In the same way, if many men had to be moved by the knowledge of man as man and by love of him in the same intention or meaning, there would not be a difference of motion in them from one and the same cause.

Moreover, because it understands the beauty and perfection of its intelligence, each of those souls loves it and seeks to become like to it according to this intention and also to make its heaven like it. Each of these intelligences is utterly immobile and in complete rest, and mobility and immobility are contraries, and contrariety is complete and maximum unlikeness and difference, as you learned elsewhere. There is, then, according to them the greatest[123] unlikeness and difference, and those souls cannot fail to know this. Therefore, those souls knowingly err in seeking through contrariety assimilation and likeness among those things in which this contrariety exists.

Moreover, if they would make or permit the bodies of their heavens to be completely immobile, there would then be true assimilation such as it is possible for there to exist between substances naturally unlike.

Moreover, the intelligences themselves neither move nor are moved, unless one perhaps says that they move as objects loved or things pertaining to love move their lovers. If then those souls which they posited for the heavens neither move nor are moved, they would be likened to their intelligences much more than they are. For they differ from them insofar as they move their bodies in such a way. It belongs to their perfection, then, not to move the bodies of the heavens in any way rather than to move them in any way. Hence,

---

[123] I read *maxima* instead of *maxime*.

they ought to have chosen this rather than that, if it was possible for them freely to choose through the will which of those perfections would help them. But if it was not free for them, they do not, then, move the heavens voluntarily. Hence, they do not seek voluntarily the perfection of such assimilation nor does the object loved move them, since every motion which comes from love is voluntary and free.

Moreover, each of these souls either understands that intelligence alone which is its own beloved or it understands others of them along with it or some of them, and it does not matter for my purposes here whether my opponent concedes this point regarding all or regarding some of them, since my argumentation proceeds in the same way whichever of these he says. But if he says that each of these souls understands only the intelligence which is its proper beloved, then our intellect is by far more noble in this wretched state than their intellect, since it is free and unimpeded for understanding all intelligibles.

Moreover, the narrowness of this misery does not even afflict (810b) one of our senses, though all the senses are particular and apprehend only particulars and singulars. How much more, then, is it impossible that it afflict the intellect which, it is agreed, has an incomparably greater amplitude and capacity. But someone might say that the strength of the love fixes it upon its beloved and holds it bound, preventing it from thinking of or understanding anything else in accord with the misery found in human souls which are at times so captivated and ensnared by perverse love that they cannot think of anything but their beloveds. To this I say that such love is perverse like the loves of our souls which I mentioned. For such loves are perverse and evil precisely because they turn souls away from the creator and prevent them from looking at him and, hence, from turning their face toward him. Hence, they have their back to the creator and their face toward the beloved objects of their soul—whatever they love in that way.[124] It is evident that nothing is more perverse than this disposition. Such love, then, is the very worst vice and is intolerably injurious to and contemptuous toward the creator.

But if someone says that each of such intelligences understands all the intelligences, it is evident that there is much diversity and multiple differences among them in terms of their perfections and nobility. For to the extent that they are like to the perfect First—which is the sublime and blessed creator—they are more perfect and noble and have a more desirable beauty. Either, then, the souls of the heavens love them by free choice and gratuitous love, or

---

[124] William speaks of the soul having two faces or as being able to face either upwards or downwards, toward God or toward creatures. See *William of Auvergne: The Immortality of the Soul*, trans. by Roland J. Teske, S.J. (Milwaukee: Marquette Univ. Press, 1991), p. 40. William says, "[T]his noble power has two faces, of which the one is enlightened from above, that is, by noble, incorporeal things, namely, those separated from matter and its appendages, and the other can be enlightened from the lower side, that is, of bodily and sensible things."

each of them is pulled by some cause and inclined toward the love of its own intelligence. If so, it is necessary, then, that each of these souls loves all those intelligences and loves one more than another in accord with the differences and comparisons of their perfections and beauties. Each of the intelligences, then, will be loved by each of these souls in accord with the comparisons and differences we mentioned. Hence, since the first intelligence is in the first degree of perfection and beauty among the intelligences, it will be in the ultimate degree of love among them. And each of the heavenly souls will have a desire to be likened to it in the ultimate degree of intention.

With the other intelligences the matter will go in accord with the levels, degrees, and comparisons we mentioned. Each of those souls, then, will not have its own solitary beloved, since each of them loves all the intelligences in common in accord with the manner and measure of its perfection and beauty. Nor will one of them have a desire or intention of assimilation that is singularly fixed upon one of them, and this same thing can be clearly seen in our souls when they are well ordered. For they love all objects of love in accord with the differences and levels and positions of the objects of love so that, for example, they love things more worthy with greater love and things equally worthy with equal love and those less worthy with less love.

Where this is not the case, the reason is perversity and disorder, and this is something self-evident for intelligent persons. Because it is unthinkable for those who posit such souls to assign them any perversity or disorder, they must make them most well-ordered and properly ordered in arrangement and virtue. Hence, in this respect they must be more ordered and more correct than our souls to the extent that they are obviously farther removed from all corruption and perversity than our souls. For it is not possible that such perversity be found in our souls when they are well-ordered so that, for example, in their love and desire to become like something, they prefer the things less lovable and less worthy of imitation to things more lovable and more worthy of imitation. And this (811a) can be clearly seen in every kind of artist—writers, painters, sculptors, and all the others. For none of these kinds of person set inferior models before themselves for imitation to portray in their works. How, then, will it be possible that one of those souls does not set before itself and choose for itself a model that is most worthy of imitation and of becoming like, if it is free and possible for it to choose whichever it wants from among the models. It is, then, evident that it follows from these points that each of these souls intends with the strongest love and vehement desire to become like the first intelligence either alone or most of all.

But if someone says that they are not free to choose in this way, they will then be much less fortunate and much more miserably confined and oppressed than our souls, even as they exist in the state of present misery. For upon none of our souls has such necessity been inflicted or imposed that it cannot imitate any of the better and more holy souls or even the angels, if it has been permitted to see them.

But if someone says that the love of such souls for their own intelligences is natural and that the desire to become like them is likewise natural, I say that, if one understands "natural" as necessary or servile, as I explained to you in the preceding parts, one is not helped in this way. For nature or naturalness does not make love or desire perverse or bad; otherwise, the creator's love and will would be in the ultimate degree of perversity and evil, since they are in the ultimate degree of naturalness, insofar as they are essential to the creator and in no sense adventitious or acquired by him or even contracted.

Moreover, I have explained to you in the treatise on the virtues[125] that every will—in whomever and whenever and for whatever it is—is of necessity most free and immune from violence and coercion. Will is, then, free in such souls. Hence, they also have the free choice which I mentioned.

But suppose that someone says that each of these souls has its intellect and desire to become like the intelligence by which it was created fixed upon that intelligence, as is the case among us, since children especially observe the conduct of their parents and imitate them most of all. I answer to this that children really do that while they are still little ones. But when they have become adults of mature age, learned in wisdom, and endowed with good morals, they respect every model of holy imitation and imitate more and more those whom they see are endowed with greater virtues.

But if one says that children's imitation of parents is natural, that is, a natural likeness in terms of the body, this is generally true, and in many cases the opposite happens. Elsewhere you learned from me the cause of this. But in morals there is frequently much unlikeness and contrariety between the children and parents. For parents are not parents of the children in this respect, that is, with regard to morals and virtues or vices, nor with regard to other dispositions of their souls. But the reason for this is that the whole of what is transferred from the parents to the children by generation proceeds and is derived from their bodies. But nothing is passed by their souls or from their souls into their bodies or souls, and I believe that I have explained this to you elsewhere with a certain explanation.[126]

But if one says that each of these souls has its own intelligence set over it as teacher or ruler or model and, for this reason, intends it singularly and alone by the ordering of the creator, but not out of a necessity of nature, which is slavery or servitude, as you have often heard, I answer to this that such confinement is not appropriate (811b) to the goodness of the creator or to the goodness of the intelligence that the soul should use it, even if it could do this

---

[125] References such as this to William's *De virtutibus* allow one to conclude that the *De universo* is a later work. For William's views on freedom in *De virtutibus*, see my "Freedom of the Will in William of Auvergne," in *Les philosophies morales et politiques au Moyen Âge*, ed. B. Carlos Bazán, et al., 3 vols. (New York: Legas, 1995), II, 932-38.

[126] See *De anima*, ch. 5, pt. 1: II, 110a-112b, where he asks whether the soul of the child comes from the souls of the father and mother.

by the permission of the creator. For no good person assigns disciples who could develop more with someone else to the teaching or instruction of a particular teacher and prevents them from learning from or listening to others, nor do any good teachers want to claim for themselves singularly and alone disciples when they are ready to develop more with other teachers. And if some do this or have done this, they are out for gain or are venal teachers or persons perverted out of evil jealousy or envy.

Chapter Five
The destruction of the preceding error by other proofs.

This love which they attribute to the souls of the heavens causes no small amount of wonder. For all love seeks for the beloved or for the lover either a benefit or a pleasure or something else which is sought by desires. But love which seeks a benefit in the beloved and is not even slight love for the beloved has not as yet properly been called love among the philosophers, but rather a business deal or venality. It is, after all, very petty and mean to calculate friendship or to twist it to gain, as a certain one of the Latin philosophers said.[127] If then the souls' love for their intelligences has such an intention, it is evident that it is not true love, but rather a business deal covered over with the false appearance of love. This is especially so, if the perfection which those souls intend flows out over them from these intelligences. And if they love them on account of such an outpouring, it makes no difference whether the benefit which is purchased at the price of love is spiritual or temporal. It makes no difference with regard to the falsity of the love, because the love is equally false in either case.

Moreover, if the intelligences pour out this perfection over such souls, intending to make them like to themselves by the assimilation of which [the Aristotelians] speak, what benefit is there for these intelligences in such likening or for these souls? What would be lost to the intelligences, if they did not pour out such motion or power of moving by that motion over those souls, especially since nothing seems to be added to those souls except the toil of constantly moving and turning such immense bodies? It is evident that none of us would want any intelligence or even the creator to pour that out over our own soul or over the soul of our horse or ass. Perhaps you could correctly want it to be poured out over your mill stone or some wheel whose constant rotation or revolution is useful to you. And if the intelligences offered this benefit to human beings, they would be rightly praised and honored with acts of thanksgiving. But what would the souls of the heavens obtain or acquire from this ceaseless whirl of their bodies, but useless and—so to speak—meaningless toil?

---

[127] See Cicero, *De amicitia* 58 as a possible source: "There is another opinion which defines friednship by equality of actions and wills. This is, of course, to calculate friendship in a way that is much too petty and parsimonious so that there is an equality between what one gives and what one receives."

Moreover, what else could those souls of the heavens seem to be, in producing their revolutions with unceasing continuity, but horses or asses set to turning a mill stone—except the horses and asses bear the toil of turning the mill stone for the obvious benefit of human beings, but the souls do this to the benefit of no one? For as a result of the daily revolution it is not better in some one of the heavens or in the parts of it than if it had been at rest during the whole period of that revolution, nor was any benefit given to someone except perhaps the day, light, warmth, and the other such dispositions came more abundantly to the lower world. But they deny this most insistently, saying that, if on account of such (812a) benefits the heavens moved, then less valuable things would be causes of the more noble things and more noble things would serve the less valuable things, that is, the heavenly would serve the earthly. They said this, however, not noticing or seeing that shepherds, who are of course human beings, serve sheep and goats with many a service, for example, of guarding and of guiding them as shepherds. Also, kings and princes and spiritual rulers serve their subjects with almost countless services.

But if one says that in serving the animals shepherds serve themselves and their masters in the guarding and guiding the animals, one necessarily has to say that these souls of the heavens serve either themselves or their masters or their master who has imposed upon them the duty of such service. But it is evident that they do not serve themselves in this, since no benefit comes to them from the dispositions we mentioned which they produce in the lower world. Hence, in this service they serve the powers which are above them and the blessed creator, if their intention is correct, just as in the governance of their kingdoms kings and princes serve not themselves, but the creator, if their intention is correct. And even if their intention is bad and perverted, and they twist their offices to the advantage of greed or to the vanity of pride, they serve the creator without knowing it, for he makes excellent use of their sins and perversities, drawing from them multiple and magnificent benefits, as you learned in the preceding treatise.[128] It is, then, no problem that better things serve less valuable ones, when they serve the creator in them. Nor can the service be worthless or the duty below the dignity of anyone of whatever excellence, when the creator has imposed it or if it pleases him. For nothing is possible for any creature which is exempt from the injunction or obedience of the creator and which ought not to be done, if the creator enjoins that it be done or if any ministers of the creator commanded it on his behalf or in his name.

---

[128] See *De universo* IIIa-Iae, ch. 12; I, 775bAB, where William answers the question why God permits the evil to flourish in this life and to dominate the good and shows the good God draws from this.

Chapter Six

That the souls of the heavens do not seek or love the intelligences as ends,
since the creator alone ought to be sought and loved on his own account.

You ought also to recall those points which you heard in the treatise on the
virtues, namely, that the creator is the end of all correct intentions, willings,
and actions and that one should not establish another end and one should
not aim at one.[129] For everything else ought to be a way to him, and the
virtues and natural habits and dispositions are certain steps and paths. But
the steps are actions, either bodily or spiritual. Nothing, then, ought to be
sought or loved as an end on its own account besides the creator, nor should
that which they call the perfection of the heavenly souls be sought by them or
by anything else on its own account only and as an end. It is, then, either
sought wrongly or with an incorrect intention, or it is sought on account of
that ultimate end which is, as I said, the sublime and blessed creator. They
ought, then, to have said this, namely, that the souls of the heavens move the
bodies of their heavens in that way on account of the creator as the end. This
can only be understood in one of these ways, namely, either because it pleases
the creator or in order that they might please the creator or because he is
exalted by it or glorified by it. Avicenna seems to have held this, when he said
that the motion of the heavens is motion in obedience to the most high God.[130]
These souls, then, move their heavens out of obedience to the most high God
or because it thus pleases the most high God, which is the same thing. The
cause of the motion, then, is not the desire for (812b) perfection or for becoming like their intelligences. But it is perhaps not necessary to posit souls
for the heavens on this account, since even without souls the heavens necessarily
have to obey the most high God in any kind of motion whatever.

Moreover, the most noble of all perfections and the most fitting for intelligent and rational substances is the perfection which consists in wisdom and
goodness. Aside from this there is neither perfection nor a part of perfection.
And when this is complete with its ultimate completion, it admits no need,
no potentiality, no lack of any desirable good in what is perfected. Since,
then, Aristotle and his followers claim that these souls are perfect in their
ultimate perfection, it is necessary that they remove from them all lack of any
desirable good. Hence, they must remove from them all desire, since desire
always accompanies a lack of that which is desired. For they did not claim
that they were perfective of our souls. They do not, then, have a desire of the
sort that he assigned to them.

Moreover, they cannot put them anywhere but in the state of glory, just like
the angels. But the state of glory has no imperfection or lack or desire of
anything not possessed.

[129] See, for example, *De virtutibus*, ch. 2: I, 109b.

[130] See, as a possible source, Avicenna, *Metaphysics* IX, 2: Van Reit, p. 461, where
Avicenna says that the movement of the heavens "is like an angelic or celestial
service."

Moreover, this desire by which they desire to become like their intelligences through their heavens is likewise unable to be fulfilled. For it is impossible that the potentiality which is in parts of the heavens with respect to each one of the ends that were mentioned be educed into act totally and at one time. For it is impossible for all parts of the heavens to obtain all such locations at the same time. But this potentiality cannot otherwise be drawn into act. Hence, it is impossible, as I said, that that potentiality be totally drawn into act so that the greatest part of it does not remain. Hence, the greatest part of the desire we mentioned remains. But a desire of this sort always involves an affliction of the one with the desire. And the greater the desire, the greater the affliction from the desire in the one with the desire. The souls of the heavens, then, are in continual affliction and in continual misery from such a desire. A proof of such affliction from the vehement ardor of this desire is the speed of their motion by which, as they claim, they try to that extent to attain this perfection. And since this motion does not cease, it is evident that this desire does not cease. So too, because the motion is not decreased, the desire is not decreased.

Moreover, every desire is a spiritual hunger, but motion is that by which one seeks to satisfy or to fill such hunger, such as the running of a hungry animal toward food or such as the leap of a lion that strongly hungers for the prey which it sees or such as the flight of an eagle or of a vulture to that for which it hungers. Hence, the motion of the heavens is necessarily like the most rapid running of such animals toward that which they strongly hunger. But the desire of each of the heavenly souls is like the strongest hunger, albeit a spiritual hunger. Therefore, just as the running or leap of a lion toward prey only occurs when there is hunger and the ardor of appetite for prey, but it ceases when the prey is caught and eaten, so it is necessary that the souls of the heavens be continuously afflicted with the mightiest and insatiable hunger, since their motion toward what they desire with such ardor is continuous. And since their motion never ceases, as they claim, it is necessary that such hunger never ceases.

Moreover, since every hunger and every desire aims at satiety and exists on its account, it is necessary that such satiety not be kept from it by any impossibility; hence, it is possible to attain it, or it is necessary that this hunger attain such satiety. Otherwise, it would be in vain, or it would exist only as a torment (813a) for the being that is hungry. Hence, it would not be natural, but hellish, as is the case with desires in hell, none of which can be fulfilled there. For the attainment of everything desirable will endlessly be prevented for those who are in hell by the justice and ordering of the creator. Hence, it is evident that such desires in the souls of the heavens are merely penal or utterly in vain. But pay careful attention to the example I shall give you of starving animals rushing for food with utter haste, because it is most appropriate to the desires and motions of the heavens. Notice that food whose consumption neither lessens the hunger nor strengthens or otherwise helps the eater is utterly useless, and thus the attainment of the object of desire which offers none of these three things to one who attains it is necessarily utterly useless. Hence, the attainment of locations is utterly useless for each of the heavens, since it is evident that none of these [three things] is acquired by parts of the heavens through this, nor is delight attained through it. For if this were the case, sadness would be obtained by the loss, and because the acquisition of each and the loss of it are and have been at the same time, there would necessarily occur at the same time in the souls of the heavens joy and sadness, and they would exist at the same time, and the souls would endlessly be in continuous joy and sadness or in a state that is a mixture of these two.

Chapter Seven
That the souls of the heavens do not intend that the heaven be renewed or that the renovation be continued infinitely.

But if someone says that there is no intention or desire of the heavenly souls for this or that state, but for the continual renovation of locations or for the continuation of the renovations, what benefit is there even in this renovation or continuation? Moreover, either there is a natural motion among the motions of the heavens or there is not. If there is, either this motion by which it moves is circular or it is some other. If it is circular, the desire and the intention of the souls with regard to this motion, then, is pointless.
[The rest of this chapter is omitted from this translation.]

(816a)

Chapter Eight
That every intellect exists on account of the intellect of the creator alone, and that he is a mirror of the whole intelligible universe.

After these points I shall try to go on and investigate more carefully that nature of the intelligences, if they exist in accord with this position; then I shall investigate their functions or operations and their number. On this last point Aristotle clearly seems not so much to have erred as to have raved most insanely. For since even according to Aristotle himself external vision was created for seeing visible things, he necessarily has also to concede with regard to internal vision, that is, with regard to the intellect, that it was necessarily created for seeing, that is, for understanding intelligibles. And the same thing must hold for the other natural forces or powers, namely, that the power of loving was created for loving lovable things, and the same way with the others. But when the intellect of one is perfect with the ultimate perfection of its intellect, the intellective power of that intellect is perfected with complete perfection so that it does not seek or desire anything more and nothing is lacking to it. Hence, it is necessary that the intellect be completed with its perfection in ultimate completion. For every created power and potency has being for the sake of its ultimate perfection, and this is its glory, as you learned in the preceding parts.[131] It is necessary, therefore, that the intellect, that is, the intellective power, was created for the sake of the understanding of the creator alone. I mean that understanding of him which is perfect with complete perfection or the completion of ultimate perfection.

But if someone says that it is necessary that the intellect understand other intelligibles; otherwise, it would not be complete with such perfection, one undoubtedly says something true. But the act of understanding or the knowing of the first and most noble intelligible, which is the creator, is not the knowing of the creator alone. Rather, it is the knowing or act of understanding of all things, the act by which all intelligibles are understood with a most noble and perfect knowing. For the creator himself is in himself the intelligible world and clearest exemplar of all things, and for this reason all things are seen most clearly in him by those who see him bare and look at him without a medium and who do not look at a mirror only. In fact, he is gleaming light that sheds light with his immediate rays, as I said, perfecting and illumining every intellect to which in his goodness he grants that it may look at him in that way.

Moreover, every intellect is by nature an intelligible, since it is naturally suited to receive in itself the inscription of the universe of intelligibles, it is evident that, when it has received this inscription, it will be like a model of the universe and like a book of its complete inscription.

Moreover, since the intellect is a mirror by nature, that is, it is naturally suited for all the intelligible forms to be reflected in it, and since the form of anything can naturally be reflected in it, it is naturally a mirror of it. Every intellect, then, is naturally a mirror of each and every intelligible and of the whole intelligible universe.

Moreover, all visible mirrors are suited to be mirrors of all visible things and of each one. Also, when every visible mirror is visible in act, that is, when some visible form is reflected in it, the mirror in act makes everything else visible, if it is clean and polished and directly opposite it. But what visible mirrors do by being directly opposite to each other, intelligible [mirrors] do between themselves by their intelligible and appropriate (816b) union, and in this way all intelligent substances by their immediate union with the first universal and most bright mirror (which is the creator) receive from his rays so that they are intelligible mirrors in act, if it is the good pleasure of the creator that they are united to him with such closeness and that he sheds rays upon them with such great illumination. For they are not activities of the creator which he does through himself, as operations of nature which are servile and in the manner of a servant, as you have often heard.[132] Rather, they are according to his good pleasure and from the ultimate degree of freedom.

---

[131] See, for example, *The Trinity, or the First Principle* (*De trinitate*), ch. 26: Switalski, pp. 149-150; Teske-Wade, pp. 172-173, where William speaks of the perfection of the human intellect as its glory.

[132] See above note 22 to the translation.

This is also the way it is between the noble, separated or immaterial substances and our souls. For by their union with them, they [i.e., the separated substances] make them [i.e., our souls] intelligible mirrors in accord with the mode and measure of such union, and on this account prophecies and revelations do not occur according to one mode or one measure. And this diversity is evident in the prophets and all those who are said truly and properly to practice divination, for some see more and see greater and more things than others, and you will hear what will be sufficient for you on these matters in what follows.

Chapter Nine
The destruction of the error of Algazeli and other philosophers concerning their claim that from the first principle there comes only one first creature, which is the first intelligence.

But from this I shall return to where I was, and I shall say that every intelligence, according to this position, is a substance that understands in act with a knowing or act of understanding that is naturally complete. It is not perfectible in potency such as our intellects are created, according to Aristotle. Every intelligence, therefore, is naturally either most close or most united to the first and universal mirror which is the creator, and it receives as a result of such a union, when the brilliance of the creator sheds his light, such intellective perfection that it is a mirror of those beings who understand or a mirror of intelligibles according to the mode and measure which the creator sets or prescribes for it. Or it is most united to another mirror by which it is made a mirror in act. I mean: an intelligible mirror, as I said. And since this matter cannot run or go off to infinity, it is necessary that an intelligence be next to the creator or without anything in between or that some other substance or other substances intervene. But you learned that it is impossible that they be infinite, for I have already destroyed an infinity of causes in every order by an irrefragable destruction in the first part of this teaching.[133]

They posit a single intellective potency and claim that it is the cause of the second, and the second the cause of the third, and so on, until their number is completed, which according to them is ten and no more. If, then, one of those intelligences is united to or next to the creator without anything in between, this is the first. For with regard to the others, if they exist, it is evident that they are after and below it where they put them and that it is between the creator and them. And since it is evident that they are far removed from all the tumult of matter, it is necessary that they be most benign, since the glory of the intellect is this union of the intellect with the creator and vision of him. For it is the ultimate perfection, but the ultimate perfection of each power is its glory, as you learned elsewhere. You also learned in

---

[133] See *The Trinity, or the First Principle* (*De trinitate*), ch. 2: Switalski, pp. 21-22: Teske-Wade, pp. 69-70.

the preceding parts that in no substance is there intellect without will and love, which are called the motive powers.[134] But the aim of love and of the will is nothing but perfect union with the ultimate object of love or will. And the ultimate object of love or will (817a) of all who will rightly and love rightly is the creator. But the ultimate union with him is the obtaining or possession of him, and it is called spiritual embrace. It is evident, therefore, that all the intelligences are most blessed since they are most united to the creator both by their apprehensive powers and by their motive powers. But this union and perfection is their ultimate glory and beatitude. Someone might say that these perfections or unions are natural, but everything natural is far beneath glory, and this is truly said in the sense of that glory by which the souls of the saints and righteous hope to be glorified in the renovation of the world by the creator. This state of glory is truly great in comparison with the state of our souls still existing in this life, but the doctrine and also the law of Christians maintain beyond the state of nature, however noble and sublime, a more outstanding and excellent state of glory. And this state is not known as yet in this world except by faith or revelation. It makes no difference with reference to my goal and intention in this treatise whether they ascribe these two states to the intelligences or only one of them.

Given this, then, we ask them whether they are idle and do nothing whatsoever, but are resting, merely intent upon the beauty of the creator and the enjoyment of his goodness and sweetness, for in these two their whole beatitude consists. But if that is so, what is the reason that the creator created only one of them, namely, the first alone. For it would not be impossible or difficult for him to create many; also his goodness is equally sufficient to make many of them happy just as it is sufficient to make just one happy. Visible beauty, after all, is not lessened or limited by a multitude of viewers. Likewise, brilliance is not, as is apparent in the sun. Envy and greed, however, are at the ultimate distance from the creator. That there are not many was, then, not due to a lessening or the smallness of the power of the creator nor due to a lack of riches nor to his envy or greed, because it is as certain as can be that he is generous in the ultimate degree of generosity. Therefore, only something that was on the side of the intelligences prevented their being many, namely, the impossibility of existing by which they were naturally prevented and removed from being or the impossibility of their being at the same time, as you elsewhere learned concerning two universes.[135] For it is wrong to say or to hold there is or was any defect or lessening of being in the creator. Likewise, it is evident that greed and envy are excluded and removed from him by every sort of impossibility. It is necessary, then, that a multitude of first intelligences is prevented from the side of the intelligence. But it is impossible that this prevention come about except in one of the ways I shall state.

---

[134] See chapter two above in this part, where William argues that the Aristotelian intelligences cannot lack will.

[135] See *De universo* Ia-Iae, chs. 11-16, where William argues that the universe is one.

One of these ways is contrariety or repugnance. And it is evident that it has no place here. For if there were many first intelligences, they would be most alike in all their essential and natural characteristics; therefore, they would be most peaceful and loving toward one another, insofar as they are good and just. There would, therefore, be no repugnance or contrariety between them which would prevent them from existing together. Also, no intelligence is in itself or through itself prevented by natural impossibility from existing. This will become evident to you, if you imagine many intelligences similar to the first intelligence. For you will find them to be most similar in the potency or potentiality for existing. But by the choice and good pleasure of the creator that one which they set first was educed from the potency of existing (817b) into act, though it was not naturally, considered in itself, closer or more prepared for the act of existing than the others. And you will see this more clearly if you imagine that it is not existing. For then it will be in every respect like the others which you imagine. Therefore, the choice of the creator, according to this opinion, fell upon this one alone in order to draw it alone from the potentiality of existing into act. It is, then, evident to you that it was not by nature alone either naturally prevented from being along with others or naturally preventing others from being.

Another way is superfluity which likewise has no place here. For if there were a million such intelligences, none of them would be superfluous or without purpose. This is evident from their operations which are to understand or to think and to know, to love, to will, and to rejoice. Something is without purpose or superfluous that is not of benefit. But such operations benefit their agents, because they bring joy to those intelligences that have them, and they glorify the creator by that much more in themselves, and they make them to be glorified and praised by those who know them. In neither of these two ways is a multitude of intelligences ruled out.

But with regard to that idea which seemed good to Aristotle and his followers, namely, that the unity of the creator precluded such a multitude, I replied to you in what preceded in the first part of this treatise on the universe.[136] But that which moved Aristotle and his followers, namely, that there could not be many substances removed from matter and separated from its appendages that are of the same rank and equal in every way and like in every respect is the worst of errors. On this account they maintained that human souls when separated [from matter] could not be many or differ in number or any other way. Every [religious] law rightly opposes this. For this is to say that all souls are one after they have been separated from their bodies and that they differ and are many only when they are in their bodies.[137]

---

[136] See *De Universo* Ia-Iae, chs. 24-27.

[137] In the 19th century E. Renan thought that William was here confronting the Averroistic doctrine of the unicity of the material or possible intellect that Thomas Aquinas would oppose later in the 13th century. Renan said of William's *De universo* that Averroism is refuted on every page (*Averroès et l'Averroïsme* [Paris, 1866], p. 225). In fact, William is arguing against a position which he either saw as a logical

Chapter Ten
The destruction of the error of Aristotle and Alfarabi and the others
who maintained that all separated souls are one and become one and
are unified by the separation from their bodies.

The explanation of this error and its most obvious destruction is this: It is self-evident, after all, that those things which are accidents of something do not produce another thing. So too, those things which come from the outside and do not belong to the substance or to the necessity or definition of its being [do not produce something else]. Because bodies do not belong to the substance or substances of their souls, it is evident that they do not make them numerically many.[138] Likewise, accidents, that is, virtues and vices, knowledge and ignorance, and emotions, such as joy, sorrow, fear, boldness, and other things of this sort do not make the souls in which they are numerically many. For on this view the soul which is now joyful could not become sad, and the converse, since it cannot become two distinct things. But joy and sadness would make it two distinct things according to this error if, for example, accidents and things coming from outside could make them this, namely, make that to which they come two distinct things. And on this view there would be no alteration or change in souls. If, then, the soul of Socrates and the soul of Plato were two distinct things while they were in their bodies, they will truly be two distinct things when they will be outside of their bodies.

Moreover, just as those things which are substantially or essentially different cannot become the same thing or the same things by the arrival of any accidents or by any likeness in qualities, so those things which are one (818a) essentially cannot become diverse things by any unlikeness or difference of accidents. If, then, all human souls are one thing essentially, they will not be made many by any difference or diversity of bodies or accidents, just as a man and an ass cannot become one by any likeness of accidents. Therefore, either all human souls are now numerically one while they are in their bodies, or they never will be numerically one when they will be separated from their bodies.

Moreover, in one and the same subject there cannot be contrariety in terms of the whole and in the same respect. But sadness and joy are a contrariety. They cannot, then, exist in one and the same subject; the subjects, therefore, are diverse. The soul which is joyous, then, is numerically distinct from the

---

implication of Avicenna's teaching or—more probably—against some Christian thinkers who drew the conclusion from Avicenna's works that human souls, once separated from their bodies, lose their individuality. See my "William of Auvergne on the Individuation of Human Souls," *Traditio* 49 (1994): 77-93.

[138] William's Latin has "*aliud et aliud*: one thing and another," just as above he speaks of "*aliud*: another thing."

soul which is sad. The soul of Socrates which is joyous is, therefore, essentially something other than the soul of Plato which is sad.

Moreover, some soul is now separate. Either it is the same as any soul existing in the body, or it is other than any soul [in a body]. For it cannot more suitably be said to be identical with one soul than with another. Hence, it is either identical with any soul existing in the body or with none. Suppose, then, that the soul of Socrates is separate from the body and the soul of Plato is not. If this is possible, since the soul of Socrates is separate from the body and since it is essentially the soul of Plato, the soul of Plato will of necessity be separated from the body of Socrates, for at least by way of accident it is true that the soul of Plato is the soul of Socrates, for the white person is a doctor and the seated person is a musician.

Moreover, if all souls are one essentially, one soul will not be better or more knowing than another, just as the one seated is not better or more knowing than the musician. That is, this person seated is not better or more knowing than this same person who is a musician.

Moreover, on this view there will not be a genuine generation of human beings, for generation occurs most of all according to form, and it is called generation especially on account of the newness of form. But in this man who is said to be generated there is no new form, since there is no new soul, and the soul cannot be called new because of a new accident or a new body, just as human beings cannot be called new because of a house which they have just begun to inhabit.

Moreover, if all separated souls were one soul and one thing, they will be something one not divisible into parts (*impartibile*), because [they are] the one soul, which certainly is not divisible into parts. Either it is possible that a human being be generated, or it is not possible. But it is evident that it is possible. Suppose, then, that some human being has been newly generated. Either that human being will be given this one soul which is separate and is all those souls which once had been in bodies and left them, or another soul will be created and given to that human being who has newly been generated. But if the person is given this one soul which is, of course, only one and something one not divisible into parts, the whole of it will be given to that human being and given as a whole. Nothing of it, then, will remain outside the body, but the whole soul will not remain outside the body, nor will it wholly remain outside it. Hence, neither the soul of Socrates nor the soul of Plato or of any one else from the dead will remain outside the body. Where then are the souls of the dead, so many thousands of whom have come before our times? But if another soul will be created, it is necessary that the same thing be said of all the others which are in bodies. Hence, all the souls which are now in bodies are other than the separated ones and will be other than those same souls when they will likewise have been separated from their bodies.

Moreover, on this view no soul would be created. For it is not possible to create a soul which already exists. But according to this error every soul is essentially in that one which is all separated souls. Besides, if it were created, it would be created either in the body to which it is united or outside of that body. If it was created outside, this is impossible, since it would have first existed in that one soul which is all the separate souls. But if it was created in the body, this would take place over some time or in an instant. (818b) Hence at that time or instant it would exist for the first time and would not previously have existed. But this is impossible, since it already existed in that one [soul] in which all separate souls were united.

Moreover, this soul which now exists for the first time, that is, which is now created, did not exist in some body, and it is impossible that it was separated from a body in which it did not exist. It was not, then, separated from some body, but that one was separated from many bodies, according to this error. This soul, then, is not that soul.

Moreover, the separation of the soul from the body and the union with it of necessity have to do with the numerically same subject. For it is not possible that something be separated unless it was united. When it is separated, therefore, it of necessity remains the same thing that it was when united. But when it is separated, it is that one soul; therefore, when it was united, it was that same one, and one must say the same concerning all other souls. Hence, all the souls which are still united to bodies are even now that one soul. From this it follows of necessity that no soul is created and that no human being is generated, as I have already said.

Moreover, by this separation there is taken from each of the souls which are in bodies not only matter, but also many of the accidents and modifications, all of which are either removed or not. If all are removed, then, knowledge does not remain, nor is there any virtue in them after death, nor any punishment. But all the [religious] laws contradict this. It is clearly seen that this is mistaken and impossible because, if it were so, the union of souls to bodies would be utterly useless and pointless, since they would leave their bodies in the same state as they entered them with no addition or gain.

Moreover, the being of souls through bodies would be utterly useless and superfluous, since they would be empty of knowledge and virtues outside their bodies, just like the being of a mirror in which no image would be reflected or the being of a tablet on which there was no writing or painting. Concerning each of these there is no doubt that its being—in terms of this potentiality—is utterly otiose and empty and likewise completely useless, unless there is some other use or utility of them. I say this because a tablet or glass can perhaps be applied to other uses than writing or painting or images. But when the being of our souls is completely deprived of knowledge and virtues and other acts and separate from the bodies, it will have no use or utility at all. But if someone says that all the accidents, all the habits, and all the dispositions are truly removed from souls in this separation from bodies, but new habits and dispositions and new qualities are given to them or ones like them in every respect are given them, this is foolish and unfair on the part of the giver. I mean that exactly the same things should be given to souls who acted well as to those who acted badly. But if different recompenses are given them according to their merits, there is, then, clearly a diversity between them when they are separate [from their bodies], because there is an obvious difference in merits and rewards or punishments and also in those new qualities and dispositions which are given to them, for though they are neither rewards nor punishments, they are different. For difference is a clear sign of plurality and diversity.

Moreover, if you would imagine one soul to have been already separated and another soul to be now separated, it is necessary according to this error that they concede that this latter is or becomes that soul. But you have already seen many problems which result for someone who says that this soul is that one. It is something quite amazing how they can say that this soul is that one, since this soul is clothed with so many habits and dispositions and emotions, but that one is deprived of everything of the sort. For they must admit regarding the same thing both its being clothed and its being naked, which are privation and possession, (819a) or both affirmation and negation, that is, both its being and its not being clothed. But if they say that this soul becomes that one, though it was not previously that one, it therefore becomes something other than it was. But this cannot be except in one of two ways, either by retaining the being it previously had or by losing it. If by retaining it, it will be one thing and another one thing, namely, that which it was first and that which it became by separation. Hence, it will be two things from which one thing does not come to be. For if one thing comes to be from two, the composite of them will be neither of the two. Then the human soul will not only be divisible into parts (*partibilis*) or divisible into two, but it will also be two different things in terms of being and, therefore, both of them. But if it loses through separation the being it previously had, it is, therefore, corrupted. Hence, the corruptibility or mortality of human souls results from this error. But this is an error which every law pursues with fire and the sword. Against this error, then, about the human soul every sort of human being ought to be armed not only with arguments and proofs, but with the sword and every kind of torment to exterminate it, since this error takes from them both the next life and the glory on account of which they were created. On this matter I have elsewhere satisfied you.[139]

Chapter Eleven
He continues to oppose the previous error
on account of the difficulties which follow from it.

Since this error is so obvious that any reasonable person—even one of slight education—is capable of destroying it, I do not want to burden you with a

---

[139] See, for example, William's *The Immortality of the Soul* (*De immortalitate animae*), a work which is entirely devoted to presenting arguments for the immortality of the soul, or his *The Soul* (*De anima*), which devotes much of chs. 5 and 6 to soul's indivisibility into parts and immortality.

greater length of proofs. But you ought to know that it detracts from the glory and magnificence of the creator in an intolerable way, because it takes from him so many thousands of souls in the next life, and he is not going to be extolled and praised by them without end. It not only obstructs or closes the mouths of those praising and singing of him, but also takes away those mouths and praises and countless songs to the creator, since it holds that he will be sung to and extolled and praised by one mouth alone. And for this reason there will be only one praise and song of him from all the souls who will be blessed, if one claims that the sum total of them will be only one soul and one sole being in essence and truth.

Nor should one show pity for the feeblemindedness or erroneousness of such a man who, because he does not grasp accidental differences in some thing, posits an essential identity in them. For he sees in all the individuals of many species all sorts of likeness in accidents, for example, in flies of the same species and same age of which there is a countless multitude. And because he does not see that they differ except by place, he thinks that, with that difference removed, there is only one thing, that is, one fly. So, when there are removed the differences which souls had from the side of bodies and which are only accidental, he thinks that all souls are one thing and one thing alone. And this is what Aristotle says: There cannot be many separate substances of the same rank and nobility, but the ten intelligences were made many on account of the differences which they have in rank and nobility, for if they were of the same rank and nobility, there would be no difference between them, and for this reason there would be no plurality.

Someone from among the Latin philosophers clearly said in his book that only a variety of accidents produces a numerical difference among individuals.[140] And by this statement some have tried to confirm this error.[141] But I have above explained to you what is the correct interpretation of this statement,[142] and (819b) let that be enough for you. For you have already learned

---

[140] In his *De trinitate* Boethius said, "*Sed numero differentiam accidentium varietas facit*: the variety of accidents makes a difference in number" (*The Theological Treatises*, ed. H. F. Stewart and E. K. Rand [Cambridge: Harvard Univ. Press, 1946], 6, lines 24-25.

[141] The identity of these people to whom William refers simply as "*aliqui*: some" is intriguing. It would seem that they were contemporaries or near contemporaries of William who knew both Avicenna and Boethius. The Paris-Orléans edition has in the margin: "*Intellige Albertum magnum*: Understand Albert the Great," but it is at least ten years too early for it to have been Albert. Roland de Vaux finds in William's discussion of the individuation of the human soul the clearest evidence for the existence of a Latin Avicennism; see his *Notes and textes sur l'Avicennisme latin aux confins des XIIe-XIIIe siècles* (Paris, 1934), p. 42, note 1.

[142] In *De universo* IIIa-Iae, ch. 29: I, 802aE, William explained that Boethius intended by his statement only to exclude a specific difference or other substantial differences. He says, "His meaning, therefore, in this statement was that only a difference of accidents, that is, not the species or a substantial difference or anything of all the common essential characteristics, makes a difference in number,

in logic that accidental differences do not make something else, but only something changed, and for this reason there is no generation or corruption, but only alteration with respect to them. Hence, if the whole variety of accidents were removed from Socrates, he would on this account be Socrates no less than he is or was previously. Nor would he be something else, but he could perhaps be said to have become someone changed or of another sort. But he could in no sense be said to have become corrupted or generated or to have become something else or even another man. Otherwise, after he had become old and wise and a man of a renowned goodness, Socrates would be another man than he was when he was a boy. And this would be to say that no man can grow and increase in wisdom or morals. It also follows from this that Socrates was not born and did not learn anything and countless other things in which the conclusion from what has already been said is sufficient for you.

It has already, then, been explained to you that likeness—no matter how great—and equality do not prevent a multitude and a diversity and that accidental differences do not prevent identity, though they are in the same individual at diverse times. For likeness—no matter how great it may be—does not preclude a society, but would rather draw together a society, if a likeness pertained to it, and it does not demand that there be a solitariness or singularity. And a multitude of like things does not of necessity introduce a superfluity. From these arguments it has become clear for you that from the side of the intelligence which they posit as first and most noble there is no prevention of plurality in the nature of the intelligence. Nor is it prevented by nature that there be an accompanying multitude of like substances, nor is this multitude of like substances excluded from existence by a natural impossibility. It has also been shown to you that from the side of the creator there was no defect or impediment that prevented him from creating so noble a multitude.

From these arguments it becomes known to you that Aristotle and his followers have taken much from the magnificence and glory of the creator in the assertion of the solitariness and singularity of the first intelligence and also in the assertion of the small number of all the intelligences which he restricted and limited to the number of the heavens, namely, ten, and of the heavenly motions. He paid little note to how much more the creator is magnified and glorified by countless intelligences than by one or than by the ten he mentioned. From this it is apparent that he either did not believe the philosophers or did not examine their books, unless he has perhaps retracted and corrected this error elsewhere.

But it is worthy of wonder that he claimed that the first intelligence was incompatible with likeness and companionship, if he did this for the reason which I mentioned, since the nature of goodness favors companions and is

---

that is, diversifies the individuals or makes for us a numerical distinction of individuals; for we do not distinguish individuals by species, but we rather unite them by the complete essential likeness which they have in their species."

friendly toward companionship, and goodness itself is in its truest sense the principle of union and assimilation. Aristotle heard this from his teacher, Plato, who speaks of the creator in the *Timaeus*, or in the book he called the *Timaeus*. He said, "He was the best, but from the best envy is far removed, and therefore he wanted to make all things like himself,"[143] that is, good, to the extent that the nature of each would be capable of beatitude, that is, of goodness. And yet, Aristotle does not say that a multitude of like things was prevented by the envy of the first intelligence, but because of the fact that such noble and such separate substances could not be many. I have, however, already shown you that a natural impossibility of existing did not prevent such a multitude from existing, and a natural repugnance or envy did not prevent it either. But I now add that the dwelling of the creator did not prevent this by its smallness, as if it were unable to receive so great and so noble a multitude.

(820a)

Chapter Twelve
Concerning the 'where' or place of the first intelligence and of the others according to the view of Aristotle.

But since Aristotle claimed that this and the other intelligences exist, it is right to examine where he located them, whether in the heavens or outside the heavens.

[The remainder of this chapter is omitted from the translation.]

(820b)

Chapter Thirteen
The destruction of the error of certain philosophers concerning the location of the intelligences.

In none of the heavens, however, is there something that is not in motion—I mean: the ten moveable heavens. But when we move, those things which are in us are moved, as Aristotle says.[144] They are moved, I say, at least accidentally. Therefore, the soul of each heaven is moved, in whatever part of its heaven it is. Hence, the intelligence will be moved, if it is in it or is with it or is even in its own heaven, wherever it is in it. Its state, therefore, will be most wretched as a result of this rapid rotation. Besides, its movement has been and will be useless in every way, since it does not benefit it or anything else. But if this intelligence is not moved, the soul which is so strongly in love with it is moved. Therefore, the soul is separated from its intelligence by its motion and, necessarily, with severe pain. Hence, it is necessary that it not move its heaven voluntarily, just as it is not voluntarily separated from its intelligence.

---

[143] See Plato, *Timaeus* 29E.
[144] See, as a possible source, Aristotle, *On the Soul* I, ch. 3, 406b1-3.

But if someone says that such separation, that is, in place, does not in any way impede the souls of the heavens or other spiritual substances, and that one spiritual substance does not see less or look less at another spiritual substance because of bodily distance and does not see more because of nearness, that person speaks the truth, if the one sees the other in a revealed vision, that is, in a vision so lofty. But if knowledge is aided by the body, the situation will be different, just as it is in the mutual knowledge of our souls which know one another only through their bodies and what belong to their bodies. But it is clear that the perfections which are infused or poured into bodies by spiritual substances are generally impeded and helped by motion and distance. But the heavens are bodies, and these intelligences pour into them (821a) loves and desires from which their motions arise. Regarding our bodies, however, and ourselves it is clear that our bodies are not moved except by the souls which are in them, because, if our intellective power by which our motions and operations are governed were not most close and united to our souls, it would not be able to govern them of itself. If then the intelligences govern the motion of the heavens and do so of themselves, it is necessary that they be most closely united to them. For this reason the perfections which the souls seek from them must be in the ultimate degree of perfection. Hence, if the strength of their love for them is so great, they are totally carried off to them, and it is not possible for them to be occupied with some other concern. For when a mighty lover is suitably united to his beloved in a union which is perfect and beyond which no greater can be sought, he clings to her with his whole thought and whole love so that he forgets not only his own business and possessions, but also even himself. Hence, it is not possible that the souls of the heavens be occupied with the rotations of their bodies, especially when such movements are so great and involve such great bodies and such speed that they cannot be cared for with moderate attention.

There is the same question about these intelligences, because, if they have the nobility which they must have according to that position, it is necessary that their intellect be totally fixed upon the contemplation of the creator and that they are so carried off by mighty love of him and so cling to his beauty and goodness that, removed from all other cares, they think of and desire nothing other than the creator, unless the most dominant will of the creator should perhaps enjoin some other duty upon them, as most certainly occurs in visions of the holy angels. This is apparent from the books of the prophets, and I shall speak of it in the following parts, if God wills it.

But if the intelligences are separate from these souls, it is not unreasonable to ask whether they are outside the heavens or in the heavens and in which parts of them and whether they are arranged according to the proportion and likeness of places so that the last one which they call the agent intelligence and the sun of our souls and the intelligible light of this earthly world, that is, of our dwelling, is closest to us.[145] In second place and rank there is the intel-

---

[145] In *De universo* William speaks almost exclusively about an agent intelligence, that is, that tenth of the separate substances; in *De anima*, however, he also speaks of an

ligence which is the beloved of the soul moving the first of the movable heavens, and above it there is only the creator, who is God most high. And if he does not have a spiritual and noble family, his life is not far removed from the life of a lion and a wolf, as a certain one of the Latin philosophers has said. He said that life without a companion is the life of a lion or a wolf.[146] I shall examine in the following, that is, after I have dealt with the intelligences, what this family of the creator is and other things which must be asked about this question. I shall begin, then, with the agent intelligence which they ranked last, that is, lowest in nobility and in dignity.

Chapter Fourteen
An inquiry concerning the agent intelligence which they claimed was the lowest in nobility and rank. And the reason that forced Aristotle and his followers to maintain this intelligence.

Aristotle, therefore, said about it, as I have already stated, that it is like the intelligible sun of our souls and the light of our intellect, making to be reflected in it in act the intelligible forms which Aristotle claimed were in it in potency, and he said that it draws them from potency into act (821b). In the same way the sun draws into act by its shining, that is, by the outpouring of its light, the potentially visible colors, that is, those which are in potency in colored bodies. But the reason that forced him to maintain this intelligence was the position of Plato concerning the forms or concerning the world of species. This world is called the archetypal world and the world of the principal forms and the world of species and the intelligible world or world of intelligibles. For Aristotle could not defend himself without being forced to grant this position of Plato's, but [the work of Plato's] in which his arguments and proofs were found has not come into my hands. I shall, then, set down the arguments which he seems to have had or could have had. For this purpose, then, I say that one should not believe the intellect about intelligibles less than the senses about sensibles. Because, then, the testimony or witness-

---

agent intellect, that is, a part or the whole of the human soul. William, I have argued, has no use for either an agent intellect or agent intelligence. He rejects an agent intellect on the grounds that the soul cannot have parts and, if the whole human intellect were active, it would be perfect in knowledge. Though he does admit the existence of separate substances—in fact very many of them—he does not attribute to any of them the functions which Avicenna attributed to the agent intelligence. See my "William of Auvergne's Rejection of the Agent Intelligence," in *Greek and Medieval Studies in Honor of Leo Sweeney, S.J.* (New York: Peter Lang, 1995), pp. 211-235.

[146] William uses this quotation twice in *De universo*; it also appears in IIa-IIae, ch. 91: I, 945aB, where he attributes it to "the noble philosopher of the Latins." The text seems to be a variation of a fragment of Epicurus quoted by Seneca; see *Letter* 19, 10, 5f, where Seneca says, "For a banquet without a friend is the life of a lion or a wolf."

ing of the senses forces us to maintain the world of sensible things and the sensible world itself, a world of particular or individual things, the intellect ought to force us for far better reasons to maintain the world of intelligibles. But this is the world of universals or species. For our intellect in this life does not of itself grasp in the proper sense particular or singular things, but only universals, that is, genera, species, and other common things, which Plato seems to have called immaterial forms and species.

Moreover, all of our knowledge is a certain assimilation to those things which are known according to that power or part by which they are known, so that, if they are known by the senses, there will be an assimilation of the sense to those objects, as is obvious in touch and sight and in all the senses. For it is necessary that a likeness of that which is sensibly known or perceived through the sense be imprinted on the organ of each sense. And the sensible thing is generally not known through the sense in any other way than through its action upon the organ of that sense and its impression of its likeness upon the same. And it seems that the situation is necessarily the same with the intellect. Hence, it is not possible to understand an intelligible object except through the action of the intellect which is passive or receptive of such passions or impressions or likeness in it. And Aristotle seemed to hold this when he said that it is impossible to understand without a phantasm.[147] Our intellections, that is, our acts of understanding by which we are understanding, are in act only passions or likenesses of intelligibles impressed by those same things upon our intellect. But what does not exist cannot act or impress anything. It is necessary, then, that intelligible things exist which imprint such likenesses or passions on our intellect. But these are the only things which we understand here, that is, in this life. It is necessary, then, that such intelligibles exist. Hence, it is necessary that these common forms, namely, genera and species and other appropriate things of this sort not only exist in some way, but exist as they are understood. In the same way, it is necessary that sensible and particular things not only exist without qualification, but that they exist as they are perceived.[148]

Moreover, how are the senses to be regarded as truer witnesses than the intellect? If things are in their being—I mean: sensible things—as the senses testify concerning them, it is necessary for far better reasons that intelligible things are the way the intellect testifies concerning them. But it testifies that

---

[147] Aristotle, *De anima* III, ch. 7, 431a16.

[148] It is striking that Thomas Aquinas says just the opposite in such similar language. He says, for example, "Plato, however, seems to have departed from the truth for, because he thought that all knowledge takes place through the mode of some likeness, he believed that the form of the known is of necessity in the knower in the same mode it is in the known. But he considered that the form of the thing understood is in the intellect universally and immaterially and without change. . . And so he thought that the things understood exist in themselves in this mode, that is, immaterially and without change" (*Summa theologiae* Ia, qu. 84, a. 1c.).

they are common, everlasting, apart from generation and corruption and from all the tumult of changes. Therefore, it is necessary that they exist in that way.

Moreover, if things were otherwise, only the senses would be true and truthful, and the intellect would be a total liar, because it lies about all things, about the being and truth of intelligibles and about their mode of existing and about the way they are.

Moreover, since the intelligible forms are passions or impressions, it is necessary (822a) that there be an agent or agents impressing them. But by their natural operation and of themselves sensible things impress only likenesses of themselves which cannot but be signs of those things by which they are impressed. Hence, they are naturally only signs of sensible things. They will not, then, be signs of intelligible things, but it is not possible to know any things except through their own proper signs. There will, therefore, be intelligible signs proper to intelligible things, and they will be impressed by those things. Otherwise, intelligibles, that is, intelligible things will not be knowable by us in the present state.

But if someone says that the intellect strips and lays bare from particular conditions the forms which are impressed by sensible things and that it in that way makes those forms intelligible and signs of intelligible things, it follows, first of all, that nature has neglected the intellective power in us and has cared for the sensible powers much more diligently than for it. For nature has provided them with so great a supply of sensible signs and of things impressing them, but has situated the intellective power in such poverty that it needs to beg for the signs necessary for itself from sensible signs, and nature has provided for it only out of the remains of them. Also, what is this stripping or laying bare? Does the intellective power have it in its power to remove or scrape off something from the sensible signs? And what sort of garments are these which it removes from them? Although I do not approve this statement and view of Aristotle's, because, nonetheless, one reads of it so often in his books and in those of others who have followed him, and this so frequently is uttered by the lips of certain people who suppose that they are philosophizing, I shall explain to you this statement about stripping and laying bare.

Chapter Fifteen
How the stripping and laying bare of things by the intellect is understood.

Know then that our intellective power removes nothing, takes away or subtracts nothing at all from sensible signs, but rather something is taken from it, since such signs do not reach it in their totality, but only a part of them, as it were, and they do not reach it with their integrity or totality. Rather, it is as I shall tell you. Suppose that someone sculpts or paints an image of Socrates and makes it like Socrates to the point that, for everyone who knows Socrates and looks at it close up, it is obviously seen as an image of Socrates. It is clear that for someone who looks at it from afar it would not be seen as an image of Socrates in particular, but an image of a man indeterminately or indefinitely, that is, in the universal. It is, then, clear to you that neither sight nor the seer removes something from the image of Socrates and does not take away or scrape away anything from it. Likewise, if one draws near to the image so that, seeing it fully and completely, one recognizes that it is an image of Socrates, there is no addition to or subtraction from the image on this account. Know that the intellective power behaves in the same way toward particular sensible signs as someone looking at the image of Socrates from a distance, and this is the meaning of stripping and laying bare, namely, the shortsightedness of the intellect because of which it cannot attain to the particular conditions by which those signs are proper to the particular things they signify, as I told you with regard to the person looking at the previously mentioned image of Socrates from afar. And this is shortsightedness of our intellect, while it is here in the body, unless it is illumined by prophetic brightness or by another light coming to it from above.

(822b)

Chapter Sixteen
The error of Aristotle and others concerning the agent intelligence is further destroyed, and it is asked whether something flows out from it over our intellective power.

But I shall return to this point in order to continue what I began concerning the view of Aristotle concerning the agent intelligence. I say, then, that in the visible sun there is not the power that it may by itself, that is, by the outpouring of its light alone, make some sensible form to be reflected in act in a mirror of glass or of some other material. There will not, then, be in the agent intelligence for such a reason alone the power to make some intelligible form to be reflected in the mirror of our intellective power. But, as he himself sufficiently explained, the intelligible forms are in the intellect in proximate potency, but in a visible mirror the visible forms are only in remote potency and have a much greater need and imperfection. And for this reason it is necessary to use visible forms which are in act in order that the light of the sun should make them to be reflected in act in such mirrors. But from the statements of Aristotle it is clearly seen that Aristotle himself thought that our intellective power was able to be illumined both from the inferior side, that is, from the side of sensible things through the stripping or laying bare which I explained, and from the superior side, that is, by the agent intelligence. It is also evident by sensation itself that prophetic splendors and illuminations of our souls which are in rapture and ecstasy and other states and dispositions which will be reported to you and listed in the following chapters cannot possibly be produced by the senses or through sensation.[149]

[149] In *The Immortality of the Soul* (*De immortalitate*): Teske, pp. 30-31, William appeals to states of ecstacy and rapture as the clearest proofs of the soul's independence from the body. He thinks of ecstacy as the soul's quite literally standing outside of the body and of rapture as the soul's being taken out of the body.

I, therefore, ask Aristotle here whether what is received from the agent intelligence upon our intellective power, when it is illuminated or irradiated by it in that way, is an intelligible form or forms or something else. But if it is the intelligible form itself, then it is not educed from potency into act in the way he said, just as from the potency of the visible mirror the form reflected in it is not educed into act, after it was in it in potency or potentially, unless one understands this potency to be only the potency to receive. But it is not that way in colored bodies or their colors. For they do not receive colors from the sun, but are helped by the activity of the sun so that they bring into act what they have in potency. So too, seeds do not receive from warmth and moisture the forms of plants or of animals. For warmth or moisture can in no sense impress those forms; rather, their potentiality is helped by warmth and moisture, and the impediments are removed which keep such forms from passing into act. It remains, then, that what the agent intelligence impresses or what flows out upon our intellective power is something other than an intelligible form. But many questions follow upon this statement. For the agent intelligence pours out naturally only a likeness of itself or of what it has. But it has within itself only intelligible forms in act. Hence, what the agent intelligence pours out upon our intellective power is either the substance of itself or an intelligible form like one of the forms which are in it, since—as you heard elsewhere—every intelligence is, according to them, full of forms.[150] But the reason for what I am saying is that the agent intelligence acts only by shedding its rays, namely, upon our intellective power, (823a) only through its substance or through its form. And if it does so through its substance, it ought to impress a likeness of its substance, that is, a substance like to it. But if it acts through its form, it ought to impress a form like to its form.

Moreover, because the sense is illumined for sensible knowledge through the likeness of the sensible form alone which is impressed upon the organ of the sense, for much better reason will our intellect be illumined for intelligible knowledge through the intelligible form alone. That, then, which the agent intelligence impresses upon our intellective power is nothing but an intelligible form and likeness of what is understood, that is, of the thing which is understood. But it is evident to every sentient person—not to mention: to every intelligent person—that the sun does not impress colors on colored bodies, since colors are not within the sun, nor did Aristotle think this. And he did not attribute this to the power of the sun, especially since he knew that this operation of the sun is natural and takes place, therefore, through likeness. Aristotle, then, was not unaware that the light of the sun does not impress or give color to colored bodies.

Moreover, since every likeness comes from the truth and every copy comes from an exemplar, but the intelligible forms which are received by our intellect or by our intellective power are likenesses, they come, therefore, from the

[148] See Aristotle, *On the Soul* III, ch. 4, 429a27-29.

truth in relation to which they are said to be likenesses. But this truth is either with the agent intelligence and in it, or there is only a likeness of such truth [in it]. But if this truth is within the agent intelligence, there will be in it the true mode of species and of true forms, and there will not be within it only a likeness of the truth, but the truth itself, and it will be this way with the other forms. Aristotle, then, falls back into the view of Plato which he thought he had escaped through this position. But if there is only a likeness with the agent intelligence, every likeness, as has already been said, comes from its truth. In that way the truth is within that other thing, and since it is impossible that the matter run on to infinity, we must come, by one step or by a definite number of more intervening steps, to something else with which the truth of this likeness exists, and likewise of all the others. But this is what Plato maintained, namely, a world of the truth of things and species and forms. He, however, held that this sensible world was a world of copies and likenesses, claiming that this is not true fire which is found among us, and that [true] fire or true earth is not found among us, but the fire-like or earth-like, and not true humanity, but the human.[151]

But if someone says that the truth of the likenesses and forms which are with the agent intelligence is found in particular things, I say that this man contradicts Aristotle: First, because the agent intelligence receives nothing from particular things, especially according to him, since he maintains that every intelligence is immaterial and cannot be acted upon.[152] Second, because every truth is prior to its likeness, but in the order of the created universe or totality, he himself placed the intelligences first after the creator in the order which I reported. You ought also to know that the same question is raised against Aristotle concerning the creator who is blessed and ever to be blessed, namely, whether with him there are only likenesses of things or their truths. For if they are only the likenesses which Plato seems to have called ideas, it is necessary that likenesses be prior to their truths, and this seems absurd.

Moreover, these likenesses were either created by the creator or not. If they were, such causation by the creator will be, therefore, disordered and backwards. For it seems that one ought to have begun from the truth which in the most correct order is in every case prior to every likeness of it, just as every exemplar is prior to its copy. (823b) But if they are not caused by the creator, since every likeness is caused, they will, therefore, be caused by their truths. And from this it follows that he received something from creatures, and in that way he would have been helped by them to create them, and it is un-

---

[151] William used the translation of Plato's *Timaeus* by Chalcidius; see Plato, *Timaeus a Calcidio translatus commentarioque instructus*, ed. Jan H. Waszink (London: E. J. Brill, 1975), p. 47: "Hence, with regard to all changeable things of this sort one should think this: this which seems to us to be formed differently at different times and is often not in accord with the form of fire is not fire, but fire-like, and not brass but brass-like. . . ."

[152] I read "*impassibilem*" for "*impossibilem*."

speakable and a wicked blasphemy against him to say or even to think that. But to avoid seeming to indulge in sophistry and to argue against Aristotle merely for the sake of argument, I say that a likeness in one sense is said to be that which arises from the truth and exists only to designate it, such as, an image of Socrates or of Caesar which undoubtedly comes after each of them and exists only to designate each of them. And this likeness is not prevented from being the truth in relation to its likeness which is imprinted upon the soul of one who looks at it. And that likeness which was impressed upon the mind of the one looking at it can be the truth and the exemplar in relation to another image which the person who saw the prior one can fashion in himself, and then the likeness which such a artisan has in his mind will be the exemplar of that second image. But that likeness is the copy of this one, and nothing prevents this one from being called the truth in relation to that one. But in another sense anything like is called a likeness, though not with equal propriety and correctness. In that way the ideas of all things are called their likenesses and are said to have been in the mind of the creator from eternity, but especially according to Plato, who seems to have said this first. According to this sense it is not necessary that every likeness be posterior to that of which it is the likeness or that it have its origin from it.

Chapter Seventeen
What is the conception of the archetypal world according to the doctrine of the Christians and that in the agent intelligence there is a plenitude of exemplary forms according to Aristotle.

With regard to the archetypal world which is the reason and exemplar of the universe, know that the doctrine of the Christians understands it to be the Son of God and the true God, and by its faith and law that people call it the image of God the Father in the ultimate degree of likeness and of the clear representation of the same. Hence, God the Father is in relation to him the truth in this comparison, and he is the image in relation to the Father, because he has his origin from him, and he is most truly called the Son of the Father on this account. He is the exemplar of all things which are truly and naturally good. Hence, he is said to be the likeness of the universe as the exemplar, and the universe shines back toward him with all its wonderfulness and beauty, and with every virtue and power and with every goodness and sweetness which is in it, though from a far, beyond all measure and comparison, so that it should be called only the thinnest shadow and slight vestige of him. But he is the complete Word of the Father by which the Father eternally spoke himself in the most complete utterance and all things in it and through it. The universe,[153] however, is to be considered only his least nod, as is explained in the first part of the sapiential knowledge which is called comparative, because it discloses to those who contemplate it the glory and magnifi-

---

[153] I read "*universum*" for "*universis.*"

cence of the creator by comparing the universe and parts of it to the creator, to the extent it is possible. This is the fourth part of contemplative wisdom.[154]

One must state that, according to Aristotle, the agent intellect has within itself likenesses of things, that is, exemplars which are naturally implanted and innate in that intelligence from the sole first exemplar which I mentioned. Hence, it is the book of all things which are naturally knowable in which it is possible to read them in the manner I shall mention (824a). As I said, it is the clean mirror in which all those things are reflected most brightly. It is not, then, necessary that the truth of particular things be with it or in it essentially, that is, so that Socrates is with it or in it, and it is this way with other things. But according to the position of Aristotle it is somehow the truth of particular forms, both spiritual ones and bodily ones. Because it is according to Aristotle the creator of even our souls and the fashioner of our bodies, and it has produced all the things which are after it and it produces those things which come to be, as Aristotle thought. And as I already told you in the preceding parts, it does not act except by understanding and willing in the likeness of the creator.

Chapter Eighteen
Why Aristotle did not assert many agent intelligences, and it is asked why according to him many intelligences cannot be caused by one intelligence.

For good reason it seems puzzling why he maintained that single one and not many, since it could not act where it was not itself present. Since, then, it produces in this whole earthly world so many souls and so many bodies, it is necessary that it be everywhere in the earthly world or that there be many like it which likewise act with it. They will, then, be in India, likewise in Britain, in Ethiopia, in Italy, in Armenia, and in Ireland, and it is no small difficulty to see this.

Moreover, since it fashions this body here and at the same time infuses the soul into it here, and it does this through itself, that is, through its own essence and power, it is necessary that it be in this body which it fashions and in this soul which it makes, as he himself said. How then is it in so many bodies and in so many souls at the same time?

Moreover, how can it act upon so many souls, that is, so that it produces them or causes them in some other way, and yet it cannot in that way act upon substances of its own species so that it causes them as well? And in that way there would be many agent intelligences.

---

[154] It is not clear what William is referring to. Though it is possible that he is referring to a part of the *Magisterium divinale et sapientiale*, it seems more likely that he is referring to a stage or level in contemplative knowledge of God. See *De universo* Ia-Iae, ch. 18 for William's use of such comparisons with creatures to rise to the contemplation of God.

Moreover, every species has naturally more power over a multitude of its own kind than of some other kind and has more power and is freer with respect to it, because every giver is more powerful for giving what it has than what it does not have. Nor is there an objection from the side of the creator for many reasons, especially according to the law and doctrine of the Christians, since he gave both the deity and the omnipotence which he had to his Son and to the Holy Spirit. Nor is there an objection from the side of the Son and the Holy Spirit, because they too give what they have, but according to the receptivity of those to whom they give. For no creature is able to receive omnipotence or deity essentially. Human beings, nonetheless, are called gods among the Christians, and according to their faith they are deified. It is evident to you that these names are said equivocally, for omnipotence is said and can be said of no creature. But power and might are multiplied in creatures and are increased according to their good pleasure.[155]

Moreover, it is evident that rational souls are not only of another species than the agent intelligence, but also of another genus. How then does this diversity proceed from it through itself?

Moreover, how does such a multitude and diversity proceed from that one intelligence, especially since that principle forced them to maintain a single first intelligence, that is, because it came from one creator and insofar as he is one and the same?[156]

Moreover, if this intelligence which is, of course, the last and lowest among the intelligences in nobility and dignity and power (824b) can produce so great a multitude of rational souls which are all noble and intelligent substances, how could the intelligence which the soul of the heaven of the moon intends not produce a multitude of noble intelligent substances whose dwelling is the heaven of the moon, just as our dwelling is the earth and the air around it? In the same way how will the intelligence which he set to rule over the heaven of the sun not cause a multitude of noble substances as close as possible to its own nobility? And it will be this way with the other intelligences so that from each of them there will be a multitude of noble substances that approximate, as is appropriate, its nobility?

Know then that the philosophers who were called "magi" posited these.[157] They said that each of the heavens has a multitude of spirits serving it which they are accustomed to invoke in their activities. If, then, it were certain that these ranks of spirits and these multitudes exist and behave in that way, they

---

[155] William must mean: according to the good pleasure of the Son and of the Holy Spirit who bestow these gifts.

[156] The principle to which William appeals is Avicenna's claim that from what is one insofar as it is one there comes only what is one. See my "William of Auvergne's Use of Avicenna's Principle: 'Ex Uno Secundum Quod Unum, Non Nisi Unum,'" *The Modern Schoolman* 71 (1993): 1-15.

[157] William offers no clue to the identity of those to whom he refers as "magi." He probably has in mind astrologers in general rather than the biblical Magi, though it is possible that he is referring to the followers of the Zoroastrian religion.

could be seen as the benefits coming from the intelligences on account of which they were posited or ought to be posited. That is to say: just as the multitude of human beings comes from the one and through the one [intelligence], so each of these multitudes or ranks also comes from one and through one intelligence, and they perhaps understood that these intelligences were the princes and rulers of such ranks or hosts.[158] But if this holds for all intelligences in this way, it will of necessity come to the creator so that his generosity not only flows out below himself over the first intelligence, but also around himself in otherwise creating the multitude of countless noble substances that befits the supereminence of his glory. And this is perhaps the army of his hosts who are divided into those who stand before him and those who serve him, as we read in the books of the Hebrew prophets.[159]

If, however, it is not that way, but he is alone and solitary, they have him sit on the throne of his glory in ignominy. And this ignominy is a solitude as yet unheard of and unspoken. For this is as though a king were said to be and dwell alone in his huge and splendid palace and to have no crowd of soldiers or of other servants, though no madman as yet has imposed this upon any head of a family. But whatever is the case with the ranks we mentioned which the magi claimed dwelled in the heavens, even if all the intelligences were so sterile and impotent that no multitude arose from them, this solitude and solitariness would in no sense befit the magnificent affluence and most omnipotent power of the creator. Nature shows us this in every kind of animal. And the reason is that every kind of animal—to the extent it is possible for it—multiplies for itself a family and fills its dwelling with its offspring or children, and this comes from its natural generosity or abundance. How, then, will the goodness and generosity of the creator be so confined and restricted? In the following I shall establish for you the ranks of such heavenly hosts in many other ways and explanations, if God wills.[160]

Chapter Nineteen
That the multitude or diversity of our souls
cannot be created by the agent intelligence.

I shall return, then, and say that the agent intelligence that causes and perfects our souls, as they claimed, does nothing except through understanding and willing, in the manner of the (825a) other intelligences. By understanding itself it has this power to cause them and also to perfect them, and this power produces by its willing that on account of which it was given to it. Not allowing it to be idle, it causes them and perfects them. Since this causation comes from it through itself and according to itself and since there is no difference in its causing, all our souls are, for this reason, caused to be in one

---

[158] I have read "*militiarum*" instead of "*miliarum.*"
[159] See Matthew 4:11 as a possible source.
[160] In *De universo* IIa-IIae William deals with the angelic powers.

rank essentially, and they are, therefore, not naturally different in dignity from one another. Likewise, they will not be different in perfection. Hence, as they are caused as equals in natural and essential dignity, so they will be caused as equals in natural perfections. But you see that the facts are just the opposite. For some are caused to be naturally quite suited for knowledge and the virtues and close even to prophetic lights and other sublime illuminations. Others, however, are barely suited for the mechanical arts; some are quite ready for all the vices. Because, then, from one and the same thing, insofar as it is one and the same, there cannot arise, according to them, a multitude or a diversity, they necessarily have to claim that such a multitude or diversity does not naturally arise from the agent intelligence, nor does it arise voluntarily. For it would undoubtedly be evil, if it destroyed some human souls and in some way subjected them to vices.

But if someone says that this comes from the side of bodies, since they claim that it is the fashioner of our bodies, the same problem occurs. For if it fashions them naturally, it fashions them of one disposition, and according to them a multitude and a diversity does not arise from one power and art. But if by will it fashions bodies so harmful to our souls, all the evils of our souls must be attributed to it, just as [one must attribute all the evils of the inhabitant] to one who builds a plague-ridden house for some inhabitant and who knowingly and willingly introduces him into it and makes him dwell there. For death and all the corruption which comes to this inhabitant of the house is not to be attributed to the inhabitant, but to the builder.

Every natural power and every potency, of course, acts as far and as wide and as abundantly as it can, as it is clearly possible to see in the operation of the solar light and heat. Hence, if this intelligence acts naturally in causing and perfecting our souls, it causes them to be as great and as many as it can, and it pours into them as great and as many perfections as it can. It, then, causes all of them equally, but this is evidently false.

But if someone says that it, of course, does what lies in it, but some are more receptive and others less receptive of its influences, there will perhaps be no less a question about a receptivity of this sort. For the whole of what each human soul has as natural it has from its cause. Hence, if such receptivity is given to the souls by the natural operation of the intelligence, it will be equally present in all of them. Hence, it will be necessary that all the natural influences of the intelligence upon them will be equal. This intelligence, therefore, does not by a natural operation diversify its influences upon our souls, but it does not do so by a voluntary action for the reason I stated. It is evident, then, that it does not make them or act upon them by its power or choice.

Moreover, if it should cause our souls outside bodies, since a multitude and diversity cannot come from the will or from an identity, there would be no multitude or diversity among our souls. For then nothing would be or come to be in them from the side of their bodies; they would, therefore, have everything which they have from the one intelligence which causes them in one and the same way. Hence, they would all be one and the same and in the same way. But in whatever relation they are considered, bodies are able to bring nothing of diversities or essential difference to souls (825b). For whether they are considered to be organs or instruments of their souls, it is evident that a diversity of instruments does not diversify the activity in them. After all, one and the same cithara player now uses one cithara, now another. And one and the same woodworker now uses an ax and now a plane, now a knife and later an awl, and there are not four artisans or woodworkers on this account.

The situation is the same in natural organs and natural operations. One and the same soul now uses the eyes, now the tongue or lips, now the hands and then the feet, and it is on this account not one soul when it uses one of its natural organs for its natural operation and another when it uses another, nor is it many when it uses many. It follows of necessity that our souls are not diversified from the side of their bodies. But from the side of the intelligence that causes them, they are all one and the same; therefore, simply and without qualification it is necessary that all our souls be one and the same soul essentially, and nothing more insane than that can be said. And on this point you have heard much in the preceding parts.

On account of the unity and identity of the agent intelligence they said that souls separated from bodies return to the intelligence from which they proceeded in the way that they claimed in accord with their opinion, and they return to the same and are united with the unity that I mentioned. For this reason they claimed that the soul returns to its own higher world, that is, to its intelligence by which it was caused, and that it receives the final perfection there, that is, in its higher world, and that it does not ascend higher or look forward to another perfection. This error undoubtedly follows for them because of the false foundation of their position, for they cannot suppose that it is right that they should ascend beyond their cause or that they even can do so or that they ought to hope for a greater perfection than it has and they find in it.

Chapter Twenty
That when human souls are separated from their bodies, they do not return to the agent intelligence so that they receive from it perfection in their higher world.

According to the faith and law of the Christians the impossibility of this error is easily shown. For it is evident that every good king and prince gives to his servants greater and more noble possessions than would come to them from their paternal inheritance, and he exalts them above their parents and far above their own nature in honor and glory, if they earned this by their gratuitous services. And at times he even elevates them above his own children in riches and power. For you could see many of the servants of the king elevated by royal favor above their nature and above their parents in honor and glory and set above or preferred to the children of the kings in power and riches and at times made equal to them and adopted as children. For how much greater reason, then, is this so in the case of the king of all ages! No thought attains the excellence of his goodness and generosity; no tongues are sufficient to tell of it. For how much greater reason, then, ought one to think that the king of all ages will in accord with his good pleasure magnificently reward those who serve him in the likeness and proportion of these examples.

Moreover, who among earthly kings does not reward and crown his warriors and conquerors according to his own magnificence? Who does not enrich, extol, and exalt them beyond what they are or even what they deserve? They, therefore, thought ignominiously and poorly of the creator and intolerably detracted from his magnificence and glory (826a), who thought that God's chosen and beloved servants, who serve him in a praiseworthy manner, that is, at his good pleasure, ought not to expect from him greater things than they are or than they naturally have and ought not to hope to become greater in the palace of that king than in the houses of their own parents.

Chapter Twenty-One
That the felicity of our souls does not come from their conjunction or union
with the agent intelligence, and
why this lowest intelligence did not beget another intelligence.

I shall show the appropriateness of this example and parable to these examples and parables when I shall present for you, according to their opinion, the intelligence and the everlasting world and its home in contrast with the creator and that splendid dwelling or palace of his glory, the king with his rewards, his house or court. But they believe in or perceive no reward for their service or of their services despite the great and good things which are offered to so renowned and magnificent a king.[161] But, in accord with their position they located the whole hope and goal of their perfection, that is, of all their future goods in the last of his servants, that is, the agent intelligence. For the agent intelligence is the last and lowest of all the noble separate substances. But they seem to posit no other intelligence for it, since they assert that only one comes from the creator and that only one comes from it, and so on until they come to this last one. On this point their philosophy is a laughing stock, and it should even be regarded as ridiculous. For they see substances incomparably less noble, namely, bodily ones, act naturally and pour forth their powers in every direction. But they claim that these intelligences act only downward and that through a lessening of their effects, as if their power had been thinned out, they come to the lowest and at last fade away to nothing, though it is evident that in every species of animals parents produce offspring as their equals and the parents make them like them, and at times even beget better and more powerful offspring. They cannot see that a fire often gives rise to one larger than itself and that it is prevented from always doing this on account of the parvity of material from which it might generate such a fire.

The very blessed creator made himself an exemplar of these, for he eternally begot from himself a Son equal to himself and eternally poured forth a gift

---

[161] This sentence seems hopelessly corrupted in the Latin.

equal to himself from the immensity and abundance of his generosity. Following the pattern of this exemplar all who are truly givers give with a total outpouring of what they have, and though they cannot give gifts equal to themselves, they give themselves to everything and for everything, and they know this benefits the receivers. All who are truly fathers strive to make their sons better and wiser than they are, and all true and good teachers desire to make their disciples better and wiser than they are. Also all true friends want those whom they genuinely love to be better than they are. How, then, can the agent intelligence be naturally unable or unwilling, whether confined by avarice or perverted by envy, immediately to make equal and to liken to itself our souls with a perfect likening, since they say that it causes them by a wonderful and awesome kind of causation?

Moreover, this opinion clearly verges upon the impiety of idolatry when they claim that there is no other author and no other rewarder of our souls than it. For this opinion does not assign any other glory to our souls than to return to that intelligence or any other perfection than it is going to receive with it after separation from its body and union (826b) with it, nor does it hold out for them another paradise than that higher world which I told you about. For this is the language by which they speak of a spiritual paradise. They cannot, therefore, understand the ultimate felicity and perfection of our souls, according to this position, save as the conjunction and union with it and the dwelling with it. They try to persuade us in this way that this intelligence should be regarded as the single author, reformer, perfecter, and rewarder of our souls. Hence, we should serve it alone, and our souls should worship it alone as their proper and sole God. For they make to our souls no promise or even give them an idea of the vision of the creator or of the enjoyment of his goodness or of dwelling with him. For if they had understood this or had thought that our souls return to the creator and would ascend above all these heavens and would dwell with him and in his house, they would undoubtedly have said so. But now on the basis of that opinion it follows that they will not even ascend to or be able to attain the lunar heaven, since this higher world which they refer to in that way is not above that intelligence. Since they say that it is alone the spiritual and intelligible sun of this earthly world, they necessarily claim that it is only in this earthly orb where alone it shines and, and that it only illumines it to the extent that it is receptive of light. In the same way it is evident that the sun and the moon have been fixed in their orbits, and we have never heard that anyone has as yet said that they will come down from there or go up from there.

But since the agent intelligence is in itself most perfect and, for this reason, most blessed and, hence, does not look forward to perfection or some complement of its perfection, when it would ascend from its orbit to something higher and go somewhere else, it is posited utterly to no purpose and to no benefit, unless it will perhaps lead with itself the multitude of souls which have been here directed and perfected by it and through it by its illumination and unless it will present them to the creator as evidence of its good rule and administration and will offer them to him as earnings from the allotment of brightness and perfection received from him. But if that is so, it acts through the most dominant command of the creator and his injunction which it is not permitted to transgress.

Hence, it will be like one of the servants of God most high and like the guardians and ministers of kingdoms and provinces which are committed to them. But such ministers are angels dispatched for various ministries. This intelligence, then, will be like one of the angels, except perhaps in this respect that greater administration has been committed to it and greater power given to it than to many of the holy and blessed angels. They will, therefore, be seen to have invented the novelty of such a name to no purpose, since there is no new reality present. For no law has any doubt that there are many armies and ranks of angels and that there are many levels among them of dignities, principalities, and powers.

Moreover, all individuals of the same species have the same natural powers and potencies and are even naturally equal. Either this agent intelligence, then, is of the same species with the intelligence from which it was generated or—as they say—created, or it is not. If it is, then it is not only like it in natural powers and potencies, but also naturally equal to it. Hence, if by its natural power or potency that the former could generate or create an intelligence, this one too could necessarily do the same thing. Hence, there will come from it another intelligence. And the process will go on to infinity. But if it is not of the same species as it, then it does not come from it by generation or natural (827a) causation of another sort. For all causation which is through itself is the natural transference of what is in the cause to the effect, and everything given naturally is in the giver. But this is understood according to species and likeness, not according to number. For it is not the numerically same light in the sun illuminating the air and in the air illuminated by the sun. All the ten intelligences, then, will be of the same species. Aristotle, however, refused to grant this, namely, that there can be many separate substances of the same species, because he did not even want to grant that our souls—whose multitude and diversity is so evident—are many, when they have been separated from their bodies. In fact, he claimed that they are of necessity all a single soul.

Moreover, since this intelligence is a substance indivisible into parts, how is there in it at the same time and in act so great a multitude of intelligible forms? For it seems necessary that they are present there either as confused and as mingled or as united together and forming a composite one, and a one by nature that is merely this composite one. Hence, there will not flow from the agent intelligence upon our intellective power some clear and distinct form, but rather a confusion and mixture of forms. But it is not possible to understand something clearly and distinctly by a confusion or mixture of forms. Because this question is no more against Aristotle than against those who hold the opposite view, I shall settle it for you in the following parts. For I do not intend to contradict him or anyone else except on points on which I see that he contradicts the truth.

Moreover, since this intelligence illumines and perfects each of our souls, it is either joined to each of them by some means of conjunction, or it is not. If it is, since this conjunction does not come about through motion, it is, therefore, next to each of our souls and conjoined to each of them without a medium. And for this reason it is whole or wholly in each of our souls, since it is necessary that it be indivisible into parts. For if it were divisible into parts and had a continuous magnitude like bodies, it would be impossible that it be joined to a multitude at the same time by one and the same part. It remains, then, that it is in each human soul; hence, it is necessary that it be at the same time in each region of our dwelling place.

Moreover, if it is apart from the soul which it illumines and perfects, for example, distant from it by a mile or by many miles, bodily light could shine from it through the intervening air or through some other transparent medium. But spiritual light does not require such media. Moreover, since that which acts through itself and not through something else can only act where it is, it is necessary that it be, therefore, wherever it acts. It is, then, in each of our souls as often as it illumines them. But it is impossible that it depart or withdraw through motion from any place in which it is. It is, then, necessary that it be by its essence and by its presence in each of our souls and that it remain with each perpetually.

Chapter Twenty-Two
It is shown by further proofs that there is no return of our souls to that intelligence we have been speaking about.

From this, however, a question arises about the return of our souls to this intelligence which Aristotle posited. For, since they are from the moment of their creation with this intelligence and cannot (827b) be separated from it and do not withdraw from it when they enter bodies, they cannot, therefore, return to it, properly speaking, unless "to return" means entirely to withdraw from the worry over bodies and the care and governance of them and of other things which are done through the body and to be totally at ease and to cling to this intelligence and the enjoyment of the outpourings which descend from this intelligence upon our souls when they have been separated from their bodies and thus welcomed into their higher world where they will endlessly remain.

This return has some likeness to that which the faith and doctrine of Christians asserts. But it differs, because the faith and doctrine of Christians holds that this return is the essential transference of souls from the lower world to another, that is, to the lofty world which is the dwelling of glory, or to another world which is the dwelling of the damned, or to a place of purgation, or to the place about which you have heard above, which is reserved for those human beings who have not added mortal sin to original sin, according to the doctrine of Christians.[162] But in this other return there is asserted only a spiritual transference, since there is neither a leaving of this world nor an entrance into another world or place.

Moreover, since this intelligence causes or, as they say, creates one of our human souls, it creates it only where it is. For creation is not an activity which can be done through another than through the agent, that is, the one who creates. But each of our souls is indivisible into parts. It does not, therefore, create one of our souls externally outside of itself. Hence, it creates it within itself. For it is not possible that the intelligence and the soul which it creates touch according to some part, since each is not divisible into parts. But if they touch according to the whole of themselves, the one is whole within the other. It is true, then, as I said, that it creates the soul within itself and not outside of itself. Therefore, when each of our souls is created, it is created within the intelligence and is in it. Whatever beings, then, are created by it at the same time are at the same time within it or in it. Since, then, none of our souls are created outside the body, but rather each is created in its body, it is necessary that all of them be at the same time in the agent intelligence, while they individually are in their bodies. Hence, though all our souls are scattered through all parts of this dwelling place, they are joined together and all gathered together in the agent intelligence. But it is very strange that none of them knows anything of the others, though they exist so that each is in all others and each individual is in each, especially since they are in so great a light, for their light is the agent intelligence. You ought to recall how it was explained to you elsewhere that our souls were not and could not be created outside our bodies.[163]

Chapter Twenty-Three
That though the agent intelligence, on their view, created souls, it does not cast them away from itself to tie them to or shove them into bodies.

But if someone says that, once the agent intelligence has created each of our souls within itself, it immediately dismisses each from itself and sends it into a body, I say, first of all, that this person admits that our souls are caused outside our bodies and, secondly, that it sends them into bodies not merely for no purpose, but also to their harm. For when it casts them away from itself, it casts them from a paradise of their happiness and glory and sends them into the darkest, filthiest, and most horrible prisons of bodies. They are

---

[162] That is, William refers to heaven, hell, purgatory, and limbo. Purgatory is a temporary state of purification for souls ultimately destined for heaven, while limbo was a state for those who died with only original sin.

[163] This seems to be a reference to William's *De anima*, which is usually dated along with *De universo* as somewhat late in William's career, perhaps in 1231-1236. William discusses this point in *De anima*, ch. 5, pt. 9: II, 140b-141a.

most dark (828a), because they are there immediately ignorant of everything, and whatever they are going to know they must learn bit by bit. They are most filthy not only with a temporal, but also with spiritual dirt, for it is evident that in bodies our souls are stained with the filth of all vices and sins. They are most horrible because a person is hard to find who is not almost intolerably horrified to look upon bodies of the dead after their souls have withdrawn from them. For as a result of the presence of the souls, that is, when their souls are in them, our bodies are pleasing and attractive to sight.

Moreover, since our souls merited nothing bad in the intelligence, inasmuch as they never sinned and could not sin on account of the purity and holiness of this intelligence, as well as on account of the happiness of its state in which they were in it, how is it possible that our innocent souls that lack absolutely all sin receive such an injury from this most holy and blessed intelligence that they are shoved into such great miseries and into such hard prisons?

Moreover, how do our souls, in departing from the intelligence, enter our bodies? Is it by motion, or by a leap, or suddenly? Concerning motion or a leap you have already heard in Aristotle that neither is possible in substances indivisible into parts.[164] But if it is sudden, that is, so that they depart from the intelligence and enter their bodies at the same time, they will either be in the intelligence and in their bodies at the same time and, for this reason, in happiness and in misery at the same time—which is obviously impossible— or they will be only in the intelligence when they enter the bodies, or only in bodies when they leave the intelligence. How then do they leave the intelligence, if they were not in the intelligence—not even a part of them—or how do they enter their bodies if they are not themselves in the bodies—not even a part of them?

Moreover, on this view, this departure of the souls from the intelligence will be violent, and their entrance into bodies will be violent. For who could suppose that they voluntarily abandon the paradise of their happiness and enter prisons of such great misery and punishments willingly.[165] The union of our souls and bodies, therefore, will not be [natural].[166] Hence, neither the life nor the vivification of our bodies will be natural.

Moreover, the goal of the creation of our souls is their perfection and happiness. But they receive each of these as a result of their relation to the agent intelligence. Since, then, the agent intelligence intends their perfection and happiness alone and creates them only for this reason, it also undoubtedly knows that they can obtain this perfection and this happiness nowhere else and from nothing else than from it and from their dwelling with it. How is it

---

[164] As possible sources, see Aristotle, *The Gait of Animals*, ch. 8, or *On the Soul* III, ch. 10, 433b11- 21.

[165] I have read *volentes* for *nolentes*.

[166] I have supplied "*naturalis*" as the basis of the following sentence.

possible that it separates them from this goal which is the only goal it intends for them? But it does separate them and keep them from the perfection and happiness which it intends for them, when it casts them away from itself and ties them to and shoves them into these prisons.

Chapter Twenty-Four
How, according to them, there can be a multitude of intelligences.

Substances separated from matter and from the conditions of matter and its appendages are not in themselves able to be numbered (*numerabilis*), according to the opinion of these people, and for this reason, as I told you, they also claimed that our souls are not able to be numbered, that is, to be more or many, except when they are in bodies, as if they have plurality and multitude or number only through bodies and the conditions of bodies (828b) or through accidents. Hence, it is right to examine how they maintain number or plurality in the intelligences, though they are entirely free from matter and its conditions. But suppose that they say that they number one another and that the relations of cause and effect make them to be many. If this were the case, namely, that cause and effect made a plurality in those things to which these terms are applied, since these two relations are found at the same time in Socrates, Socrates will of necessity be many men at the same time. For Socrates is the cause of his son through the generation by which he generated him and at the same time the effect of his father through the generation by which he was begotten by him.

Moreover, it has already been explained to you elsewhere that relation does not diversify or give number to things;[167] otherwise, each thing would not only be many, but would even be countless and infinite, since to each thing there come countless comparisons and infinite relations. But if someone says that cause and effect are relations which the same thing cannot have toward itself, I say that likeness also cannot be a relation which the same thing has to itself, and the situation is the same with infinite relations, that is, with relative terms. But likeness and unlikeness do not make things many, nor do they give them number or plurality. Otherwise, as I have told you, Socrates would not be the same man who he was as a boy or when he was born.

Moreover, since by as many causations as there are human souls, the agent intelligence has a causality appropriate to each one through which it is its cause, the intelligence would be as many as our souls are. But Aristotle seems to have counted intelligences by the heavens and their motions and souls, because, as he thought, they were the causes of their motion and in the way I told you. But this is by far more absurd and more removed from reason than it would be [if he counted them] by their bodies and relations. For water is

---

[167] See *The Trinity, or the First Principle* (*De trinitate*) ch. 28: Switalski, pp. 158-160; Teske-Wade, pp. 180-82, where William argues that relations are not the causes of a plurality, even in the persons of the Trinity.

not to be called many because it moves many millstones, nor are winds many because one wind moves many ships. Suppose, however, that he says that the wind does not move ships as something loved, nor does water move the mill- stones in that way, but by a violent impulse, whereas the intelligences move the heavens as objects of their love, and on this account they are made many or found to be many. Then, it turns out for Aristotle first of all that the blessed creator, who, as I have explained to you, is one in the ultimate degree of oneness, is more multiple than countless armies, for he moves countless men as the object of their love, not only in a spiritual, but also in a bodily way, not only by one motion, but by as great a variety of motions as can be found or be done in his worship and service.

Moreover, who does not see that one and the same object of love every day moves countless lovers to itself, for example, one and the same food moves many animals, one and the same prey moves many predators, one and the same betrothed woman moves many lovers, one and the same money moves many greedy men, and one and the same honor moves many ambitious per- sons?

Moreover, it is necessary that all the intelligences be equal and like in every way. For if they are of the same species, since they are separated from matter and its appendages, what is the source of diversity among them, since with our souls, after they are separated from their bodies, there will be no diversity according to these men; in fact there will not even be a plurality?

Moreover, since each thing comes from its cause by an operation that is natural and through itself, but an operation that is natural and through itself takes place through likeness, as I have often told you, what will the source of an unlikeness or diversity between cause and effect, especially according to these people who (829a) maintain this?

Moreover, every power and potency and, in general, every cause that oper- ates through itself alone and of itself alone and according to itself alone makes its effect equal to itself and makes it like to itself with a perfect likening and adequation. For if the brightness of the sun would cause according to itself alone the light which it pours into the air, it would of necessity make it equal to itself. It does not, however, do this, but acts according to the receptivity of the air and according to the nearness or distance of the air to the sun. An example of this sort is evident in mirrors that are alike in form, polish, and cleanliness; when you set them opposite to each other in suitable opposition and nearness, the appearance reflected from the one in the other will be equal in every respect and like the appearance which is reflected first and is in the first, and this equality and likeness would run on infinitely, if infinite mirrors of this sort, that is, equally polished and clean and of the same form in every respect could be set opposite to one another. Because the first intelligence causes the second in this manner, it of necessity makes it equal to itself and makes it like itself in every respect, and it is necessary that the situation be the same with the second and the third and so on until one comes to the last one, which they call the agent intelligence. All the intelligences, then, will be equal to one another in every respect. Hence, no one of them would be more worthy to be the first or the highest and nearer to the creator or to proceed from him first. And in this way it is evident that there ought not to be an order of nobility or sublimity or even of any perfection among them; from this it follows that there is no order among the souls of the heavens and, consequently, also not among the heavens on account of the proportionality, that is, the likeness of the relations of the intelligences to them and to their heavens.

Moreover, the creation of intelligence by intelligence which they maintain is either done by the intelligence within itself [or not]; that is to say, either the first intelligence creates the second within itself or outside. But if it creates it within, the second intelligence was created by the first within the first.

Chapter Twenty-Five
It is asked how they claim that one intelligence creates another, and it is shown that creation is only done by the power of the omnipotent creator.

From this there arise these questions which you will hear. For example, did the second intelligence create the third as soon as the second intelligence existed, or did it postpone creating it for some time or period?[168] But if it then created the third, it is necessary that the third created the fourth. The matter runs on in this way to the last. In the same way it is possible also to ask whether the first heaven was created with this intelligence or before. If with it, is the situation the same with the other heavens or not? If not, there was a time, then, when the first heaven alone existed and none of the others, nor were there any other bodies, since they claim that the matter of the first heaven and the form of the same were created by the first intelligence. It remains then that there was only a vacuum beneath that heaven. Hence, the whole lower world did not then exist, but such a great vacuum and empty space was contained and surrounded by the first of these heavens. But you have already heard the destruction of a vacuum by Aristotle and by me. But if the first intelligence created that whole heaven at that time, that is, the soul and its body and also the matter and form of the body of the same heaven, this creation occurred only by a spiritual word, that is, by an act of knowing, and by a spiritual command or order, which is nothing but the will in act or willing. But it is evident that to produce in this way so splendid and so (829b) magnificent a work as is the first heaven in its integral perfection and to cause so sublime an effect as is the second intelligence is the work of only the supereminent and almighty power of the creator.

Moreover, on this view the creator was idle in all things and in every respect and did nothing at all and is still such. And he will be at rest from all work forever and ever, except that he created the first intelligence, but left the other

---

[168] Though there is no question mark in the Latin, the sense seems to require that the sentence be read as a question.

intelligences, the souls of the heavens, their bodies, and all other things to be created by it. Such men honor the creator at least in this respect that they say that he entrusted some things to others to be created. You see, then, that every [religious] law contradicts this claim, since [the laws] call God himself the creator of all things and confess that he created, fashioned, stretched out, and made firm the heavens. But if at the command and injunction of the creator the first intelligence acted and the others acted as a result, it is evident that one should attribute to them only the ministry of creation, but not the authority in any sense, though it is evident that "creation" according to the common meaning is in no sense a work of servitude or ministry, but one of the highest and first authority. For this reason neither idolaters nor men of this sort have as yet dared to call one of such substances the creator, but have rather attributed the name "creator" in the singular and incommunicably to the one which they maintained is the author of all things and the most dominant king of the ages.

Chapter Twenty-Six
On the above point, namely,
that the power to create is not present in the intelligences.

I shall return to the place where I was and I shall say that, if the first intelligence created a substance in itself and so on with the others, it would equally come down to the lower heavens, and in the same way it is possible to ask about our souls.

Moreover, if each of the intelligences created another and its own heaven, except for the last which they call the agent intelligence, how was that one unable or unwilling to create a heaven suited to itself?

Moreover, to whom would the creation of this lower world be attributed? For if it were attributed to the creator alone, it is evident how ineptly and contemptuously they say this, since they attribute more noble and more sublime works to the intelligences and they leave the least and most vile of such works to the creator. But they honor the agent intelligence to the point that they attribute to it the creation and perfection of our souls. How then do they cast it down and lower it to the point that they do not attribute to it at least the creation of the sublunar world or at least of the earth?

Moreover, either such men confess that there are holy and blessed angels in accord with the words of the prophets of the Hebrews and the law and doctrine of both Christians and Saracens, or they do not. But if they do confess this, they must confess that there are many thousands, in fact thousands upon thousands of separate substances and intelligences. Among these intelligences it seems to be impossible that one can distinguish, except in terms of more or less, the offices and dignities committed to them by the creator. Here they seem to approach at least to some extent the common truth. But if they say that the creation of intelligences and of heavens did not have a beginning and that none of them were made in time or in an instant of time, but that all the intelligences and all the souls of the heavens and the heavens themselves rather exist from eternity and eternally (830a), it is not necessary that I repeat what you have heard me say on this in the preceding parts.[169]

Chapter Twenty-Seven
The destruction of the errors of the previously mentioned philosophers on the statement they make that the intelligences create through the intellect.

But we must not pass over the manner of operation by which they say that the first intelligence created the second, namely, by understanding the creator. For from this it follows for them that every intelligent substance creates a creator. For if from its understanding the creator it was or is possible for the first intelligence to create the second, or rather if its very understanding of the creator is for it to create the second intelligence, then every similar act of understanding the creator—in whatever it is found—will be to create another intelligence, unless one would say that the understanding of the creator was so noble and perfect in the first intelligence that so noble and so excellent an effect had to proceed from it, namely, the second intelligence. I say, then, that from each act of understanding the creator there ought to be an effect appropriate to the act of understanding, that is, in accord with the differences and relations of the acts of understanding. That is to say, the relation or proportion of the one act of understanding the creator to the another is the relation or proportion of the effect of the one to the effect of the other. And just as from the previously mentioned act of understanding of the first intelligence there resulted that sublime and excellent effect which they call the second intelligence, there should result from every other act of understanding the creator a like and equal effect of the same nobility.

Moreover, in no artisan is it possible that one find this sort of thing, namely, that a person who understands or imagines a house makes a statue or a box. For [one always makes things] from an understanding or imagining and from a form or concept, and not from anything else, and a product of an art always has a form which the artist gives or impresses on it. But the first intelligence could create the second intelligence only by understanding it; it did not, therefore, create it by understanding the creator, unless someone should perhaps wish to say that, by understanding the creator it understood it in a more sublime and better way than if it understood the second intelligence in itself and immediately directed the fine point of its intellect to it. But if this were their meaning, then it would be true that, by understanding it properly and by itself, the first intelligence created the second. This, then, ought to have been their statement, namely, that by understanding the second intelligence the first intelligence created it. But their statement concerning the creation of the soul of the first heaven seems more incongruous and contrary to reason,

---

[169] See *De universo* IIa-Iae, chs. 8ff.

since the forms of the first intelligence and the soul of that [first heaven] are different not only in species, but also in genus. And on this account this statement of theirs amounts to their saying that by understanding or imagining a sword an ironworker fashions an ax, or the converse, since, as I said, the form which the artisan gives or impresses is necessarily produced from the form that is understood or imagined within the artisan.

What they said concerning the creation of the corporeal form of this heaven is far more irrational. And the reason is that it has a far more distant likeness and greater difference with respect to everything which is in the intelligence [except] the matter of the heaven. And on this account far less could it come from the imagination or understanding of anything that was within the intelligence, since every form impressed by the intellect or imagination or art is necessarily like the form which is in the intellect or imagination of the one who impresses it. And with regard to the creation of the matter of the heaven it is further evident in this way that (830b) their opinion was very improbable and unthinkable. But the reason for this is that on account of its lack of form matter itself could not have a form like to itself in the intelligence, but it is necessary, as I have already told you, that everything which comes to be through the intellect or imagination has being in accord with the likeness of a form, as a result of the understanding or imagination of which it exists. Hence, it was not possible that matter proceed in this way from the first intelligence.

Moreover, since I have already explained to you that in immaterial substances and things possibility is nothing but the power of the efficient cause of that intelligence.[170] Therefore, possibility or potency in the first intelligence is only the understanding of the potency of the creator. But the potency of the creator is neither less than nor other than he, and it is not possible that there be any failure or impotence in him. Hence, from the understanding of his potency it was not possible that something imperfect or something that exists only in potency should proceed, and it was not proper or fitting that what proceeded from the understanding of his potency should be less perfect than what proceeded from the understanding of his essence, since his potency is in no way less or less perfect than his essence.

Moreover, the potency of the creator is only active and only influencing; it is in no sense passive or receptive or receiving, as the potency of matter clearly is. And matter is receptive only, and in no way is it active or influencing. Through the understanding of the first potency, then, matter ought not to have proceeded from the first intelligence, but rather an active and influencing substance.

---

[170] See *The Trinity, or the First Principle* (*De trinitate*), ch. 8; Switalski, pp. 48-54; Teske-Wade, pp. 92-97, where William argues against the Aristotelian view that the possibility of anything lies in its matter.

Chapter Twenty-Eight

That in the intelligences there is no possibility, and that only in God is there the power productive of them, and that they can create nothing by understanding the creator or something apart from themselves.

But there is no possibility in such substances, that is, immaterial ones, except their active or effective potency, that is, the potency from which or by which they exist through their mode of production. This point will be explained to you clearly and easily, when you suppose that one of these substances does not exist. For example, let one of them be called A. I say that the possibility by which A is a possible being is not something else in A or within A, when A is not yet existing. For in that which is not yet existing it is not possible that something exist which truly is. Hence, the potency of A by which it is a possible being is, according to the truth, nothing, since it is not in A or in something on the side of A, that is, not in the matter of A, since A is immaterial, nor in something else on the side of A, since there is as yet nothing at all on the side of A. Therefore, possibility of this sort is absolutely nothing, since there is nowhere for it to be on the side of A. Either it will be through itself, that is, without a subject—which is impossible—or it will be in the efficient cause of A. But in the efficient cause there is no potency but the potency productive of A or some other active potency. But this is to say that the potency by which A is able to be created by the creator is, before it is created, nothing but the potency by which the creator has the power to create A, just as the potency by which it can be understood that [A] does not yet exist is nothing else in it or within it, since in that or within that which does not yet exist nothing can as yet exist, but there is only the intellective potency which is only in him or with him who can understand it.

And the same thing holds for what can be supposed and what supposes, for the praiseworthy and what praises, and for the like, especially those terms which signify apprehensions or passions which come from appetites. And I explained this for you in many ways (831a) in the singular treatise on predication and the ways of predicating,[171] because in all such cases, both in the present example and in ones like it, the same thing is predicated by way of action and by way of passion, and by way of potency and of possibility. In this way, when one thing is said to love another and the latter is said to be loved by the former, by each verb, that is, by the active and by the passive verb, one predicates only the love which exists only in the lover and within him. Likewise, when Socrates is said to know something and it is said to be known by him, one predicates only the numerically one knowledge which is in Socrates alone in both cases, that is, by each verb, the active and the passive.

---

[171] See *The Trinity, or the First Principle* (*De trinitate*), ch. 32: Switalski, pp. 181-183; Teske-Wade, pp. 201-202, though William seems to refer to the long final chapter of *The Trinity*, in which he deals extensively with predication about God.

Moreover, an intellect insofar as it is understanding does not act upon the thing understood.[172] Nor does it act upon something else, for to see is not to act upon, and Aristotle in his treatises often said that to understand is in a sense to be acted upon and a sort of being acted upon,[173] and he commonly called the intelligible forms reflected or reflecting in the mirror of our intellect passions, as he said in the book, *On Interpretation*, that words are marks of those passions which are in our soul.[174] One who understands, then, insofar as he is understanding and one who knows insofar as he knows is acted upon according to Aristotle and receptive rather than active or influencing. Or he at least has something in himself. Nor has anyone extended the meaning of such a statement to the blessed creator or to one of the noble immaterial and separate substances. As for them, Aristotle and his followers did not think that they receive anything, since they claimed that they existed from eternity in all their perfections and that nothing new ever came to them or would come to them. But this statement or opinion does not free them or allow them to escape the fact that understanding or knowing is being acted upon or receiving or having something within one, namely, knowledge or understanding. Hence, it is universally true that one who knows or understands in the sense of one who knows or understands, that is, in the way in which he is knowing and understanding, does not act upon or influence something else. Foolishly and falsely, then, did they claim that the first intelligence or any of the others created or acted upon something in the manner in which it was understanding, that is, through its act of understanding.

Moreover, if one who understands or knows in the sense of one who knows or understands were acting upon or influencing, he would act upon or influence the thing known or understood rather than something else. For if one who sees a man or anything else, by reason of the fact that he is seeing, were acting upon or having any influence, it would be more proper or more fitting that through such vision or sight one should be acting upon the man or having an influence upon him than upon something else. And if through vision one were not acting upon or having an influence upon the thing seen, even less would one act upon or have such an influence upon something else. But you have heard their claims, and you clearly read in them that no intelligence has caused or created something except by understanding itself or some of those things which belong to it—either its actuality or potentiality—or the creator himself. Nor did they say that one of them did something to or had an influence upon one of these, that is, to one of the intellective things. Rather it is as if someone said that by understanding or imagining a box any artisan or worker built a bridge which does not help or pertain to the construction of the box in any way.

---

[172] I read "*intellectam*" for "*intelligentem*."
[173] See Aristotle, *On the Soul* III, ch. 4, 429a13-17.
[174] See Aristotle, *On Interpretation* ch. 1, 16a3-5.

Moreover, it is apparent that they did not know that in every agent who works through art or wisdom the art is only like a lamp and that it does not produce something else, but only shows what one should do or how one should do it, just as sight stands in relation to walking. (831b) It does nothing by way of production, but only shows the way and dangers of the way. But the will commands walking, and the power to walk, which is in the feet and legs and other members that aid in walking, effect or accomplish the walking. Since understanding—at whatever degree of nobility or excellence it is—contributes no more to the activity of the one who understands than the seeing of the same person, it is evident that none of the intelligences produces or has produced from its act of understanding something else in the manner of production. Hence, the first intelligence did not create or cause the second, nor the second the third, and so on with the rest, nor did the agent intelligence create our souls by its act of understanding or cause them in another way in the manner of production, as I said. From these points it will be clear to you that it is never truly and properly said among us that an artisan produces something by art or makes something from art in the manner of production. The law of the Christians calls the art of the creator the Son of the same creator and teaches and proclaims that all things are or have been made from and through him, and it undoubtedly does this with complete truth. I have already explained to you that this art is not only art, but also the word and command of the almighty God the Father whom those things which are not obey no less than those which are, as you have heard from one of the prophets of the Hebrews.[175] He says that God calls those things which are not as well as those which are.[176]

Moreover, when the agent intelligence causes one of the souls, it either causes it by understanding the creator or by understanding itself or by understanding something apart from itself in accord with the manner that they posited for the other intelligences. If one says that the agent intelligence causes one of our souls by understanding the creator, another intelligence ought to be caused from this intellection or act of understanding, as they said about the other intelligences. Otherwise, what cause of the difference could they assign here? Unless they should perhaps say here that the understanding of the creator in the other intelligences is more sublime and noble and, for this reason, more sublime and more noble effects come from it than from the understanding of the creator which is found in the agent intelligence.

I say to this that they speak correctly in accord with this position. But like causes are always proportionate to their effects, and since the causes do not differ except in terms of more and less, as they claim, they necessarily have to maintain that their effects differ only in the same way, and that is only ac-

---

[175] In *De universo* Ia-Iae, ch. 27, William argued that the Word of God is not merely a word that states something, but a word of command by which God most freely created the world. See above pp. 81-82.

[176] William refers to Romans 4:17.

cording to more and less. Since, then, the act of understanding by which the agent intelligence understands the creator does not differ from the acts of understanding by which the other intelligences understand him, except according to more and less, the effects which comes from such acts of understanding do not differ except in the same way. An effect, then, which proceeds from the agent intelligence from the act of understanding by which it understands the First, that is, the creator, will be of the same species as the effects likewise existing from the other intelligences. It will, then, be an intelligence.

They say, however, that the agent intelligence does not cause any noble substance apart from our souls. But if one says that by understanding itself the agent intelligence causes our souls, just as by understanding themselves the other intelligences cause or caused the souls of the heavens, it follows in the same way that our souls do not differ at all from the heavenly souls, except in the way that such acts of understanding and objects of understanding differ. They do not differ in species, but according to more or less, as if by degrees of nobility and sublimity and perfection. But it is evident that this is impossible, since the souls of the heavens are naturally perfect and have operations far different from the operation of our souls. (832a) The magnitude of the diversity between the heavenly bodies and our bodies indicates the magnitude of this diversity, for they differ from one another in genus and in shape as well as in motion. It is evident that they differ in shape and motion and also genus even to those who have little training in natural things. It is evident that the shapes of animal bodies are diverse in accord with the diversity of the souls, and at times their compositions are also diverse.

But if someone objects regarding a lion and a dog that their bodies seem to have like configurations, though they clearly differ in species, I reply to this that the person who said this did not sufficiently consider the shapes of the body of the lion and of the dog, especially in the claws and the teeth. Nor does the statement of Aristotle by which he said in his book on souls that a lion inwardly is a dog and a dog inwardly is a lion force us to grant that a dog and a lion are the same in species.[177] He said this more in accord with the interior shape of a lion and a dog than in accord with their nature. This is clearly apparent from another statement of the same man in the same book where he said that fire leaps forth from the bones of a lion when they smashed together. But this does not happen with the bones of a dog. The same diversity between the souls of the same animals is apparent from the natural ferocity and rage and wildness of a lion and their dwelling apart from human beings and from the natural tameness of dogs and their guarding, adulation, and manifold services to humans as well as their dwelling inseparably from human beings. The cause for such things, however, is that all natural characteristics always pertain to all the individuals of the same species.

---

[177] An electronic search of Aristotle's works turned up nothing of the sort.

Chapter Twenty-Nine
That the agent intelligence does not cause our souls by understanding,
nor does the first intelligence cause the second or anything else.

But if someone says that the agent intelligence causes our souls by understanding something apart from itself, the same problems result which you heard in the preceding chapters concerning the other intelligences.

Moreover, according to this position there is no doubt that it causes all our souls by understanding one and the same thing and in the same way. What is the source, then, of so great an unlikeness in them, of so great a diversity, and of so much not merely variety, but even opposition and contrariety of arts, functions, and all kinds of operations?

Moreover, the understanding of the creator has never ceased, never ceases, and never will cease to be within the first intelligence, and its understanding of itself does not cease to be with the same, and the situation is the same with the other acts of understanding, that is, with the understanding of its own actuality and the understanding of its own possibility.[178] The actions or effects of another mode of causation, which come from intelligibles of this sort ought, therefore, never to cease. Each one of such causations will, then, be continuous and eternal; hence, each of them will not cause one single intelligence, but infinite intelligences through the understanding of the creator.

And it ought to be this way with the other intellects and their effects. For if from one act of understanding by which the first intelligence understood the creator for one hour or one day, the second intelligence proceeded, since its act of understanding of the creator has the same perfection and power and is equal in every respect in any hour or day whatever, it is necessary that there proceed from it without qualification another intelligence. For why should an equal and like act of understanding in the same intelligence at another hour or day be idle and void of an equal and like effect? Unless one should perhaps say that by that first causation or generation or even creation (832b), the first intelligence expended and spilled forth absolutely the whole of its power, and for this reason it became unable and powerless to create or otherwise cause or generate something further. It is evident that things are this way in certain animals, because in their case the number of generations and the time for generating are determined. But it is impossible that things be this way with the intellective power. For in animals it is this way on account of the weakness of the generative power which the frequency of generating produces, but in the first intelligence or any other one of them such weakening or other manner of failure has no place.

Moreover, every intellective power is strengthened and perfected by an understanding of the creator, and if it is receptive of increase, it is increased as a result of it.

---

[178] I have read *possibilitatis* instead of *passibilitatis*.

Moreover, the act of understanding of the first intelligence is not lessened and does not fail, nor does it admit any kind of loss. Hence, it continuously remains unimpaired in its power and perfection in every respect. Therefore, either an intelligence never proceeds from it or through it, or an infinite number of intelligences flow from it incessantly, one after another. An example of this sort is found in a source of absolutely unfailing abundance that admits of no diminishment in any way. For just as in that case the abundance of the source remains in the same power and perfection without any manner of decrease, so with unceasing perseverance there overflow from it emanations without number and end. In no way, then, can the second intelligence be solitary.

Moreover, every intellective power is illumined by its most noble and greatest intelligible object in the knowledge of it and is set afire with love for it, and these two are the first outpourings of the object upon the intellective power. From these two outpourings there flow from it, as a result, the operations of servitude and services by which it knows that it pleases such an object of knowledge and of love or with regard to which it considers itself in debt to such an object of knowledge and love. And this has no opposition except where some evil perverts an intelligent substance of this sort.

It is, then, evident to you that as a result of such love and knowledge there proceed praises and acts of thanksgiving and pleasing services toward such an object of knowledge and love, but from these two influences such a knower and lover is in no way impregnated, nor does this knower and lover receive anything so that an intelligent substance proceeds from it, except perhaps in the manner of merit or grace, as is reported in the law of the Hebrews and in the law of the Christians regarding some by whom the blessed creator was so well pleased that, though they were sterile, he gave them children even in their old age.[179] But it is not that way in the first intelligence according to the opinion of these people who make no mention and even have no thought of any grace or merit in this area. There are also other influences upon our souls from the understanding and knowledge of the creator, namely, fear, honor, reverence, and holiness, by which people commit themselves totally to his honor and worship, unless the perversity of some corruption turns them aside from this.

Chapter Thirty
That the first intelligence did not proceed from the creator
by a natural procession, nor did the second so proceed from the first.

But one might say in accord with their opinion that the power of nature is such that like is procreated by like and, for this reason, when the first intelligence proceeds from the creator by a natural procession, there is transferred to it by the creator the power of creating a substance like to itself, just as by

---

[179] For example, Elizabeth and Zachariah in Lk 1:36 and Sarah and Abraham in Gen 17:15-16.

the light of the sun there is poured forth into the light which proceeds from it the power of causing similar light (833a) and so on until it comes to the last receptacle of light. I reply to this and say that it is not universally true that everything that is within the parent is poured forth into the child. For it is not fitting or possible that the child have everything which is in the parent, and the faith and doctrine of Christians clearly teaches this point in the first father and the first son and the first giver and the first gift, as you learned in the first part of this teaching.[180]

I also say that the first intelligence did not proceed from the creator in the way that they say, that is, by natural procession, but rather by the most free creation and choice of his good pleasure. I also add that, in the way in which it is permitted to speak of a multitude in the creator, there are many things in him which cannot be transferred to creatures or communicated to them. One of these is omnipotence, and another is universal domination, neither of which is it fitting or possible that a creature possess. And there are many other things of this sort which it is quite easy for you to see for yourself.

Moreover, if the second intelligence went forth from the first by a natural activity, as these men seem to say, you have already heard from Aristotle that nature operates in the manner of a servant.[181] But every activity of this sort comes from another and through the manner of one who commands. The creation, then, of the second intelligence is by the creator himself through the manner of one who commands, according to their opinion.

Moreover, a servant in the manner of a servant can do nothing in an operation by himself: I mean in an operation which he does in this way. Nor can he stop doing it by himself or speed it up or add or lessen anything in it. Such an operation, then, in terms of its being or its non-being, totally consists in the good pleasure of the one who commands—both with regard to its being and its non-being, with regard to its acceleration and its retardation, and with regard to everything else that belongs to it. It should be attributed and credited to him alone, and in our conduct we preserve this very thing, as if we were interpreting the servitude of nature and the command of the creator over nature. To him alone we offer thanks for the services of his servants, for by his good pleasure and command alone they are offered to us. So too, we return thanks to those who send us gifts, not to those who bear them, and we consider ourselves in debt and obligated to them alone in return for such gifts or services. The second intelligence, therefore, owes its whole creation to the creator alone and nothing at all of it to the first intelligence.

---

[180] See *The Trinity, or the First Principle* (*De trinitate*), ch. 17: Switalski, pp. 100-02; Teske-Wade, pp. 134-35 for the equality of the Son to the Father and ch. 22: Switalski, pp. 118-19: Teske-Wade, pp. 148-150 for the equality of the Spirit to the Father and the Son.

[181] See above, note 22 to the translation.

But if one says that the first intelligence created or otherwise caused the second intelligence by the command of the creator and did this voluntarily and not under coercion, I say to this that one who said this already admits that the second intelligence proceeded from the first by a natural operation, just as a voluntary operation does not proceed from a servant in the manner of nature or even of servitude. It is, moreover, evident that we do not attribute or credit voluntary gifts sent to us by others to their bearers, especially when only the will of the sender inclined or induced the will of the bearers to bring them to us. It is right and quite appropriate to hold this with regard to each intelligence, according to those people who extol them with such great excellence of nobility and perfection. For nothing can be more correctly or magnificently thought regarding them than that they are subject to the creator in the ultimate degree of subjection and servitude.

Chapter Thirty-One
In how many ways and meanings the name creation is used.

You ought, however, to know that the verb "to create" and the noun "creation," when translated into the vernacular (833b) Spanish, has almost the same meaning and signification as the word for generation or birth. Hence, among the Spaniards one who is born or begotten of a house, that is, of a line or family is said to be "created" of it. But God the most high is not commonly said to be the creator in this meaning, nor is creation used in this meaning. Rather, creation is the activity of the creator alone, because at the good pleasure of his will alone without any means or help he bestows being upon what he wills. And in this way or meaning he is said to create only non-bodily or incorporeal substances, with the sole exception of the heavenly ones. For other substances are generated through actions and passions, and they are generated through many conflicts of agents and patients. But the heavens and the other heavenly bodies are created in the previously mentioned way and meaning.

With regard to the four elements it is evident that they are constantly being generated and corrupted in part, even if not in terms of their totality. But although the custom of Christians admits that human beings generate other human beings and that human beings are parents of human beings, it does not accept that human beings create other human beings or that human beings are creators of other human beings. It also shrinks from hearing, as if impious and unspeakable, the verb "to create" used of anything other than the creator, except in a transferred signification and meaning, as kings or priests are said to be created among that people. This is undoubtedly said with a far different meaning. This activity, then, that is, of creating in this meaning is made proper to the creator among this people in this meaning and usage. As I said to you regarding certain other things, its power and creation itself are not transferred from the creator to some creature, nor is it shared with something else.

Chapter Thirty-Two
A report of the marvelous powers of certain animals and its application.

It is appropriate, however, that in this chapter you recall the powers of intelligent and even of sentient substances which produce amazing impressions outside themselves and outside the bodies to which they are joined or bound. You will, nonetheless, find none that generates or creates a substance like itself either in itself or outside itself. Of this kind is the fish—as I have elsewhere told you—which is called the sting ray (*torpedo*). By mere contact with it it makes the hand of the one who touches it so numb that it can do nothing at all for a whole hour. And what is even more amazing: if it is touched with a lance of whatever length, it produces the same numbness in the hand of the one who touches it—I do not mean: in the lance. Among these is the fish called sucking fish (*echeneis*). It clings on the outside to the hull of a ship, and no matter how big the ship and how agitated by the blast and impulse of the winds, it forces it to remain stationary. Among these is the basilisk which kills human beings, as is said, by its look alone. Among these is any man or a woman who has an evil eye, if one believes common speech, especially that of old women. Among these is the wolf, if one can believe the words of men who say that, if it sees a man before the man sees it, it naturally makes him hoarse, but if it is first seen by the man, it does not do that to him. There are countless other things of this sort which the books of secrets and marvels contain. I have, then, made mention of these to you so that you will not be led by the example of these into the opinion of the creation or generation which they assign to the intelligences. That is to say, so that, because they claim that the intelligences have incomparably more noble and greater powers than the souls (834a) of the animals I mentioned, you do not believe that you are forced to hold or concede that the intelligences ought to be able to produce such creations as they assign to them, since you have often heard that the souls of dogs or spiders can do many things which our souls cannot, though in nobility and perfection they are naturally incomparable. But a common example is found in iron and gold. It is clear that iron can do many things that gold cannot. So too, the ear can do what the eye cannot, though the eye is much more noble than the ear. And from these a countless multitude of examples is offered to you.

Chapter Thirty-Three
The resolution of the contradiction between Plato and Aristotle concerning the archetypal world and that the names which denote excellence belong properly and truly to God alone, but equivocally and under some condition to creatures.

After this I shall return to the contradiction between Plato and Aristotle, and I shall settle it for you. I shall state the common truth in which all laws agree and to which the words of the prophets attest. I say, then, first of all, that the creator is truth through himself and in himself, and he is most correctly and most suitably called the first truth. He is also truth in relation to the universe which was created, established, and ordered by him in a most beautiful order, and the universe is a very empty and very thin shadow in relation to him and in comparison to him. Avicebron taught this in his statement by which he said that creatures have raised themselves up to the creator and produced a shadow of him.[182] But the explanation of my meaning in the word "shadow" is this: When you consider the immensity and sublimity of the creator in all predications and each one of them that indicate his magnificence and care and glory, you will clearly find that those same predications, when they refer to the universe and its parts, signify only slight shadows and nods and vestiges and tiny signs of those things which they signify in the creator when they are said of him. For example, pay attention to the meaning of "powerful" and "power" when the creator is said to be powerful or when his power is mentioned. Consider likewise the meanings of the same terms when a creature is said to be powerful, and compare the power of the creator to the power of the creature, and you will clearly see that the power of the creature in relation to the power of the creator is not worthy to be called power, but only a sign or slight trace of it, since it is impressed by it. For many reasons there is no comparison between them of the sort that can be thought between a most abundant and unfailingly overflowing fountain and one of the drops of its water or between the abyss or the sea and even one small drop of its water.

The first of these reasons is this, namely, that each of these is called water and is so called univocally and according to one and the same meaning. For the whole of the water flowing from such a fountain and each drop of it are called water; so too, the abyss or sea and each drop of it. But it is not that way with the power of the creator and the power of each creature.

The second is that each drop or particle of the whole emanation from the fountain is a part of it. Likewise, each drop or particle of the abyss or sea is a part of the same. But it is not that way with any power of a creature, no matter how great it might be, and the power of the creator, namely, so that the former is part of the latter or even something comparable to it.

The third reason is that drops or particles amassed or gathered in a number (834b) are something comparable, that is, they can undoubtedly constitute an amount of water comparable in magnitude to the total emanation we mentioned or to the whole abyss—or even an equal amount of water. For the whole abyss is constituted from equal drops finite in number, and as you learned elsewhere, no magnitude is put together from infinite things of its own kind. For example, no line comes from infinite lines, no surface from infinite surfaces, no body from infinite bodies, regardless of the quantity they are shown to have. But when you gather together in your imagination or intellect all the powers of each and every creature and think of the aggregate of them all as one power of them all or as the power of the universe, the whole

---

[182] See above, note 28, where the text from Avicebron's *Font of Life* (*Fons uitae*) III, 55, p. 201, ll. 6-8, is cited.

of this assembled power will not be comparable to the power of the creator. The explanation of this is that, if you suppose either that all things are infinite or that such power is gathered or multiplied from an infinity, neither infinity will be able to resist the power of the creator even at a single point of them.

In this way consider the wisdom of the creator in relation to each of the other wisdoms and the infinity assembled from them, and you will find that each one of them and the infinity assembled from them is not something comparable to the wisdom of the creator. The situation is the same with the goodness of the creator and other goodnesses. So too, with his sweetness and other sweetnesses, with his generosity and other generosities, with his beauty and loftiness and nobility and all those other things whose predications in some way make known to us, as I said, the magnificence or excellence of the creator and are used in reference to creatures in accord with their appropriate smallness. But with these comparisons and considerations pay careful attention to how they are truly imposed and what they are made properly to signify by human beings, and you clearly find that no term for color properly names or denominates a color unless it is pure and unmixed with its contrary, just as "whiteness" does not name the color unless it is free from blackness, nor does "white" denominate properly and truly anything but that which participates in whiteness that is pure and unmixed with blackness.

For this reason Aristotle said that some things are called white which seem not to be white at all, undoubtedly meaning that they should in no sense be said to be white, if even the slightest mixture of blackness were seen in them.[183] Hence, it is evident that in such cases the naming or denominating is done through error or ignorance. The term "power," therefore, when it is imposed truly and signifies in its proper sense, names only power that is free from impotence in every way and unmixed with the same. In this way "powerful" only denominates one who has power in the true sense, and the situation is the same with being and entity, true and truth, good and goodness, beautiful and beauty, wise and wisdom, lofty and loftiness, and noble and nobility. It is, therefore, obvious from these and through these that the true and proper significations of such predications belong only to the creator and apply to other things only equivocally (*aequivoce*) and to some extent (*secundum quid*) or by relation (*ad aliquid*) or in some likeness that is very small and most far from the creator. With respect to these namings and denominatings, their truths—so to speak—are in the creator. But in creatures there are only likenesses of such truths according to the way in which it is possible and appropriate to think that there are likenesses between the creator and creatures.

---

[183] See Aristotle, *Topics* III, ch. 5, 119a27-31 as a possible source.

(835a)

Chapter Thirty-Four
The destruction of the error of Plato who maintained that the denominations of things of this world are not made through the truth, but only through likeness.

But Plato extended such likenesses further than was necessary and further than the truth demanded. He stated in his conversation in the book which he called *Timaeus* that all naming of creatures takes place only through likeness and no naming of them is done through the truth.[184] Hence, he obviously maintains that there is neither true fire nor true water nor true air in the sensible world, not noticing that there are many namings of creatures which are made without any comparison or likeness to the creator. For earth is not named earth, as it is denominated good, nor is it denominated black as it is denominated good. Nor is it denominated bodily or the residue of elements, as it is called a creature or work of the creator. Likewise, it is not named the matter of earthly bodies or the dwelling place of humans and walking animals in that way. Concerning these namings it is obvious that they of themselves indicate nothing that belongs to the creator. Therefore, these namings and those like them belong to creatures in accord with their being and truth and in accord with their proper differences without any comparison and reference to the creator. For if true earthiness or fieriness were not in this sensible world, there would not be true earth or true fire in it either. And so there is no true earth or true fire in this world. It is necessary, nonetheless, that Plato concede regarding the earth which is in this sensible world that it is something in truth or in accord with the truth or that it is nothing. But if it is something in accord with the truth, when we impose names upon it, Plato will of necessity return to that very point which he denied. For if it is named earth, then he necessarily concedes that earth according to the truth is in this sensible world and that this is the true earth which we see in it. But if he does not agree that we should name it earth, let him name it A or B. And then the question will be whether true A is in this sensible world. Because he must accept that true A exists in this world, he will of necessity be forced to concede that the truth of A is here, not merely the likeness of it.

Moreover, what would Plato answer, if he were asked whether he is the true Plato who holds this opinion and whether the truth of Plato is in him and in this sensible world? If he answers that he is really the true Plato and that the truth of Plato is in him and in this world, how will he escape from being forced likewise to concede that this is true earth and the truth of it is in this world? But if he says that he is not the true Plato and that the truth of Plato is not in him, but that he exists only according to some likeness of the true Plato and that the true Plato is in the world of species, then true individuals or particulars do not exist in this sensible world, that is, neither true men nor

---

[184] See Plato, *Timaeus* 48E-49A, though William uses the Latin translation of Chalcidius. See above note 151.

true horses nor true asses. Hence, this world is not truly sensible, nor a true world. It follows, then, that there is nothing at all in this sensible world in accord with the truth and that the world itself is nothing in truth or in accord with the truth. But what is nothing in truth is likewise nothing and truly nothing. I do not want to use against him that statement of Aristotle's by which he said in the book of the *Metaphysics* that each thing stands in relation to the truth as it stand in relation to being,[185] because (835b) an adversary is not a good witness against a person.

Moreover, there is, according to Plato, at least a likeness of earth in this world, if not the truth, and this likeness does not make it truly or essentially earth, but only earth-like. Likewise, he will say that in this earth there is not true corporeality, but only a likeness which likewise does not make it to be a true body, but only body-like. He must, therefore, eventually come to this point that it is not truly or essentially substance, but it is also not something else. Hence, it will not truly and essentially be something. And the situation is the same with each of the others. It will, therefore, truly and essentially be nothing of all singular and particular things. But you might say that this is the being of earth, namely, to be earth-like, and likewise that the being of fire or to be fire is only to be fire-like, and that the situation is the same in all the other predicables of this sort.

But it is clear that earth-like and fire-like do not express a what, nor are they predicated in the manner of "what it is."[186] Nothing then is predicated among us, that is, in this world, and nothing can be predicated as a what. Hence, there is no what, nor is there anything definable, since it is not possible to say of anything what it is.

Moreover, since truth and the true always exist together, just as whiteness and white—and the same way with other things, for example, the truth of humanity is where there is a true man and only where there are true men, just as there is true whiteness only where there are true white things. Therefore, true men and true horses[187] and all other true things will only exist in the world of species. Hence, true individuals or particulars are all in that world, and none are with us, that is, in this world. It is clear to you from these arguments which things have their truth with the creator and the sort of truth it is and which things have their likeness with us, that is, in this world. Also, those things which have their truth with us have only their likenesses with the creator. This is evident from the sharing or participation of names; I mean the sharing which I mentioned to you, which is really by equivocation, not univocity, that is, of one meaning in our world, while only the likeness is found in the creator. But understand "likeness" in the way I told you, namely, in the way in which the exemplar is a likeness of the exemplification. In that way you see that the house is really the external one, namely, the one which is

---

[185] Aristotle, *Metaphysics* II, ch. 1, 993b30-31: "Each thing has truth as it has being."
[186] William's Latin would very literally read: "in that which is what is."
[187] I have read *equi* instead of *aequi*.

seen externally with bodily eyes and which is built essentially from wood and stones. But the likeness or exemplar is within or interior, that is, in the mind of the workman. You see also that the name "house" is imposed on that which is outside, outside, I mean, of the mind of the workman, and it is in no sense imposed upon that which is in the workman or in his mind. And it only names that which is seen externally, that is, the dwelling or receptacle of human beings. But in no sense does it name something that is in the workman. No one has ever dared to call the exemplar a house except through an intolerable abuse. In accord with this manner earth is the name of that which is and is seen around us and in no sense of something which is with the creator or in his mind. Nor has anyone called anything but those around us earth or fire or water.

Chapter Thirty-Five
The destruction of Plato over the fact that he claimed that the truth of particular things is in the archetypal world.

But when you more carefully consider the words of Plato, the impossibility of them will be clearly evident to you. First, because the exemplar (836a) cannot be truly and properly be said to be the truth of the exemplification. For the truth of each thing is nothing but the substance or essence or being of it. And this is what the account or definition unfolds. This is the residue from the whole clothing of accidents. But it is evident that in none of these ways is the exemplar the truth of the exemplification. Nor can a thing be said to be truly and properly the truth of its sign. For the truth of a thing is said to be with that or in that being with or in which is found the account or definition and upon which the name is first and principally imposed. This is seen in a man and his picture or image. For the name "man" is principally and first imposed on a man who is a walking, two-footed, rational animal. And with him and in him is found the whole account or definition which I set forth. And he it is who is truly and properly and singularly, that is, alone said to be a true man. But the picture or image of him is in no sense said to be a true man. It is called a man, but equivocally, as you heard in Aristotle. The archetypal or exemplary world, then, is in no way the truth of particular things, that is, is in no way the substance or essence or being of them, unless through an intolerable abuse one should want to say that every image to whose likeness another image is made is the truth of it.

Moreover, when he said that the world of species is the exemplar of this sensible world of particulars, either Plato understood the species which we say are predicated of many numerically different things in the "that which is what is," or he understood the likenesses or ideas of things or exemplar images of things. But if he understood it in the first meaning, Plato himself clearly contradicts this statement in his book which he called *Timaeus*, when he says that this which is with us is not earth, but the earth-like, and that true fire is not with us, but the fire-like.[188] For example, according to Plato himself, true earth and fire are not predicated essentially or in the "that which is what is" of these things which are around us, for in that previous statement of his he removes true fire and true earth from the things around us.

Moreover, a species of this sort is the whole being of individuals, for whatever Socrates has besides man—that is, besides those things by which a man is constituted—is accidental to him. But what he has as a residue from accidents is his whole being; hence, his whole being is the species, that is, the species "man," as it is said or predicated of him, when one says, "Socrates is a man." Because, then, the whole being of all individuals is in the individuals and not outside them, it is clear that such a species is entirely in its individuals or singulars and not outside them.

Moreover, where there is the truth of each thing, there it is, and the other way around. Hence, if the truth of earth and the truth of fire are in the exemplary or archetypal world, it is necessary that true fire and true earth are in it, but countless problems follow upon this. First, that true fire will not be a body, neither will true earth. Hence, "body" will not be the genus for fire and earth: I mean, for true fire and true earth.

Moreover, on this view a true body will not be in this world, but in the archetypal world. And in the same way it follows that a true substance will not be in this world either. Hence, a true accident will not be here for the same reason, and in that way there will be nothing true in the world of particulars. Hence, there will be in it neither the true sun nor the true moon, neither the true Socrates nor the true Plato. So too, no true heat nor true cold; hence, neither the truly hot nor the truly cold will be anything in our world. But where true cold is found, there is what is truly cold; likewise, where true heat (836b) is found, there is what is truly hot. Truly hot and truly cold things, then, exist in the archetypal world alone, and in the same way truly white and truly black things exist there alone. Hence, truly visible and truly tangible things are in it alone, and on this account truly sensible things are only there. Hence, truly particular things are in it alone. It is, then, alone truly the world of particulars.

Moreover, if true whiteness is in it alone, how can true whiteness exist where nothing is truly white or even white? But it is evident according to the view of Plato that there is nothing sensible in the intelligible world. Hence, there is nothing either white or black, nothing either hot or cold, nothing either soft or hard. Hence, the truth of sensible qualities is not there, since things truly sensible are not there.

---

[188] See above note 151. In Chalcidius' translation of the *Timaeus*, ed. Jan H. Waszink (London: E. J. Brill, 1975), p. 47, we read: "Hence, with regard to all changeable things of this sort one should think this: this which seems to us to be formed differently at different times and is often not in accord with the form of fire is not fire, but fire-like, and not brass but brass-like. . . ."

Moreover, according to this, there is no true motion around us, but in the archetypal world. But he claims that that world is most at rest, immobile, and eternal.

Moreover, since the truth of each thing is its being which its account or definition explains, none of those things which are in this world are definable; that is, none of them has an account or definition that explains its being. And for this reason none of them will have created or caused being, since every being of this sort is inexplicable, and in that way none of those things which are in this world will have being. But everything which does not have being does not exist. Hence, none of all those things which are in this world exist.

Moreover, since Plato could not but maintain that that world was without parts, he cannot maintain that there is in it something that has three dimensions. For in something without parts there cannot be three dimensions, nor can there be something that has three dimensions.

Moreover, true earth which is found there is neither cold nor dry nor heavy nor weighty. For such dispositions have no place in the intelligible world. How, then, is that earth which has none of these dispositions true earth?

Moreover, how is it earth from which there cannot be made a single clay vessel or single pot?

Moreover, that earth is either one numerically and singular or not. If it is, the situation is the same with fire and with each of the other things. Hence, whatever is in the archetypal world is one numerically and singular or particular. That world, then, is a world of particulars or of singulars, and all those exemplars which are in it are singular or particular. Hence, all the things which are in this world were made according to the patterns which are singular and particular.

Moreover, that earth is either composed and with parts or simple and without parts. But if it is simple and without parts, how is it true or a true body? But if it is composed and with parts, it follows that it is either heavy or light; hence, it is sensible, and on this account it is like our earth in every respect.

Moreover, on this view, it will also be in place in the same way. By the same path they must say the same thing about fire and about the other bodies of this sensible world. Hence, the archetypal world will be nothing but another sensible world like this one. It is evident, then, through these arguments and others which have come earlier, that Plato did not understand what he said about the archetypal world and about species which are predicated about individuals or singulars essentially. For it is necessary that they be in their singulars and with singulars. For where Socrates exists, it is necessary that man exist, and where man exists, it is necessary that there be some man. He, therefore, understood his statements concerning the ideas or external forms which are eternally in the mind of the creator.

(837a)

Chapter Thirty-Six

Another destruction of the error of Plato where it is taught that the ideal entity and that of things in our world differ essentially and that they are not said of the same thing and that names of these things of our world are true and essential and truly name things which truly exist and that they are transferred to the creator or to spiritual substances through a likeness, not properly.

But in this respect he either spoke with an intolerable abuse or he clearly erred, because he said that the names of earth and fire and others of the sort are not predicated of bodies that are in our world according to the truth or according to essence, but only by likeness. For no one could doubt that such names are essential and are names in the true sense, not denominations or adnominations,[189] and that they were created for expressing the essences or substances, but not the likenesses of things or other dispositions or comparisons of them, as has been shown to you.

Moreover, neither Plato nor anyone else could ever have had a doubt that every exemplar and any exemplification of it are two things according to the truth and essentially, just as a cause and its effect and also as prior and posterior. Of these it is evident that, since they are mutually related, it is impossible that they be said of the same thing. For in this comparison or consideration they are contraries. Hence, it is clearly impossible that the earth which is in our world and the exemplar earth, namely, that of which this world is an exemplification, have one truth or essence. Because, then, each of them exists according to the truth, it is necessary that they be two and that they have two beings and two truths, since each thing stands in relation to being as it stands to truth, as you have heard in Aristotle in the Book of the Metaphysics.[190] And it is clearly true through itself that the truth of each thing is its being, and the other way around. It is evident, then, that this bodily world is the true world and has true being, not merely the being of a likeness. Because, as I have told you, the names of the parts of this world are not names of likenesses, neither denominations nor adnominations imposed from accidents, but are names in the true sense and of true nomination, they name those things which are truly and essentially. On this account essential names are imposed by us on things to name them what they are truly and essentially, such as, sun, moon, earth and each of the other such things. And such nominations are proper to them according to these meaning, and they are in no sense transferred to the creator or to spiritual and separate substances, but rather by some likeness, as the prophets at times speak of the sun of justice

---

[189] William distinguishes between "nominations," "denominations," and "adnominations." As becomes clear further on, these indicate the difference between naming substances, naming qualities and quantities, and naming relations.

[190] Aristotle, *Metaphysics* II, ch. 1, 993b30-31.

and the sun of intelligence.[191] But the reasons why this is done are evident to you in that case. But with earth, whether the prophets speak of the earth of the living or whether the law of the Hebrews speaks of the earth flowing with milk and honey according to the likenesses taken from the language of prophets and philosophers, it is understood through some likenesses. For he, that is, the creator, is like a fatherland or city of the holy angels and holy souls who live blessedly in it. And he is like a region overflowing with spiritual delights from which a torrent of pleasures and streams of spiritual delights unceasingly and unfailingly pour out as emanations upon all the hosts of spiritual forces. He is, then, called earth because of his likeness to a dwelling—the dwelling of the citizens we mentioned (837b) —flowing with milk and honey as a result of the overflow of spiritual delights. But these expressions and others like them are known to those trained in the language of the prophets.

Chapter Thirty-Seven
*That certain nominations which according to the most exact truth
belong to the creator, but are shared with creatures and are truly shared,
but according to the meaning by which the names are suited to them.*

I have already told you in the preceding parts that certain nominations belong to the creator according to their most exact truth and according to the original imposition of the names. He, nonetheless, shares such nominations with all or with some creatures. Such are a being and being, powerful and power, wise and wisdom, good and goodness, beautiful and beauty, and ones like these which belong to the creator alone according to their truth which is purified and unmixed with the contrary in every way. But they are shared with other things by a certain likeness, though one far distant, as I explained to you. And when you have purified names that pertain to his supereminence and glory, such as, king and lord and those like them and remove their contraries from their concepts until they are pure, you will find that they are names of the creator alone, signifying his excellence and glory.

For example, if you purify "king" from that which belongs to being ruled and if you likewise purify the king himself from all iniquity, injustice, imprudence, negligence, and weakness or debility, the name of king belongs to the creator alone. I say the same thing of this name "lord," when you purify its concept, namely, lordship from everything which is its contrary—that is, from all subjection and debt of servitude; for one is not truly and purely lord who is subject to another or even owes service to another—and when you likewise purify the concept of lordship on its inferior side, that is, on the side involving comparison which a lord has to his inferiors or subjects. But this is power (*potestas*). You will find his power pure and free from all those things which

---

[191] See Mal 4:2 for "sun of justice." The expression "sun of intelligence" is not found in the Vulgate.

have to do with impotency, and there will occur to you the concept of lord-ship purified in both respects as belonging to the creator alone and made proper to him with an appropriation that cannot be shared.

In that way you will find in the books of the prophets that it is often said that: "Lord is his name," and in his own person, "I am the Lord; this is my name."[192] It is, then, clear to you that such names are not shared with crea-tures according to their purified meanings in which they are made proper to the creator. And for this reason they are not shared univocally, but equivo-cally and by a most remote likeness. But this diversity of meanings and inten-tions does not prevent them from being truly said of creatures and in the intentions by which they are applied to them and suited to them. For there is no doubt that the king of the Indians and the king of the Ethiopians are truly kings in these senses by which kings are commonly referred to by men, whether on account of the bare power (though they defile it with many iniquities and injustices) or on account of power decorated with justice and other royal virtues. On this account men call tyrants wicked kings, though they are not kings, that is, do not rule them rightly, but rather oppress them with tyranni-cal violence and feed off them, not guarding and defending them, but mak-ing of them plunder for themselves. In that way the wisest of the Hebrews called a wicked prince over a poor people a roaring lion and a hungry bear.[193] But you might say that "king" is the name of a right and office, and that it is [not] imposed (838a) from these things which the powerful wrongly do, but from the right or office or duty of those things which they ought to do, and that someone is not a king as a result of what he does—whatever these acts might be—nor as a result of the power to do such things, but on the basis of the office and right, or duty, of ruling, that is, of guarding, defending, pacify-ing through justice, and judging subjects.

I would agree that such a person speaks correctly. But this is in accord with the true and proper meaning of this name "king." And yet the common folk twist that name to the previously mentioned loose expressions and others of the sort. Nor should one say that there is no truth present in these statements of the common folk, for in all common statements there is present the truth[194] of the concept with regard to naming and designating things. And the mean-ing of this statement is that no trope or loose expression of any sort keeps the truth of the meaning from those applying the name in this way, that is, tropi-cally or loosely. This is to say that the common folk truly call a tyrant a king or prince in accord with their meaning. Otherwise, it would not be possible that he be called a bad king or bad prince.

---

[192] See Ps 67:5 and Is 42:8.

[193] Prv 28:15.

[194] I have read "truth: *veritas*" for "power: *virtus*," at least partially on the basis of William's use of "truth of the concept" just below.

In the same way someone who is not a man cannot be called a man and can in no sense be named a bad or a wicked man. Nor is it necessary that I here explain or report to you the childish cleverness of sophistries by which one speaks of a dead man who is no longer a man or of a false coin or of a man in a painting who is not man. For you know that in one who is said to be a dead man the principal part of that which is a man, that is, his soul, is removed by the fact that he is dead. Hence, this whole concept "dead man" does not express a man, but a part of him, that part, namely, which death leaves with us, and this is the body. This concept "false coin" likewise does not express a whole coin. The reason is that the adjective "false" removes the true matter of the coin, because it ought to be either gold or silver. The whole concept "false coin" does not express a coin, but only what is left from the matter of the coin, that is, the form of it alone, just as "dead man" only expresses the matter of a true man. But this concept "man in a painting" does not express a true man or the true matter of a man or the true form, but only a likeness or painting of him, and a man in a painting is nothing but a painting or a painted likeness of a man. The adjective "in a painting" removes the whole true man, that is, in terms of the matter and in terms of the form, as I said, claiming the appellation for itself and transferring it to its proper signification, namely, to the picture alone. The adjectives "evil" and "wicked" take nothing from the substance of the reality which the substantive names, for whether one says "a bad or wicked man" or "a bad or wicked king" the whole remains in terms of the signification of man or king—both the true matter and the true form.

I shall return to where I was and I shall say that, whether things are named in ordinary and common speech in their proper sense or by a trope or loosely or through a likeness or some other comparison, they are truly named according to the meaning of those who name them. For we do not call false illustrations or tropes or any other loose expressions insofar as they are illustrations or tropes or loose, that is, in accord with their meanings as such. It is true, then, that earth is true earth and true earth in whatever sense the term "earth" is taken, and on the basis of the meaning presented Plato too does not contradict this statement when he says that it is not earth, but the earth-like which is found in our world.

(838b)

Chapter Thirty-Eight
Whether the archetypal world is the creator himself or something other than the creator according to Plato and concerning the absurdities resulting from his position.

But the meaning of Plato on this point causes no slight wonder, and it should not be passed over. On this account we must investigate whether he understood that the archetypal world was the creator himself or something other than the creator and something made or created by him. But if he understood that it was the creator himself, he necessarily has to admit that each one of such species or ideas is the creator or part of the creator. Because, then, it was explained in the first part of this philosophy of God in the mode of wisdom that the creator is without parts in every way, he necessarily has to concede that each one of such species or ideas is the creator himself and that besides this, on this view, the creator himself is true earth and likewise true water. And it is the same way with each of the other things. Hence, it is necessary to concede that all species and intelligibles of that intellectual world are one and the same thing according to their essence and truth, and that thing is without parts in the ultimate degree of indivisibility into parts. But if it is one single thing, he ought to explain how this is a world or universe. In any case you will hear some things about this from me in the following. But if Plato understood that this intellectual world or world of species is something other than the creator, it will necessarily be created or made by him. It will also be necessary that its parts be intelligible or intellectual substances and, for this reason, ones that understand and are more excellent and more noble in all their dispositions than the angelic substances and intelligences to the extent that they are closer to the creator in natural order. It will also be necessary on this view that this world have another exemplar in the creator, to the likeness of which it was created by him. In this way the recourse will proceed to infinity. And there will be no end of exemplars or words, or Plato will be forced to admit that the creator created one of these exemplars or worlds. But this is not only impossible according to Plato, but it has also been shown to you by me in the first part of this philosophy that in every wise agent that acts through himself it is necessary that there be an exemplar of all the products which he produces through wisdom, and with him and in him it is the same thing as the art or wisdom by which and through which he acts or to the likeness of which he makes something.[195] And I should not produce for you a repetition of such an explanation.

Chapter Thirty-Nine
Another explanation of the contradiction which existed between Plato and Aristotle in which it is explained that the wisdom of the creator is the archetypal world.

Having settled these points, I shall return to the resolution of this contradiction which existed between Plato and Aristotle, and I shall say that the archetypal world, that is, the exemplar of all those things which were made or created by the creator or which will be made or even can be made is properly the wisdom eternally generated by the creator which the law, doctrine, and the faith of Christians calls the Son of God and God. It was the choice of his goodness that his magnificence and glory be known (839a) and explained by me, and concerning his generation and the other such things you have a worth-

---

[195] See *The Trinity, or the First Principle* (*De trinitate*), ch. 18: Switalski, pp 102-107; Teske-Wade, pp. 135-40.

while and noble treatise in the first part of this philosophy.[196] Wise men and teachers of the Christians call this God and Son of God the art of the omnipotent God full of living reasons,[197] and they understand living reasons as those species or ideas which Plato posited according to the conception and opinion of those who have thought well and praiseworthily in this matter concerning Plato and his philosophy. The blessed and venerable Son of God, then, is the exemplar and world or universe of such species and ideas and the art full of living reasons, which are all one in it, according to the statements of the wise men and teachers of the Christians, and these reasons which we mentioned are the Platonic species or ideas or forms. In the same way the philosopher says that every intelligence is full of forms;[198] on account of this fullness of reasons and the innumerable multitude of such ideas or forms it can be rightly called and seen to be multiform in the law and doctrine of Christians. You ought also to know that an intelligent substance whose intellective power is perfect in its complete perfection is made to be an intelligible world or intelligible mirror, as I have already told you, and such perfection is the glory and excellence of our intellect and the first part of the future beatitude and of perpetual happiness which the blessed creator promised to his elect. You have already heard something about this from me. But it will be clearly explained to you, if God wills, in accord with your abilities how the wisdom of the creator is one in the ultimate degree of oneness and how it is multiform, how in it those innumerable multitudes of ideas are one and how they are many, as well as how they are in the blessed and holy angels and also in our souls when they are beatified with that glory, when I investigate the nature of spirituality and things proper to it. This is the question which Plato ought to have explained above.

Chapter Forty
That in every intelligence there is a fullness or multiformity of ideas or exemplars.

You ought to know that this intellective and multiform perfection ought not to belong in any sense to the agent intellect alone, but to all the other intelligences—if there are any—and to all the blessed angelic substances. But this perfection in them is divided into two, one of which is natural and innate, the other added on by the gratuitous generosity and beneficence of the creator. This latter is called by Christians both grace and glory: grace on account of its gratuitous bestowal, but glory on account of the supereminence

---

[196] Again William refers to *The Trinity, or the First Principle* (*De trinitate*); from ch. 14 on the work deals with the generation of the Son and the procession of the Holy Spirit.

[197] See Augustine, *The Trinity* (*De trinitate*) VI, 10, 11: CCL 50, 241, where he speaks of the Word as "the art of the omnipotent and wise God full of all the living and unchangeable reasons. . . ."

[198] See Aristotle, *On the Soul* III, ch. 4, 429a27-28 as a possible source.

of its perfection beyond which no other is sought or hoped for. In the following I shall try to investigate and determine, with the help of God, what the amplitude or largeness or capacity this natural perfection has in terms of objects that can be known or cognized. That is to say, are they all or only certain ones, or a part of them, knowable or cognizable before this capacity or within it?

Let the simplicity or partlessness of such a substance or even of the creator, then, not bother you, as if it would exclude from them this multiformity or multitude of reasons or ideas or exemplary forms. In the following (839b) I shall make you know, if God wills, that the simplicity and partlessness in such substances is their intellective amplitude and capacity. Once this is established, then, for these substances, it is evident to you how, according to Aristotle, the agent intelligence is the sun or light of souls,[199] and this is necessarily true of every such substance, that is, one that is immaterial and perfect with the perfection we mentioned. And it is the more true of the higher ones to the extent that they must have greater brightness than the lower ones. For spatial distance does not exclude such substances from their brightness, as is evident to you in bright bodies since the shedding of their rays is thinned and weakened in other bodies in accord with the greatness of their nearness and distance to them, and not according to the dispositions of the intervening bodies between those that shed rays and those that receive them. These dispositions, as you learned elsewhere, are rarity and density; but in spiritual substances nearness and distance are of another sort, and perhaps bodily nearness and distances help and impede them at times from such reception of rays. For it is likely, though not as yet proved through demonstration by me or by someone else whose explanation has come to me, that good and bad angels do not all know things near them and distant from them equally. I mean near and distant by local nearness and distance.

For who supposes that the angels, whether good ones or bad, who are in the city of Arim know those things which happen in farthest Thule as well as they know those things which happen in Arim? This is one of those questions which arouses and upsets many. So too with saints who are caught up in the spirit for visions and revelations, it must be investigated with no less of an investigation whether this happens through local motion or in some other way. But I have already told you about the sun and its brightness that it does not imprint through it colors upon the surfaces of the bodies on which it shines, but it helps the colors which exist in the bodies in potency. In the same way the warmth of the sand or dust does not impress upon the egg of the sturgeon the form of the sturgeon, but it helps the matter so that it proceeds into actuality in that form of the sturgeon. For the potency which is in that matter is incomplete and not sufficient by itself to educe into actuality the form of the sturgeon without the help of warmth, as you clearly see in the

---

[199] See Aristotle, *On the Soul* III, ch. 5, 430a14-17

warmth of the sun, since it does not impress the forms of plants, but helps the seeds so that from them there are educed into the actuality those things and their forms which are potentially in the seeds.

Chapter Forty-One
Whether from above the light of knowledge is shed upon our souls by the agent intelligence, and whether this irradiation or illumination is produced by every other spiritual substance.

The explanation of this is as follows: nothing imprints naturally or through itself a form or likeness of a form which it does not have. But the operation of the sun in natural things is through itself. Moreover, the examples and likenesses in Aristotle for the perfectability of our souls in no way are in harmony with these statements of his. For in the tablet of a picture or of a writing there do not exist potentially those things of which the tablet is receptive. Rather, they come to and are imprinted upon it entirely from the outside by the agent, or the (840a) one who writes on it, and they do not in any sense proceed from it either partly or as a whole.

[The rest of the chapter and of the work are omitted from this translation.]

Bibliography

Primary Sources

William, of Auvergne. *Opera Omnia.* 2 vols. Edited by F. Hotot, with *Supplementum*, edited by Blaise Le Feron. Orléans-Paris, 1674; repr. Frankfurt am Main: Minerva, 1963.

————. *De trinitate.* An Edition of the Latin Text with an Introduction by Bruno Switalski (Toronto: Pontifical Institute of Mediaeval Studies, 1976).

————. *The Trinity, or the First Principle.* Translated by Roland J. Teske, S.J. and Francis C. Wade, S.J.; introduction and notes by Roland J. Teske, S.J. Medieval Philosophical Texts in Translation, Vol. 28. Milwaukee: Marquette University Press, 1989.

————. "Tractatus Magistri Guilielmi Alvernensis de bono et malo." Edited by J. Reginald O'Donnell. *Mediaeval Studies* 8 (1946): 245-99.

————. "Tractatus Secundus Guillielmi Alvernensis de bono et malo." Edited by J. Reginald O'Donnell. *Mediaeval Studies* 16 (1954): 219-71.

————. *De immortalitate animae.* Edited by Georg Bülow. In *Des Domininicus Gundissalinus Schrift von der Unsterblichkeit der Seele nebst einem Anhange, enthaltend die Abhandlung des Wilhem von Paris (Auvergne) "De immortalitate animae."* In *Beiträge zur Geschichte der Philosophie des Mittelalters* II 3. Münster: Aschendorff, 1897.

————. *The Immortality of the Soul.* Translated by Roland J. Teske, S.J., with an Introduction and Notes. Mediaeval Philosophical Texts in Translation, Vol. 30. Milwaukee: Marquette University Press, 1991.

————. *Il "Tractatus de Gratia" di Gugliemo d'Auvergne.* Edited Guglielmo Corti. Rome: Lateran University, 1966.

Secondary Sources
Books

Avicebron. *Avencebrolis Fons Vitae.* Ex arabico in latinum translatus ab Johanne Hispano et Dominico Gundissalino. Edited by Clemens Baeumker. In *Beiträge zur Geschichte der Philosophie des Mittelalters* I (Münster: 1892-1895).

Avicenna. *Avicenna Latinus: Liber de Anima seu Sextus de Naturalibus.* Edition critique de la traduction latine médiévale par Simone van Riet. Introduction sur la doctrine psychologique d'Avicenne par Gerard Verbeke. 2 vols. Louvain: E. Peeters; Leiden: E. J. Brill, 1973 and Louvain: Editions Orientalists; Leiden: E. J. Brill, 1968.

————. *Avicenna Latinus: Liber de Philosophia Prima sive Scientia Divina.* Edition critique de la traduction latine médiévale par Simone van Riet. Introduction doctrinale par Gerard Verbeke. 3 vols. Louvain-La-Neuve: E. Peeters; Leiden: E. J. Brill, 1977, 1983, 1983.

Boethius, *The Theological Treatises.* Translated and edited by H. F. Stewart and E. K. Rand. Cambridge: Harvard University Press; London: Wm. Heinemann, 1946.

Borok, Helmut. *Der Tugendbegriff des Wilhelm von Auvergne (1180-1249)*. Eine moralhistorische Untersuchung zur Ideengeschichtliche Rezeption der aristotelischen Ethik. Düsseldorf: Patmos-Verlag, 1979.

Duhem, Pierre. *Le système du Monde. Histoire des doctrines cosmologiques de Platon à Copernic*.. Vol. 5. Paris: Librairie scientifique. A. Herman et Fils., 1917.

Kretzmann, Norman and Anthony Kenny and Jan Pinborg, eds. *The Cambridge History of Later Medieval Philosophy from the Rediscovery of Aristotle to the Disintegration of Scholasticism 1100-1600*. Cambridge: Cambridge University Press, 1982.

Marrone, Steven P. *William of Auvergne and Robert Grosseteste. New Ideas of Truth in the Early Thirteenth Century*. Princeton: Princeton University Press, 1983.

Masnovo, Amato. *Da Guglielmo d'Auvergne a S. Tommaso d'Aquino*, 3 vols, 2nd ed. Milan: Vita et Pensiero, 1946.

Quentin, Albrecht. *Naturkenntnisse und Naturanschungen bei Wilhelm von Auvergne*. Hildesheim: Gerstenberg, 1976.

Roland-Gosselin, Marie Dominique .*Le "De ente et essentia" de S. Thomas d'Aquin. Texte établi d'après les manuscrits parisiens*. Introduction, notes et études historiques par M.-D. Roland-Gosselin. Paris: J.Vrin, 1948.

Rohls, Jan. *Wilhelm von Auvergne und der mittelalterliche Aristotelismus*. München: Chr. Kaiser, 1980.

Schindele, Stephan. *Beiträge zur Metaphysik des Wilhelm von Auvergne*. Munich, 1900.

Valois, Noël. *Guillaume d'Auvergne, Évèque de Paris (1228-1249): Sa vie et ses ouvrages*. Paris: Picard, 1880.

Articles and Chapters in Books

Allard, Baudoin C. "Additions au *Répertoire des maîtres en théologie de Paris au XIIe siècle*." *Bulletin de la société internationale pour l'étude de la philosophie médiévale* 5 (1963): 147-49.

_____. "Note sur le `De immortalitate animae' de Guillaume d'Auvergne." *Bulletin de philosophie médiévale* 18 (1976): 68-72.

———. "Nouvelles additions et corrections au *Répertoire* de Glorieux: A propos de Guillaume d'Auvergne." *Bulletin de philosophie médiévale* (Louvain). 10-12 (1968-70): 98-118.

Anciaux, P. "Le sacrament de pénitance chez Guillaume d'Auvergne," *Ephemerides theologicae lovaniensis* 24 (1948): 98-118.

Barzán, Bernardo C. "Pluralisme de formes ou dualisme de substances?" *Revue philosophique de Louvain* 67 (1969): 30-73.

Bernstein, Alan E. "Esoteric Theology: William of Auvergne on the Fires of Hell and Purgatory." *Speculum* 57 (1982): 509-31.

———. "Theology between Heresy and Folklore: William of Auvergne on Punishment after Death." *Studies in Medieval and Renaissance History* 5 (1982): 4-44.

Caffrey, Mary Carol. "Realism and Knowledge according to William of Auvergne." Ph.D. dissertation, Fordham University, 1944.

Caster, Kevin J. "The Distinction between Being and Essence according to Boethius, Avicenna, and William of Auvergne." *Modern Schoolman* 73 (1996): 309-32.

———. "The Real Distinction in Creatures between Being and Essence according to William of Auvergne." Ph.D. dissertation, Marquette University, 1995.

———. "William of Auvergne's Adaptation of Ibn Gabirol's Doctrine of the Divine Will." *Modern Schoolman* 74 (1996): 31-42.

Contenson, P.-M., de. "La théologie de la vision de Dieu au début du XIIième siècle. Le 'de retributione sanctorum' de Guillaume d'Auvergne et la condamnation de 1241." *Revue de sciences philosophiques et théologiques* 46 (1962): 409-44.

Corti, Guglielmo. "Le sette parte del *Magisterium diuinale et sapientiale* di Guglielmo di Auvergne." In *Studi e richerche di scienze religiose in onore dei santi apostoli Petro et Paulo nel XIX centenario del loro martirio*, 289-307. Rome: Lateran University, 1968.

Davis, Leo D. "Creation according to William of Auvergne." In *Studies in Mediaevalia and Americana*. Edited by G. Steckler and L. Davis, 51-75. Spokane: Gonzaga University Press, 1973.

De Porter, A. "Un manuel de prédication médiévale. Le ms. 97 de Bruges." *Revue néoscolastique de philosophie* 25 (1923): 192-209.

Forest, Aimé. "Guillaume d'Auvergne, critique d'Aristote." In *Études médiévales offertes à Augustin Flictie*, pp. 67-79. Paris: Presses Universitaires de France, 1952.

Gauthier, René A. "Notes sur les débuts (1225-1240) du prémier 'averroisme.'" *Revue des sciences philosophiques et théologiques* 66 (1982): 321-34.

Gilson, Etienne. "La notion d'existence chez Guillaume d'Auvergne." *Archives d'histoire doctrinale et littéraire du moyen age* 21 (1946): 55-91.

―――. "Les 'Philosophantes.'" *Archives d'histoire doctrinale et littéraire du moyen age* 19 (1952): 135-140.

―――. "Les sources gréco-arabes de l'augustinisme avicennisant." *Archives d'histoire doctrinale et littéraire du moyen age* 4 (1929): 5-149.

―――. "Pourquoi saint Thomas a critiqué saint Augustin." *Archives d'histoire doctrinale et littéraire du moyen age* 1 (1926) 5-127.

Glorieux, Palemon. "Le tractatus novus de poenitentia de Guillaume d'Auvergne." In *Miscellanea Moralia. Bibliotheca Ephemeriarum Theologicarum Lovaniensium*. Series 1, Vol. 3, 551-65. Louvain: Nauwelaerts, 1949.

Heinzmann, Richard. "Wilhelm von Auvergne," *Lexikon für Theologie und Kirche*. 2 ed. Freiburg im Breisgau: Herder, 1965. Vol. 10, 1127.

―――. "Zur Anthropologie des Wilhelm von Auvergne," *Münchener Theologische Zeitschrift* 16 (1965): 27-36.

Jüssen, Gabriel. "Wilhelm von Auvergne." In *Contemporary Philosophy. A New Survey. Volume 6. Philosophy and Science in the Middle Ages*. Part I, 177-85. Dordrecht: Kluwer Academic Publishers, 1990.

―――. "Wilhelm von Auvergne und die Entwicklung der Philosophie in Übergang zur Hochscholastik" and "Von Wilhelm von Auvergne zu Thomas von Aquin― und zurürk." In *Thomas von Aquin im philosophischen Gesprach*, 185-203 and 262-265. Ed. Wolfgang Kluxen. Freiburg and Munich, 1975.

―――. "Wilhelm von Auvergne und die Transformation der scholastischen Philosophie im 13. Jahrhundert." In *Philosophie im Mittelalter. Entwicklungslinien und Paradigmen*. Ed. by Jan P. Beckmann et. al., 141-64. Hamberg: Felix Meiner, 1987.

―――. "Die Tugend und der gute Wille: Wilhelm von Auvergnes Auseinandersetzung mit der aristotelischen Ethik," *Philosophisches Jahrbuch* 102 (1995): 20-32.

Knowles, David. "William of Auvergne," *The Encyclopedia of Philosophy*. 8 Vols. New York: Macmillan, 1967. Vol. 8, p. 302f.

Kramp, Josef. "Des Wilhelm von Auvergne 'Magisterium Divinale,'" *Gregorianum* 1 (1920): 538-613, 2 (1921): 42-103 and 174-95.

Landry, Bernard. "L'originalité de Guillaume d'Auvergne," *Revue d'histoire de la philosophie* 3 (1929): 441-63.

Landgraf, A. "Der Tracktat de 'De errore Pelagii' des Wilhelm von Auvergne." *Speculum* 5 (1930): 168-80.

Lewis, Neil. "William of Auvergne's Account of the Enuntiabile: Its Relation to Nominalism." *Vivarium* 33 (1995): 113-36.

Longpré, Ephrem. "Guillaume d'Auvergne et Alexandre de Halès," *Archivum Franciscanum Historicum* 16 (1923): 249-50.

———. "Guillaume d'Auvergne et l'Ecole Franciscaine de Paris," *La France Franciscaine* 5 (1922): 426-29.

Masnovo, Amato. "Guglielmo d'Auvergne e l'universita di Parigi dal 1229 al 1231." In *Mélanges Mandonnet* II, 191-232. Paris: Librairie J. Vrin, 1930.

Michaud-Quantin, P. and M. Lemoine. "Pour le dossier des 'philosophantes.'" *Archives d'histoire doctrinale et littéraire du moyen age* 35 (1968): 17-22.

Moody, Ernest A. "William of Auvergne and his Treatise De Anima." In *Studies in Medieval Philosophy, Science, and Logic*, pp. 1-109. Berkeley and Los Angeles: The University of California Press, 1975.

O'Donnell, J. Reginald. "The Rhetorica Divina of William of Auvergne. A Study in Applied Rhetoric." In *Images of Man in Ancient and Medieval Thought*, 323-33. Leuven: Leuven University Press, 1976.

———. "William of Auverge (of Paris)," *The New Catholic Encyclopedia*. 15 Vols. New York: McGraw-Hill, 1967. Vol. 14, p. 921.

Smalley, Beryl, "William of Auvergne, John of La Rochelle and Saint Thomas on the Old Law." In *St. Thomas Aquinas 1274-1974 Commemorative Studies*, II, 11-71. Toronto: Pontifical Institute of Medieval Studies, 1974.

Teske, Roland J. "William of Auvergne." In *Dictionary of Literary Biography*: Vol. 115: *Medieval Philosophers*, 344-53. Detroit: Gale Research, 1992.

———. "William of Auvergne's Rejection of the Agent Intelligence." In *Greek and Medieval Studies in Honor of Leo Sweeney, S.J.*, 211-35. New York: Peter Lang, 1995.

———. "William of Auvergne on the Eternity of the World," *Modern Schoolman* 67 (1990): 187-205.

———. "The Identity of the 'Italici' in William of Auvergne's Discussion of the Eternity of the World," *Proceedings of the PMR Conference* 15 (1990): 189-201.

———. "William of Auvergne on *De re* and *De dicto* Necessity," *Modern Schoolman* 69 (1992): 111-21.

———. "The Will as King over the Powers of the Soul: Uses and Sources of an Image in Thirteenth Century Philosophy," *Vivarium* 32 (1994): 62-71.

———. "William of Auvergne and the Manichees," *Traditio* 48 (1993): 63-75.

———. "William of Auvergne on the Individuation of Human Souls," *Traditio* 49 (1994): 77-93.

———. "William of Auvergne on Freedom of the Will." In *Moral and Political Philosophies in the Middle Ages*. Proceedings of The Ninth International Conference on Medieval Philosophy, II, 932-38. New York: Legas, 1996.

———. "William of Auvergne's Use of the Avicennian Principle: 'Ex Uno, In Quantum Unum, Non Nisi Unum,'" *Modern Schoolman* 71 (1993): 1-15.

———. "William of Auvergne on the 'Newness of the World,'" *Mediaevalia: Textos e Estudios* 7-8 (1995): 287-302.

Vannest, Alfred. "Nature et grâce dans la théologie de Guillaume d'Auxerre et de Guillaume d'Auvergne." *Ephemerides theologicae lovanienis* 53 (1977): 83-106.

Vaux, Roland de. "La première entrée d'Averroës chez les Latins," *Revue de sciences philosophiques et théologiques* 22 (1933): 193-245.

Vernet, F. "Guillaume d'Auvergne, Évèque de Paris. In *Dictionnaire de théologie catholique*, VII, 1967-1976. Paris: Letzouy, 1923-1950.

Viard, P. "Guillaume d'Auvergne." In *Dictionnaire de spiritualité* VI, 1182-1192. Paris: Beauchesne, 1937—

Weisheipl, James A. "Albertus Magnus and Universal Hylomorphism." *Southwestern Journal of Philosophy* 10 (1979): 239-60.

Subject Index

abstraction, 25, 124

absurd, 172, 185

abundance, 72-73, 79, 176, 180, 196

accident, 35, 37, 42, 54, 56, 60, 107, 160, 205

accidental, 25, 36, 40, 100, 131, 163-164, 205

accidents, 25, 159, 161, 163-164, 185, 204-205, 207

act of understanding, 19, 83-85, 87-91, 95, 142, 155-156, 189, 192-196

action, 40, 47, 69, 87, 126, 168, 177, 191

actuality, 69-71, 75-76, 85-86, 89, 93, 113, 133-134, 143-144, 192, 195, 213-214

adnominations, 207

age, 9, 17, 62, 101, 112, 116-117, 149, 163, 196, 217-218

agent intelligence, 10-12, 19, 25-26, 28, 84, 166-167, 170-173, 175-181, 183-185, 187-188, 193-195, 213-214, 218

amplitude, 20, 77-79, 89, 97, 103-105, 112, 123-124, 147, 213

angels, 24, 28, 34, 38, 58, 93, 105, 140, 148, 152, 166, 181, 188, 208, 212-213

anti-perpetual, 110

antiquity of the world, 21, 71, 99, 117, 125, 135

archetypal world, 10-12, 25, 27, 167, 173, 199, 204-206, 210-211

argument, 17, 21-22, 24, 35, 64, 118-119, 121-123, 126, 128-130, 136-137, 173

arguments, 7, 9, 17, 19, 21-23, 27, 33-35, 42, 52, 54, 108, 122, 126-127, 129, 132, 135, 137, 143, 162, 164, 167, 203, 206

art, 14, 18-19, 27, 69-71, 73-74, 76-78, 88, 90-91, 97, 120, 177, 189-190, 193, 211-212, 225

artisan, 8, 68-71, 74, 85, 88, 120, 173, 189-190, 192-193

assimilation, 146-148, 150, 165, 168

authority, 15-17, 23, 46, 188

beatitude, 26, 67, 100, 157, 165, 212

beauty, 32, 50, 66-67, 81, 91, 94, 104, 139, 141, 146-148, 157, 166, 173, 201, 208

beginning, 9, 14-15, 19-21, 23, 33, 48, 99-100, 102-103, 106-111, 114, 117-119, 121-123, 125, 132-133, 135-136, 188

being, 7-8, 17-20, 22, 24-27, 34-44, 46-47, 52-54, 56-57, 65, 67, 70, 72-76, 80, 82, 84, 86-87, 90-92, 96-100, 102-115, 118, 120-121, 124-135, 145, 147, 153-155, 157-163, 167-170, 173, 190-192, 197-198, 201-209, 216, 225-226

being of time, 102, 107, 110, 113

being necessary through itself, 34-40, 42, 47, 108, 135

blasphemy, 173

bodies, 8, 10-11, 23, 25-26, 50, 54-56, 62-63, 73, 80-82, 85, 100-101, 104, 106-107, 115, 122, 125, 132, 137, 140, 143-146, 149-150, 152, 158-163, 166-167, 171, 174, 177-178, 181-188, 194, 198-200, 202, 206-207, 213

body, 18, 21, 23, 37, 49-50, 62-63, 65-66, 70, 80-81, 84, 87, 92, 107, 111, 121-122, 124, 135, 140, 144-145, 149, 160-161, 166, 170, 174, 180, 182-183, 187, 194, 200, 203, 205-206, 210

causal order, 115

causality, 27, 75, 114, 185

causation, 83, 95, 134, 172, 176, 180-181, 195

cause, 11, 18, 21-22, 26-27, 35, 43, 45, 53, 56-58, 60, 68, 72, 75-77, 79, 82-83, 86-88, 90, 92-97, 101, 114, 118, 120-121, 125-126, 131, 135, 145-146, 148-149, 152, 156, 175-178, 181, 185-187, 190-191, 193-195, 207

ceasing to be, 102-103, 132

children, 26, 73, 149, 176, 178, 196

circle, 31, 53, 98, 113-114, 126, 137, 145

coercion, 41, 149, 198

cognition, 142

colors, 25, 81, 130, 167, 171, 213

command, 19, 26, 45, 69, 77, 93, 96-98, 181, 187-188, 193, 197-198
comparison, 60, 67-68, 85, 95, 99, 104, 122, 141, 157, 173, 200, 202, 207-208, 210
comparisons, 8, 21, 66, 82, 105, 110, 131, 148, 174, 185, 201, 207
concomitance, 20, 103, 111
contrariety, 37-39, 45, 60, 83, 103, 108, 129, 131, 146, 149, 158-159, 195
contrary, 33, 38-41, 44-47, 49-51, 56, 60, 62, 64, 75, 77, 81, 85, 89, 102-103, 108, 117, 125-126, 134, 145, 189, 201, 208
copy, 171-173, 227
corporeal world, 17, 19
corruption, 36, 40, 42, 60, 98-99, 134-135, 148, 164, 169, 177, 196
creation, 8, 11, 18-19, 21-23, 26-27, 64-65, 68, 72-73, 80, 82-84, 86, 90, 99, 110, 116, 118-119, 121-123, 125-126, 128-129, 132, 134-135, 182-184, 187-190, 195, 197-199, 217
creator, 8, 10-12, 15-24, 26-28, 31-32, 43, 58, 64-101, 103-105, 108-125, 127-131, 133-135, 139, 141-143, 147, 149-158, 163-167, 172-176, 179-181, 186-204, 206-213
creature, 10, 18-19, 24, 27, 39, 41, 68, 82-83, 85-86, 97, 118, 121, 135, 151, 156, 175, 197-198, 200, 202

darkness, 7, 17, 34, 38, 40-41, 43, 47-50, 56, 59
death, 13, 52, 55, 60, 62, 96, 161, 177, 210, 216, 225
defectability, 132
definition, 20, 37-38, 61, 81, 102, 104, 106, 108, 146, 159, 204, 206
deity, 42, 59, 61, 109, 175
delights, 23, 208
demons, 24, 28, 34, 140
demonstration, 213
denominated, 202
denominations, 12, 57, 202, 207
determine, 31, 57, 108, 131, 140, 213
diameter, 64, 130, 132

difference, 20, 36, 39-40, 62, 67, 76, 101, 119, 146, 150, 157, 159, 162-163, 176, 178, 190, 193, 207
dignity, 50, 151, 167, 175, 177
dilemma, 21
disciples, 150, 180
disposition, 49, 120, 147, 177
dispositions, 28, 44, 67, 80, 120, 124, 126-127, 135, 143, 149, 151-152, 161-162, 170, 206-207, 211, 213
diversity, 10, 26, 62, 67, 76-77, 83, 86, 88, 91, 98, 147, 156, 159, 162, 164, 175-178, 181, 186, 194-195, 209
doctrine, 10, 18-20, 23-25, 27-28, 73, 85, 90, 157-158, 173, 175, 182-183, 188, 197, 211-212, 215-216
duration, 19-20, 23, 55, 102-103, 106-107, 110-111, 114-116, 118, 122

earth, 25, 27, 38, 49-50, 80, 92, 99-100, 110, 114, 116, 143-144, 172, 175, 188, 202-208, 210-211
ecstacy, 170
effect, 19, 21-22, 35, 44, 64, 73, 79, 82-83, 86, 95, 114, 118, 121, 126, 181, 185-187, 189, 193-195, 207
efficient cause, 75, 114, 135, 190-191
emanation, 19, 26, 65, 73, 200
end, 15, 19-21, 23-24, 26, 31-32, 43, 64-65, 74-75, 85, 101-103, 105-111, 114, 116, 119, 132, 136, 138, 152, 163, 196, 211
ends, 10, 106, 152-153
entrance, 183-184
envy, 44-45, 51, 54, 58, 67, 150, 157, 165, 180
equivocal, 27
equivocation, 36, 203
error, 7-10, 12, 18-19, 32-34, 36-37, 40, 42-43, 48, 50, 52-53, 57, 65, 69, 82, 84-85, 89-91, 93-94, 96, 117, 120, 127-128, 144, 150, 156, 159-165, 170, 178, 201-202, 207
eschatology, 26
essence, 35-36, 40-41, 44, 81, 85, 90-91, 101-103, 107-108, 118-119, 121, 163, 174, 182, 190, 204, 207, 211, 216, 225-226

Name Index

Adam, 133
Albert the Great, 163
Alfarabi, 10, 159
Algazeli, 10, 156
Alkindi, 65-66
Aquinas, Thomas, 20, 23, 27, 35, 103, 158, 168, 218
Arabs, 82, 90. 141
Armenia, 174
Arim, 213
Aristotelians, 18-19, 24, 26, 56, 82-83, 87, 150, 158-159, 164
Aristotle, 8-12, 16, 18-22, 24-28, 73, 82, 84, 96, 107, 115, 117, 126-128, 139-140, 143-144, 146, 152, 154, 156, 158-159, 163- 165, 167-174, 181-182, 186-187, 190, 194, 197, 199, 203-204, 211
   The Gait of Animals, 184
   Metaphysics, 27, 203, 207
   Nicomachean Ethics, 43, 141
   On the Heavens, 22, 105, 129-132
   On Interpretation, 192
   On the Soul, 168, 171, 184, 192, 212-213
   Physics, 22, 75-76, 105, 122, 124-125, 129, 135
   Politics, 61
   Posterior Analytics, 118, 136
   Topics, 43, 201
Augustine, 17, 20, 27, 33-34, 44, 66, 103, 212, 214
Aurillac, 13
Auvergne, 13
Averroes, 159
Avicebron, 18, 34, 67, 90, 93, 104, 200
Avicenna, 9, 17-22, 25-27, 33-35, 56, 68, 73, 75, 82, 84-85, 94, 115, 117-127, 129, 139, 143, 152, 159, 163, 175

Baeumker, Clemens, 67
Bartholomaeus, 13
Bazán, B. Carlos, 141, 149
Bjørnbo, Axel, 65
Boethius, 20, 35, 39, 130, 163
Bonaventure, 23
Britain, 174

Caesar, 173
Caster, K., 18, 35, 90
Cathars, 17, 34
Chalcidius, 67, 172, 202, 205
Christians, 10, 24, 27, 44, 97, 116, 133, 157, 173, 175, 178, 182-183, 188, 193, 196-198, 211-212
Christian people, 19, 33, 90, 99
Cicero, Marcus, 101, 108, 128, 150
Corti, Guglielmo, 14-15, 33

Dales, Richard, 117
Davidson, Herbert, 118, 135-137
Davy, M., 14
De Poorter, A., 14
De Vaux, Roland, 163

Elizabeth and Zachariah, 196
Elysian Fields, 17, 62
Epicurus, 167
Ethiopia, 174
Ethiopians, 209

Ferguson, E., 34

Genesis, 19, 116
Gerard of Cremona, 66
Gilson, Etienne, 33
Greeks, 24, 34, 116, 140
Gregory IX, 13
Grosseteste, Robert, 13-14, 25, 117

Hamilton, Bernard, 34
Hebrews, 96-97, 99, 115, 133, 188, 193, 196, 208-209
Hebrew people, 34, 69, 90, 140
Hebrew prophets, 176, 188
Hermes Trismegistus, 90

Ibn Gabirol, see Avicebron
India, 174
Indians, 209
Ireland, 174
Italy, 174
Italians, 101, 108, 128

Jupiter, 94, 138

Mediæval Philosophical Texts in Translation
Complete List

Grosseteste: *On Light.* Clare Riedl, Tr. ISBN 0-87462-201-8 (Translation No. 1). 28 pp. $5

St. Augustine: *Against the Academicians.* Mary Patricia Garvey, R.S.M., Tr. ISBN 0-87462-202-6. (Translation No. 2). 94 pp. $10

Pico Della Mirandola: *Of Being and Unity.* Victor M. Hamm, Tr. ISBN 0-87462-203-4. (Translation No. 3). 40 pp. $10

Francis Suarez: *On the Various Kinds of Distinctions.* Cyril Vollert, S.J., Tr. ISBN 0-87462-204-2. (Translation No. 4). 72 pp. $10

St. Thomas Aquinas: *On Spiritual Creatures.* Mary C. Fitzpatrick, Tr. ISBN 0-87462-205-0. (Translation No. 5). 144 pp. $15

Guigo: *Meditations of Guigo.* John J. Jolin, S.J., Tr. ISBN 0-87462-206-9. (Translation No. 6). 96 pp. $10

Giles of Rome: *Theorems on Existence and Essence.* Michael V. Murray, S.J., Tr. ISBN 0-87462-207-7. (Translation No. 7). 128 pp. $15

John of St. Thomas: *Outlines of Formal Logic.* Francis C. Wade, S.J., Tr. ISBN 0-87462-208-5. (Translation No. 8). 144 pp. $15

Hugh of St. Victor: *Soliloquy in the Earnest Money of the Soul.* Kevin Herbert, Tr. ISBN 0-87462-209-3. (Translation No. 9). 48 pp. $5

St. Thomas Aquinas: *On Charity.* Lottie Kendzierski, Tr. ISBN 0-87462-210-7. (Translation No. 10). 120 pp. $15

Aristotle: *On Interpretation: Commentary by St. Thomas and Cajetan.* Jean T. Oesterle, Tr. ISBN 0-87462-211-5. (Translation No. 11). 288 pp. $20

Desiderius Erasmus of Rotterdam: *On Copia of Words and Ideas.* Donald B. King and H. David Rix, Tr. ISBN 0-87462-212-3. (Translation No. 12). 124 pp. $15

Peter of Spain: *Tractatus Syncategorematum and Selected Anonymous Treatises.* Joseph P. Mullally and Roland Houde, Tr. ISBN 0-87462-213-1. (Translation No. 13). 168 pp. $15

Cajetan: *Commentary on St. Thomas Aquinas' On Being and Essence.* Lottie Kendzierski and Francis C. Wade, S.J., Tr. ISBN 0-87462-214-X. (Translation No. 14). 366 pp. $20

Suárez: *Disputation VI, On Formal and Universal Unity.* James F. Ross, Tr. ISBN 0-87462-215-8. (Translation. No. 15). 132 pp. $15

St. Thomas, Siger de Brabant, St. Bonaventure: *On the Eternity of the World.* Cyril Vollert, S.J., Lottie Kendzierski, and Paul Byrne, Tr. ISBN 0-87462-216-6. (Translation No. 16). 132 pp. $15

Geoffrey of Vinsauf: *Instruction in the Method and Art of Speaking and Versifying.* Roger P. Parr, Tr. ISBN 0-87462-217-4. (Translation No. 17). 128 pp. $15

Liber De Pomo: *The Apple, or Aristotle's Death.* Mary F. Rousseau, Tr. ISBN 0-87462-218-2. (Translation No. 18). 96 pp. $5

St. Thomas Aquinas: *On the Unity of the Intellect against the Averroists.* Beatrice H. Zedler, Tr. ISBN 0-87462-219-0. (Translation No. 19). 96 pp. $10

Nicholas of Autrecourt. *The Universal Treatise.* Leonard L. Kennedy, C.S.B., Tr. ISBN 0-87462-220-4. (Translation No. 20). 174 pp. $15

Pseudo-Dionysius Areopagite: *The Divine Names and Mystical Theology.* John D. Jones, Tr. ISBN 0-87462-221-2. (Translation No. 21). 320 pp. $25

Matthew of Vendome: *Ars Versificatoria.* Roger P. Parr, Tr. ISBN 0-87462-222-0. (Translation No. 22). 150 pp. $15

Francis Suárez. *On Individuation.* Jorge J.E. Gracia, Tr. ISBN 0-87462-223-9. (Translation No. 23). 304 pp. $25

Francis Suárez: *On the Essence of Finite Being as Such, on the Existence of That Essence and Their Distinction.* Norman J. Wells, Tr. ISBN 0-87462-224-7. (Translation No. 24). 248 pp. $20

The Book of Causes (Liber De Causis). Dennis J. Brand, Tr. ISBN 0-87462-225-5. (Translation No. 25). 56 pp. $5

Giles of Rome: *Errores Philosophorum.* John O. Riedl, Tr. Intro. by Josef Koch. ISBN 0-87462-429-0. (Translation No. 26). 136 pp. $10

St. Thomas Aquinas: *Questions on the Soul.* James H. Robb, Tr. ISBN 0-87462-226-3. (Translation No. 27). 285 pp. $25

William of Auvergne. *The Trinity.* Roland J. Teske, S.J. and Francis C. Wade, S.J. ISBN 0-87462-231-X 286 pp. (Translation No. 28) 1989 $20

Hugh of St. Victor. *Practical Geometry.* Frederick A. Homann, S.J., Tr. ISBN 0-87462-232-8 92 pp. (Translation No. 29) 1991 $10

William of Auvergne. *The Immortality of the Soul.* Roland J. Teske, S.J., Tr. ISBN 0-87462-233-6 72 pp. (Translation No. 30) 1991 $10

Dietrich of Freiberg. *Treatise of the Intellect and the Intelligible.* M. L. Führer, Tr. ISBN 0-87462-234-4 135 pp. (Translation No. 31) 1992 $15

Henry of Ghent. *Quodlibetal Questions on Free Will.* Roland J. Teske, S.J., Tr. ISBN 0-87462-234-4 135 pp. (Translation No. 32) $15

Francisco Suárez, S.J. *On Beings of Reason. Metaphysical Disputation LIV.* John P. Doyle, Tr. ISBN 0-87462-236-0 170 pp. (Translation No. 33) $20

Francisco De Vitoria, O.P. *On Homicide,* and *Commentary on Thomas Aquinas: Summa theologiae IIaIIae, 64.* Edited and Translated by John Doyle. ISBN 0-87462-237-9. 280 pp. (Translation No. 34) $30. Available as e-book.

William of Auvergne. *The Universe of Creatures.* Edited, Translated, and with an Introduction by Roland J. Teske, S.J. ISBN 0-87462-238-7. 2XX pp. (Translation No. 35) $25. Available as e-book.

Mediæval Philosophical Texts in Translation
Roland J. Teske, S.J., Editor

This series originated at Marquette University in 1942, and with revived interest in Mediæval studies is read internationally with steadily increasing popularity. Available in attractive, durable, colored soft covers. Volumes priced from $5 to $30 each. Complete Set (33 softbound titles) [0-87462-200-X] receives a 40% discount. John Riedl's *A Catalogue of Renaissance Philosophers*, hardbound with red cloth, is an ideal reference companion title (sent free with purchase of complete set). New standing orders receive a 30% discount and a free copy of the Riedl volume. Regular reprinting keeps all volumes available. Very recent volumes are available as e-books. See our web page.

Order through:
> Bookmasters Distribution Services
> P.O. Box 388
> 1444 U.S. Route 42
> Ashland OH 44805
> Order Toll-Free (800) 247-6553
> FAX: (419) 281 6883

Editorial Address for Mediæval Philosophical Texts in Translation:
Roland J. Teske, S.J., Editor MPTT
Department of Philosophy
Marquette Univesity
Box 1881
Milwaukee WI 53201-1881

Marquette University Press office:
Marquette University Press
Dr. Andrew Tallon, Director
Box 1881
Milwaukee WI 53201-1881

Tel: (414) 288-7298 FAX: (414) 288-3300
Internet: andrew.tallon@marquette.edu. CompuServe: 73627,1125
Web Page: http://www.marquette.edu/mupress/